THE SAN FRANCISCO FERRY PLAZA
FARMERS' MARKET
COOKBOOK

A COMPREHENSIVE GUIDE TO IMPECCABLE PRODUCE
PLUS 130 SEASONAL RECIPES

by Christopher Hirsheimer and Peggy Knickerbocker

Foreword by Alice Waters

Photographs by Christopher Hirsheimer

CHRONICLE BOOKS

SAN FRANCISCO

Dedications

For Frani, Verity, Nash, Lillie, and Henry
–Christopher

To Marti and Jack
–Peggy

Text copyright © 2006 by Christopher Hirsheimer and Peggy Knickerbocker. Photographs copyright © 2006 by Christopher Hirsheimer. Front cover, top image, copyright © 2003 by Richard Barnes. All rights reserved. No part of this book may be reproduced in any form without written permission from the publisher.

Library of Congress Cataloging-in-Publication Data available.

ISBN 0-8118-4462-5

Manufactured in China.

Designed and typeset by Barretto-Co.

Distributed in Canada by Raincoast Books
9050 Shaughnessy Street
Vancouver, British Columbia V6P 6E5

10 9 8 7 6 5 4 3 2 1

Chronicle Books LLC
85 Second Street
San Francisco, California 94105

www.chroniclebooks.com

CONTENTS

Foreword

Alice Waters

The defining moment of my week is my visit to the Ferry Plaza Farmers' Market in San Francisco on Saturday morning. I know I'm going to meet pals and hang out discussing the events of the day and eating little bites of this and that; and most important, I know absolutely that I'll find something wonderful to cook, because I know the farmers and their produce. Thanks to Peggy and Christopher, if you read this wonderful book you will get to know them, too, and you will understand right away, better than I can even begin to convey here, how the way you shop depends on an understanding of food that comes from learning from the people who grow it.

At the farmers' market you'll always find people who can open your eyes to beauty. For example, in the spring I always go to Joe's stand in hopes that he'll have bouquets of radishes like he did last year; and I know I'll have to get there early or they'll all be sold. But instead, if, when I get there, I talk to him and find out that it's been too dry and his radishes have gone all rooty because they've had to work too hard to find moisture, but did I happen to taste the berries at his neighbor's stand yet?—then I've learned something and I've had a rewarding human interaction, too. I'll rush off to the bakers' stand and the tortilla maker's, before they run out of lemon rosemary bread or their tiny corn tortillas, respectively, and then I'll catch my breath and move on through the stalls of salad greens and fruits and vegetables, where if I'm lucky I'll catch sight of Peggy—dressed in some bright tropical-citrus color, and walking purposefully, wide-eyed, dazzled, and energized by the bounty—or Christopher, mesmerized by a close-up of sprouting broccoli while still listening intently to one of the farmers she loves to talk to. And then we'll all have tea together.

The point is that my visit to the market is as much about the need to see people and communicate with them as it is about buying food. And it's this communication that keeps us coming back. Real food, real people. Going to the market gives us an opportunity to make friends. It starts with a transaction that's essential, an exchange for food, but it widens to include the fundamental experience of being alive. And by providing the element of surprise, going to the market frees us from our rigid agendas and teaches us what being alive can mean.

Alice Waters

As this book makes so vividly clear, going to the market also celebrates the rhythms of the earth and supports the culture and traditions of diversified, sustainable, local agriculture. We can help stabilize local economies when we buy directly from the people who grow our food. We can give our money directly to the people who need it the most, without middlemen. When I buy food at the market I know I'm paying the real cost of food. And I'm not just making a donation to a noble cause, I'm seeing real value for money, especially when I learn directly about the actual costs to the farmers themselves—the vicissitudes of the weather, the endless work of cultivation and care, the hours before dawn spent harvesting before the long haul to the market—teaching me what human patience and strength can be.

I've traveled some around the world and nothing better expresses the essential reality of a time and a place than a farmers' market, where you can you see for yourself what's on offer from the slowly turning lazy susan of the seasons—to steal a phrase from the poet John Hollander. We help ourselves, knowing that we, too, are elements of an ever-changing edible landscape. As the poet says, our host is Time, and sooner or later, others will take our place at the table. Meanwhile, for our children's sake as well as our own, and along with Peggy and Christopher, let's enjoy the market!

Bird's-eye-view of the Ferry Building, San Francisco, circa 1909.

Courtesy of the California Historical Society, FN-25662.

History of the Market

Shoppers—in groups of one and two and small tribes—move from stall to stall at a weekend pace. They feast their eyes on the bountiful displays of seasonal produce and flowers, sampling here and there, and pause to chat with one another and with the farmers. No one seems to have a list. The regulars fill their tote bags with favorite foods of recent weeks and still leave room to discover the new finds of the season. Social life in the market plaza echoes this mix of routine and serendipitous; it's a place for meetings with friends and chance encounters with old acquaintances. Conviviality comes naturally in the exhilarating setting. The market plaza is anchored by the graceful mass of the Ferry Building and looks out over the bay—sparkling or steely depending on the weather, but always good for a deep breath of salt air.

Like many successful redevelopment projects, the market has the feel of a place that has always been there. In fact, it opened in 2003, but the foundations of this vital urban market—the food culture and the location—have a long history and a fortuitous connection.

Abundant, varied local foods have always been part of what makes San Francisco a great city. Newcomers from all over Asia, Europe, and the Americas brought with them a rich array of culinary traditions. As California was settled, farmers produced an ever-increasing bounty and variety of agricultural products from the state's fertile soils and benign climate. Commodity crops became the backbone of both the agricultural and the overall economy. At first labeled "alternative agriculture," organic and specialty-crop farming emerged during the 1970s and 1980s as a movement that eschewed the mass-production ethic in favor of healthful food, healthy farms, and food with flavor. Initiatives such as the Farm-Restaurant Project introduced Bay Area chefs, longing to find more flavorful ingredients, to local organic farmers eager to find appreciative markets. The term *California cuisine* quickly became synonymous with cooking that was a celebration of ingredients. Linking farmers directly with chefs and, of course, consumers brought "hippie" produce companies into the mainstream,

History of the Market

spurred a burgeoning farmers' market movement, and made cities dream of building or reviving great public markets.

For much of a century, the Ferry Building, the grand and iconic port of entry to San Francisco, was a center of public life. Then came the decades of ignominy, as an elevated freeway cut off the city from its waterfront and consigned the building to a grimy facade and chopped-up office uses. In thirty seconds in 1989, the Loma Prieta earthquake accomplished what years of public advocacy had not. Damaged beyond repair, the freeway was demolished a year later. Much public debate followed, with the city working through how best to use this "gift" of a ten-acre urban space, a reconnection of city and waterfront, and the virtual reappearance of the landmark Ferry Building.

In 1991, the two histories converged: the saga of the Ferry Building, now ready for a new lease on life, and the San Francisco food movement, equally ready for a fitting showcase for the region's extraordinary agricultural bounty. Cosmopolitan San Francisco residents were well aware of the important role public markets play in great cities in the world. At the same time, the administration of then-mayor Dianne Feinstein had been following the emerging public-market movement in other U.S. cities.

It was the initiative of developers Joe Weiner and Tom Sargent that got the ball rolling. A few years earlier, they had developed a public-market plan as a reuse for one of the waterfront piers. Now, in the revitalization of the central Embarcadero, they saw the opportunity to create a public market in the Ferry Building. As a starting point, they proposed to the Port of San Francisco a simple Saturday farmers' market in the four-acre space left vacant by the demolished freeway. The port was skeptical but agreed to a one-time market event. Tom asked me to organize it and put up his own money to fund it.

On a glorious Saturday in September 1992, over ten thousand people streamed into the Embarcadero to buy produce from more than one hundred of the best local organic and specialty-crop farmers, to feast on "street food" made by over a dozen of the city's best restaurants, and to rediscover the waterfront. There was no turning back. In May 1993, the Ferry Plaza Farmers' Market opened as a weekly certified farmers' market. It was the city's third market—the Alemany market opened in 1942, and Heart of the City was launched in 1980—and decidedly its most upscale.

The Ferry Plaza Farmers' Market was operated by a newly created organization, the San Francisco Public Market Collaborative. The collaborative's board of directors and advisory board, brought together by Tom and me, were made up of leading restaurateurs, farmers, planners, and architects, as well as a food historian, a poet, and a farmland preservation advocate. They all shared a common dream of creating a great public market for San Francisco. It took a decade and effort on three fronts to realize that dream.

The first focus was to make the farmers' market a success. Initially, farmers complained that Ferry Plaza customers, compared to those at other markets, were mainly single people and only purchased small quantities. To attract family shoppers, the market organized a series of events with children's activities, live music, and tastings of tomatoes, peppers, or berries—whatever was at peak season. Within six months, plans to close for the off-season were scrapped and the market became year-round. Sweeping out the huge puddles of rainwater that accumulated in the parking lot became a routine winter chore.

Within a couple of years, the market had become the city's Saturday living room. Shoppers became regulars, ever-more knowledgeable about the distinctions between Brooks, Van, and Bing cherries; and *puntarella*, Treviso, and Castelfranco chicories. A breakfast of organic eggs scrambled with smoked salmon from Hayes Street Grill, one of the market's longtime food stands, extended the leisurely morning. It was the place to take out-of-town guests, especially food lovers, and election season always delivered a crop of candidates to shake hands and mingle.

In 1998, the market relocated up the waterfront to Green Street to make way for construction of the new Embarcadero Boulevard and plaza. This was a peak time for the market, especially after the F streetcar line was completed, providing convenient public transit. There were about 150 farmers, about one-third of them year-round and others attending seasonally. Many sold only organic—and almost always distinctive—products, and most had been in the market since day one. A limited number of vendors of prepared and processed foods, carefully selected to conform to the emerging sustainability principles, also had stalls. A Sunday market was added, but then dropped after two years due to lack of attendance.

The second focus was to develop educational programs about sustainable agriculture. In order to be eligible for grant funding, the market board founded a sister nonprofit organization, the Center for Urban Education about Sustainable Agriculture (CUESA). In 2000, CUESA replaced the collaborative as the market's governing organization. The programs developed by CUESA were as forward-looking and acclaimed as the market itself.

A series of regular market programs was started. Shop with the Chef, which continues to this day, was a free cooking demonstration by a local chef and featured ingredients from the market. Meet the Producer began as an element of the cooking demonstration, and then became a stand-alone forum for market producers to talk about their farming operations. Coordinated and attractive ABOUT MY FARM posters at every booth also helped shoppers learn more about who was growing the food they were buying. Market Cooking for Kids provided a fun hands-on activity for children while their parents shopped and schmoozed. It evolved to become a program that brought children from low-income community centers to the market, and then became CUESA's major community outreach effort. For several years, it offered

History of the Market

monthly cooking and horticulture classes to almost a dozen public schools in San Francisco and Oakland, though a lack of funding has since ended the program.

Open Garden Day, another long-term outreach program, was a self-guided tour of the Bay Area's hundreds of urban garden projects, publicized by means of a GIS (Geographic Information Systems) map that itself became a year-round resource. Two related one-time projects also demonstrated CUESA's emerging role as an educational resource: the publication of the *Urban Gardening and Greening Directory*, and the organization of a seminal conference, "A Garden in Every School: Cultivating a Sense of Season and Place."

In the midst of managing the farmers' market and developing educational programs, the San Francisco Farmers' Market Collaborative and then CUESA never lost sight of its dream. Establishing a permanent public market and education center remained the underlying focus and enduring mission. The vision was clear: "Imagine a spacious market hall filled with the activity of vendors selling farm-fresh, seasonal produce and local specialty foods in colorful stalls. The hall opens onto a lively plaza bordered by produce and flower vendors, cafés, and a children's play area. Beyond the plaza, ferryboats come and go on the sparkling bay." This paragraph leads off a colorful booklet produced in 1994, and is still a succinct presentation of the market's underlying principles and purpose. The vision was more deeply elaborated and substantiated in the "Education Center Study and Public Market Strategic Plan" produced a few years later. The plan assessed a number of potential sites along the waterfront, but the Ferry Building remained a favorite.

Ultimately, the success of the market and all it had come to mean to the city and its legion of supporters was persuasive. In 1999, the Port of San Francisco invited proposals for the redevelopment of the Ferry Building that included a public market as a preferred use for the public and retail spaces encompassing the entire sixty-thousand square-foot ground floor. The winning team immediately invited the Ferry Plaza Farmers' Market and CUESA to make the building their permanent home and itself assumed the ambitious task of developing the permanent market stalls. At the grand opening of the restored Ferry Building in the spring of 2003, the farmers' market was all the garland the event required.

Sibella Kraus
FOUNDING EXECUTIVE DIRECTOR, 1991–2000
SAN FRANCISCO PUBLIC MARKET COLLABORATIVE
CENTER FOR URBAN EDUCATION ABOUT SUSTAINABLE AGRICULTURE

DIRECTOR, 2001–PRESENT
SUSTAINABLE AGRICULTURE EDUCATION (SAGE)

Tuesday Market

Introduction

Every Saturday morning, a swarm of shoppers flocks to San Francisco's Ferry Plaza Farmers' Market for a culinary extravaganza arguably unequaled in the United States. Symphony conductors and chefs, filmmakers and financiers, socialites and socialists, parents and children are among the fifteen thousand visitors who gather for the communal highlight of their week, engaging in disputes over which stall carries the ripest Sacramento Delta peaches, the sweetest heirloom tomatoes, the crunchiest Mission almonds.

Shoppers wander the one-hundred-odd stalls that stretch 660 feet along the bay and the Embarcadero. By morning's end, baskets bulge with the wealth of California's fertile fields, valleys, and foothills: six types of figs from a farmer with two PhDs; a beguiling assortment of tender, prematurely harvested organic salad greens—wild purslane, oak-leaf lettuce, small-leaved cress, frisée—ten varieties of crisp heirloom apples; plump, sweet strawberries from a farmer who, by going organic, is now able to employ fifteen family members from Mexico; twenty strains of exotic peppers; big, spiky cardoons; and artichokes, large and small.

The Ferry Plaza Farmers' Market is operated by the Center for Urban Education about Sustainable Agriculture (CUESA). Its mission is to promote regional sustainable agriculture through the operation of farmers' markets and educational programs. The Ferry Plaza market is the crucial link between San Francisco residents and the farmers who practice sustainable agriculture in the area. Purchasing directly from the growers helps them earn more of the food dollar, a critical factor in their ability to stay in business.

The market, which operates Saturdays, Sundays, Tuesdays, and Thursdays, was the first tenant of the Ferry Building Marketplace. Two symbiotic entities exist at the Ferry Building: the permanent stalls of the Ferry Building Marketplace located on the first floor, and the transient, yet consistent outdoor stalls of the Ferry Plaza Farmers' Market, operated by CUESA.

The interior of the renovated Ferry Building, a former transportation hub built in 1880, is reminiscent of old, lofty European produce markets. The skylights of its soaring naves shine onto an indoor food corridor of twenty vigilantly chosen permanent stalls and restaurants with specialties such as artisanal cheeses, organic tacos, fancy wines, antique and modern cooking implements, local oysters, herbs, caviar, extra-virgin olive oils, grass-fed beef, Japanese delicacies, and an artist's palette of rare foraged mushrooms.

The genius of the farmers' market is the availability, in one spot, of the vast bounty of the region's small-scale growers. Their crops are picked in season for ripeness and ultimate flavor just hours earlier, unlike the gassed, waxed, and artificially colored foods that are typically packed into refrigerated trucks and shipped to distant supermarkets for sale days, and sometimes weeks, later. Since their financial gains are slim, these small organic farmers are instead driven by a passion for maintaining the health of the earth and for experiencing firsthand the joy of their customers.

The mission of the farmers' market, in turn, is to encourage the survival of these small farmers and thus help protect the region's endangered agricultural resources. Educational programs sponsored by CUESA focus on a variety of public issues, such as the rural-urban competition for water and the importance of organic and sustainable farming in protecting soil, water, and air quality.

Buying your food at the farmers' market can even be seen as a political statement. For example, you are saying yes to the survival of small, local farmers and no to the big industrial complexes that threaten to overwhelm everyone's future. You are also saying no to the risks of scientific procedures that include the mismanagement of potentially dangerous chemicals, no to genetically modified foods, no to monoculture that rapes the earth of its nutrients, and no to certain frozen foods that need only a spell in the microwave and are too often hurriedly eaten—sometimes even while standing up. Rather, you are saying yes to buying vivid, luscious living food, yes to the survival of farmland on the urban fringe, and yes to cooking good food for your family and friends and slowing down enough at the table to taste the difference.

The San Francisco Ferry Plaza Farmers' Market Cookbook introduces you to many of these growers and other vendors who make the market the place it is. We have organized the book by season and then, within each season, alphabetically by the fruits, vegetables, and other products that are at their seasonal peak during these months. The text for each item not only includes descriptive information and frequently some history, but often also showcases a grower or vendor and his or her wisdom and know-how about the subject at hand. We provide specifics on seasonal availability at the market, detailing the months, and give advice on choosing, storing, preparing, and sometimes even freezing items. We regret that space has not allowed us to include every farmer and vendor or everything sold at the market. Instead, we are presenting what we believe is the best of the market throughout the year.

A final chapter, "All Year Long," looks at a handful of items—grass-fed beef, bread, cheese, and olive oil—that are available at the market throughout all the seasons.

Following the description of each market item is one or more recipes featuring it. Between us we have some eighty years of continuous cooking experience and have made most of the recipes many times with great results. We are not offering groundbreaking culinary ideas. Rather, we are giving you the best recipes we know—some from farmers, some from chefs, some from friends, some of our own favorites—for the items at hand.

We have made the recipes simple, so that you can come home from the market, unload a basket, and quickly assemble a meal with your just-purchased treasures—ingredients so alive that they practically prepare themselves. Indeed, it may seem almost as if a recipe is created as the produce tumbles onto your countertop.

(opposite) Star Route Farm's spring lettuce

Apricots

Apricots are stone fruits—fleshy fruits with a hard central stone, or pit, enclosing a seed kernel. They range in color from white to almost black and vary in size from pea to peach. In the mid-eighteenth century, the Spanish carried apricots to California to plant in their mission gardens. As early as 1792, the first major harvest was recorded south of San Francisco in the Santa Clara Valley. Warm days tempered by the cool air from the Pacific that poured over the coastal range at night were ideal growing conditions for the delicate spring fruit.

With the growth of the computer industry in the 1970s, farmers were forced to move east out of what is now called Silicon Valley into the San Joaquin and Sacramento valleys. Although the climate is hotter and not as ideal, some sixty varieties are now cultivated in the area, which produces 95 percent of the apricots grown in the United States. Late frosts, heavy spring rains, and stiff winds can devastate this early blooming crop, knocking fragile blossoms from the trees. Their short season and small production make apricots all the more precious.

For fifty years, the Torosian family has been farming in the Tulare County town of Dinuba, some two hundred miles southeast of San Francisco. Fifteen years ago, when small farmers just couldn't make it growing fruit for the wholesale commercial market, Tory Torosian saw hope in the prospect of selling at farmers' markets. "It turned out to be a terrific deal for us, my wife is involved, the kids help—it's a great family enterprise," says Torosian. "We get the pleasure of seeing people enjoy our fruit besides making some bucks to survive. We get a thank-you that we'd never get from the packinghouse; folks come by and bring us preserves that they've made with our apricots. It's unbelievable."

Tory Farms grows four apricot varieties in staggered crops: the medium-sized, flavorful Poppy in early May; the large, deep-colored Earlicot in mid-May; and the Rosecot and Golden Sweet at the end of the season in June. "My God, good apricots are hard to beat," Torosian exclaims. "My favorite is the Golden Sweet. I never peel tree-ripened fruit. I just split them in half and chomp."

Season
Early May until mid-July.

Choosing
Look for plump, well-formed fruits that are just soft to the touch, golden orange, and have a delicate but distinct apricot aroma. The deeper the color, the riper and sweeter the fruit will be. If you are choosing apricots for cooking, slightly firmer fruits will hold their shape better. Avoid pale yellow fruit with a greenish tinge.

8 APRICOTS WEIGH ABOUT 1 POUND

Storing

Keep apricots in the coolest part of your kitchen, away from the stove and the heat that your refrigerator generates. Arrange in a single layer on a plate or rack. Properly stored fruit will keep for up to 5 days. If you buy a box of apricots, sort through the fruit and use them progressively as they ripen. Avoid storing apricots in the refrigerator. The cold kills their bouquet and flavor. Chill only the ripest fruit to prevent spoilage. If you find you need to ripen apricots quickly, place them in a closed paper bag with an apple, pear, or banana; the latter fruits naturally emit ethylene gas as they ripen, which hastens the ripening of the apricots.

Preparing

You don't need to peel tree-ripened fruits. Just rinse them under cool water. To split an apricot in half, slice around the seam, circling the pit; twist the halves gently in opposite directions; pull apart; and remove the pit. Eat out of hand or proceed with your recipe.

The kernel inside the hard apricot pit is similar to an almond. If you are making apricot jam, add a few kernels to the pot; they will impart a delicate almond flavor to the preserves. The kernels do carry a small amount of prussic acid, which is a mild form of cyanide that is destroyed by roasting. A small scattering of kernels for flavor is harmless, however.

Freezing

Peel apricots by plunging them into boiling water for 30 to 60 seconds, scooping them out, immersing them in cold water, and then slipping off the skins. (Peeling is advisable because the skins toughen during freezing.) Cut into halves or slices, discarding the pits. Toss the fruits in lemon juice, then portion the fruits into freezer containers or zippered plastic bags, adding enough simple syrup (heat equal parts water and sugar until sugar is dissolved; cool before using) to cover. To flavor the fruit further, add herbs sprigs, such as mint or lemon verbena, to the hot syrup and discard when cool.

Alternatively, halve apricots, remove and discard pits, put in a bowl, and toss with lemon juice, taking care not to break up the fruit. Arrange in a single layer on a parchment-lined baking sheet that will fit into your freezer. Freeze fruit until solid, about 2 hours, and then place in zippered plastic freezer bags and return to the freezer for up to 6 months.

Note: In an effort to improve the texture and juiciness of the highly perishable apricot, well-known fruit breeder Floyd Zaiger of Modesto has developed a number of apricot hybrids that are grown throughout California, including various plumcots, 50 percent each plum and apricot; Apriums, about 75 percent apricot and 25 percent plum; and Pluots, about 75 percent plum and 25 percent apricot.

Apricots

Gladys's Apricot Cobbler

Serves 6 to 8

Tory Torosian remembers eating his mom Gladys's delicate pastry as a little kid. "When you have beautiful fruit, don't screw it up with a lot of sauces," he says. "Simple roast chicken and my mom's apricot cobbler are the all-American summer Sunday dinner."

FOR THE CRUST

1 1/3 CUPS UNBLEACHED
ALL-PURPOSE FLOUR

1/2 TEASPOON SALT

1/3 CUP VEGETABLE OIL

2 TABLESPOONS MILK

FOR THE FILLING

4 CUPS SLICED, PITTED
APRICOTS

3/4 CUP SUGAR

2 TABLESPOONS UNBLEACHED
ALL-PURPOSE FLOUR

2 TABLESPOONS CHILLED
UNSALTED BUTTER, CUT INTO
SMALL PIECES

Preheat the oven to 425°F.

To make the crust, sift together the flour and salt into a bowl. Measure the oil in a measuring cup and then add the milk to it. Pour the liquids into the dry ingredients and mix with a fork until a soft dough forms. Using your hands, shape the dough into a flat disk and place between 2 sheets of waxed paper each 9 by 13 inches. Roll out the dough to the size of the waxed paper.

To make the filling, arrange the apricot slices evenly in a 9-by-13-inch baking dish. Sprinkle the sugar and the flour evenly over the fruit. Scatter the butter pieces over the top.

Carefully peel away the top sheet of waxed paper from the dough. Place the dough sheet, waxed paper side up, on top of the apricots. Peel off the remaining sheet of waxed paper.

Bake until the crust is golden brown, 25 to 35 minutes. Remove from the oven and let cool for 10 or 15 minutes, then serve warm or at room temperature.

Golden Sweet apricots

Apricot Upside-Down Cake

Serves 8 to 10

Flo Braker has been the *San Francisco Chronicle*'s "Baker" columnist since 1989. She is also a member of the Bay Area's Bakers Dozen, a group of accomplished bakers who get together to share their knowledge and find solutions to their baking problems. Simply put, Flo knows all when it comes to baking. She generously shared this delicious recipe with us.

FOR THE FRUIT LAYER

3 TABLESPOONS UNSALTED
BUTTER

1/2 CUP PLUS 2 TABLESPOONS
PACKED LIGHT BROWN SUGAR

10 OR 11 FIRM, RIPE APRICOTS
(ABOUT 1 1/4 POUNDS),
HALVED AND PITTED

FOR THE BATTER

1 1/3 CUPS BLEACHED
ALL-PURPOSE FLOUR

2 TEASPOONS BAKING
POWDER

1/2 TEASPOON GROUND
CINNAMON

1/8 TEASPOON SALT

6 TABLESPOONS UNSALTED
BUTTER

1/4 CUP GRANULATED SUGAR

2/3 CUP PACKED LIGHT
BROWN SUGAR

2 LARGE EGGS

1/2 CUP MILK

1 TEASPOON PURE VANILLA
EXTRACT

1/2 TEASPOON PURE
ALMOND EXTRACT

Position an oven rack in the lower third of the oven and preheat to 350°F. Butter and flour a 9-by-2-inch round cake pan.

To make the fruit layer, in a small saucepan, melt the butter over low heat. Remove from the heat and let cool for about 5 minutes. Add the brown sugar and stir to combine. Spread the mixture evenly over the bottom of the prepared cake pan. Arrange the apricot halves, cut side down and close together, on the sugar mixture. Set aside.

To make the batter, have all the ingredients at room temperature. Sift together the flour, baking powder, cinnamon, and salt into a bowl. In another bowl, using an electric mixer, preferably fitted with a paddle attachment, beat the butter on medium speed until creamy and smooth. Add the granulated and brown sugars and continue to beat, stopping the mixer occasionally to scrape down the sides of the bowl, until fluffy, about 5 minutes.

Add the eggs one at a time, beating well after each addition until the mixture is again fluffy. Measure the milk in a measuring cup and then add the vanilla and almond extracts to it. With the mixer on low speed, add the dry ingredients in 2 batches alternately with the milk mixture in 2 batches, combining thoroughly until smooth after each addition. Stop the mixer occasionally and scrape down the sides of the bowl. Spread the batter evenly over the fruit layer.

Bake the cake until it is golden brown and a toothpick inserted in the center comes out clean, 45 to 55 minutes. Transfer to a wire rack to cool for about 5 minutes. Using a thin-bladed knife, gently release any portion of the cake sticking to the sides of the pan. Then, wearing oven mitts, slightly tilt the pan to ensure the cake is not sticking to the sides. Invert a serving plate on top of the cake pan and invert the pan and the plate together. Let the pan remain on the cake for about 2 minutes, then gently lift it off.

continued

While the cake is warm, spoon any brown sugar "sauce" that remains in the pan into each apricot cavity. This decorative touch creates "faux pits" for the apricot halves. Serve warm or at room temperature.

Claudia Roden's Stuffed Apricots

Serves 4 to 6

In 1968, with the publication of *A Book of Middle Eastern Food*, author Claudia Roden revolutionized Western attitudes toward Middle Eastern cuisine, introducing a new world of foods—both exotic and wholesome. Among them were these luscious apricots filled with ground almonds and perfumed with rose water, a fitting homage to the great Turkish apricot belt.

12 APRICOTS
JUICE OF 1/2 LEMON
2 TABLESPOONS WATER
1 CUP SUGAR
11/4 CUPS GROUND ALMONDS
2 TABLESPOONS ROSE WATER

Slit each apricot just enough to remove its pit. Put the apricots in a deep, heavy saucepan with the lemon juice, water, and 3/4 cup of the sugar. Set aside until the sugar has melted and drawn the juices from the fruit, about 2 hours.

Place the pan over very low heat, cover, and cook, turning and basting the fruit often. Turn them carefully so that they remain whole. When the apricots are soft, after about 20 minutes, remove from the heat and let cool completely in the syrup.

Meanwhile, in a bowl, combine the almonds, the remaining 1/4 cup sugar, and the rose water, and mix well to form a paste.

When the apricots have cooled, remove them from the syrup using a slotted spoon, reserving the syrup. Stuff an equal amount of the almond paste into each fruit. Arrange the apricots in a bowl and pour the syrup over them. Serve chilled or at room temperature.

Asparagus

Asparagus is ready to harvest on Randy Johnston's farm near Fresno in late February or early March, when the temperature hits 60°F. The season lingers until the shoots flower or bolt—well into May.

Johnston, who previously raised cattle, is one of only a few farmers who bring asparagus to the market. After his cattle days, he wanted to raise a crop that was not widely available at farmers' markets, which is how he came to raise organic asparagus. The expense of intensive weeding and organic fertilizer makes growing for the larger commercial market too costly, so Johnston and his daughter, Heather, who cultivate just four acres, sell five hundred to six hundreds pounds of asparagus at various farmers' markets every week.

In contrast, large-scale asparagus grower Roscoe Zuckerman takes Sacramento Delta asparagus to market from his farm on an island between the San Joaquin and Sacramento rivers. The farm, which dates back to the 1920s, lies twelve to twenty feet below sea level. Adamant about the superiority of delta asparagus, the handsome, mustachioed Zuckerman explains, "The high water table keeps the spears turgid and robust in flavor." And judging from the fifteen hundred pounds of asparagus he sells weekly at the Ferry Plaza market, his customers agree.

Yet another highly regarded asparagus producer is Fairview Gardens in Goleta, near Santa Barbara, one of the oldest organic farms in California and an American pioneer in the growing of white asparagus. These highly prized spears, regarded as culinary gold in Europe, do not differ from green asparagus botanically, but rather in how they are raised. To achieve their creamy white color, they are kept from sunlight (and chlorophyll, which turns them green) under mounds of soil and/or sand and black tarps. This process is labor-intensive, but the delicious result—less fibrous and more subtly flavored than green spears—is worth the trouble.

Asparagus, both green and white, is expensive for good reason. It takes two to three years from the time you plant an underground crown, or mature root, to your first crop of bright green, smooth-skinned edible shoots, or stems, to develop. In other words, a lot of earth is occupied before any real production begins. And once it is producing in season, this Mediterranean plant (a perennial in the lily family) requires lots of harvesting attention, often once a day.

Season

Green and white asparagus are in season from roughly February through May.

Asparagus

Asparagus officinalis

Choosing

Select crisp, strong, smooth, bright green spears with compact, nonflowering blooms at the tips. Moist cut ends indicate the spears have been recently harvested. If the ends look split or dry, pass up the spears. Freshness is imperative, as asparagus begins to lose its natural sugars the moment it is harvested. Most good cooks agree that thicker spears provide more flavor and succulence.

Storing

Asparagus tastes best when cooked immediately. If you must wait, snap the ends off, wrap the spears in a damp cloth, and store in a plastic bag in the vegetable bin of the refrigerator for up to 4 days.

Preparing

If a bundle from the market includes thick and skinny spears, separate them by size and cook accordingly. Eat the fat ones whole and cut the skinny ones on the diagonal for a sauté or stir-fry. Break the ends where they give easily and discard or use for soup. Use a vegetable peeler or paring knife to peel off the tough outer flesh on the lower part of fat green spears, so that the whole stalk is tender. Peeling is economical and makes for faster cooking and a more elegant, smoother taste. All white spears should be peeled.

Shaved Raw Asparagus with Lemon Vinaigrette

Serves 4

Chef Jonathan Waxman serves this spring salad (pictured opposite) at his restaurant Barbuto, located in a former garage in Manhattan's Meat-Packing District. A mandoline is the best way to shave the spears. If you don't have one, use a sharp chef's knife or a vegetable peeler.

12 MEDIUM-SIZED ASPARAGUS SPEARS, TOUGH ENDS SNAPPED OFF

2 TABLESPOONS FRESH LEMON JUICE

1/3 CUP EXTRA-VIRGIN OLIVE OIL

SALT AND FRESHLY GROUND BLACK PEPPER

2-OUNCE WEDGE PARMIGIANO-REGGIANO CHEESE

Using a mandoline fitted with the slicing blade, and with the hand guard in place, carefully shave the asparagus lengthwise into long, graceful strips. Place the strips in a bowl and toss with the lemon juice, olive oil, and salt and pepper to taste. Finally, using a vegetable peeler, shave the cheese over the top. Serve at room temperature or slightly chilled.

Variation: Shave 1 large fennel bulb and 1 or 2 Belgian endives on the mandoline and toss with the asparagus shavings. You may want to increase the olive oil and cheese to your taste.

White Asparagus with Mandarin Orange Mayonnaise

Serves 4

At the market, white asparagus is less common than green, so splurge when you see it, or create a striking platter by using a mixture of white and green spears. If you are using both colors, cook the green spears separately for less time; they will take 5 to 7 minutes, depending on their size.

FOR THE MAYONNAISE

2 CLOVES GARLIC

GENEROUS PINCH OF KOSHER
OR SEA SALT

2 LARGE EGG YOLKS

1 CUP MILD EXTRA-VIRGIN
OLIVE OIL (SEE NOTE)

GRATED ZEST AND JUICE OF
1 SMALL MANDARIN ORANGE
(ABOUT 1 TABLESPOON JUICE)

1 POUND WHITE ASPARAGUS
SPEARS, TOUGH ENDS
SNAPPED OFF AND SPEARS
PEELED

To make the mayonnaise, use a mortar with a pestle for the best results. Mince the garlic and place in the mortar with the salt. Pound together until a smooth paste forms. Whisk the egg yolks into the garlic-salt mixture until it is pale and creamy. While whisking constantly, start to add the olive oil a few drops at a time until the mixture emulsifies and begins to thicken. At this point, you can begin adding the remaining oil in a thin, slow, steady stream. Continue whisking until all the oil is incorporated. Whisk in the mandarin orange zest and juice. Cover and refrigerate until serving.

Alternatively, to use a blender, chop the garlic and place in the blender with the salt. Blend briefly, then add the yolks and blend briefly until pale and creamy. With the motor running, begin adding the olive oil a few drops at a time until the mixture emulsifies and begins to thicken. At this point, you can begin adding the remaining oil in a thin, slow, steady stream. Add the mandarin orange zest and juice and pulse to incorporate. Cover and refrigerate until serving.

Divide the asparagus into 2 equal piles and secure each pile into a bundle with kitchen string. Pour water to a depth of about 5 inches into an asparagus pot or other deep, narrow pan and bring to a boil over high heat. Stand the asparagus bundles, tips up, in the pan, reduce the heat to medium, cover, and cook until the ends are tender when pierced with a fork, 20 to 30 minutes.

Using tongs, remove the bundles from the water and lay them on a clean kitchen towel to absorb excess moisture. Cut the strings and arrange the asparagus, with all the tips in one direction, on a platter. They can be served warm or at room temperature. If water accumulates under the asparagus, pour it off before serving.

Serve the asparagus with some of the mayonnaise spooned in a band over the spears and the remainder offered in a bowl alongside.

Note: Use a mild-flavored olive oil for the mayonnaise or it will overwhelm the sauce. Most Tuscan oils would not be a good choice, for example, as they are typically strong flavored. Instead, use a milder French, Tunisian, Moroccan, or Ligurian oil. Or, use a subtle California extra-virgin olive oil from the Sciabica family of Modesto (page 290), such as their spring-harvest oil made from Mission olives.

Cecilia Chiang's Asparagus with Soy-Sesame Dressing   Serves 4

Use skinny asparagus, if possible, for this recipe from Cecilia Chiang, one of San Francisco's great Chinese cooks and restaurateurs.

1¹/₂ POUNDS ASPARAGUS SPEARS, TOUGH ENDS SNAPPED OFF AND SPEARS CUT ON THE DIAGONAL INTO 2-INCH PIECES

2 TABLESPOONS SOY SAUCE

2 TABLESPOONS ASIAN SESAME OIL

2 DROPS CHILE OIL

1 TEASPOON SESAME SEEDS, TOASTED

Bring a saucepan filled with water to a boil over high heat. Add the asparagus and cook until crisp-tender, about 2 minutes. Do not overcook. Drain and then plunge the asparagus into a large bowl of ice water. Set aside to cool for a few minutes.

Drain again, then transfer the asparagus to a kitchen towel, pat dry, and place in a large bowl. In a small bowl, whisk together the soy sauce, sesame oil, and chile oil. Drizzle over the asparagus and toss to coat evenly.

Transfer the asparagus to a serving bowl, sprinkle the sesame seeds on top, and serve.

Roasted Asparagus

Serves 4

Many European cooks bundle asparagus with string and boil or steam them in salted water, but for the simplest, quickest, and tastiest preparation, roast the whole spears in the oven or, if your grill is hot, over a charcoal fire.

1 POUND ASPARAGUS SPEARS, TOUGH ENDS SNAPPED OFF AND SPEARS PEELED

EXTRA-VIRGIN OLIVE OIL FOR DRIZZLING

SALT AND FRESHLY GROUND BLACK PEPPER

PARMIGIANO-REGGIANO CHEESE FOR SERVING

Preheat the oven to 400°F.

Arrange the spears in a single layer on a rimmed baking sheet. If your asparagus spears vary in size, separate them into piles of thick spears and skinny spears and keep them divided on the baking sheet. This makes it easy to remove the skinny ones first, as soon as they are ready. Drizzle with olive oil and season with salt and pepper.

Roast until the ends are easily pierced with a knife, about 7 minutes for skinny spears and 10 minutes for thick ones. Transfer to a serving platter, drizzle with a little more olive oil, and, using a vegetable peeler, shave some cheese over the tips. Serve hot.

Blueberries

"Blueberries are a native fruit, so they are not bothered by most pests," explains John Carlon of Sierra Cascade Blueberry Farm, who decided to raise blueberries because they are "hard to farm and easy to market." He figured that fact would keep competition at bay and give him a crop he could always sell. The family farm, on just eight acres near Forest Ranch in the Sierra foothills, is tended by forty workers who harvest continuously for six weeks, or slightly longer.

The pitifully short blueberry season comes in late May, but during that time the indigenous berry provides a tart-sweet flavor unparalleled in any other fruit, with an affinity for baking and an empathy for lemon and peaches. The berries promise health benefits, too, with their high concentration of antioxidants and vitamin C.

Although prized by Native Americans, blueberries weren't commercially cultivated until the 1920s, in New Jersey. Since then, they have been excellent candidates for sustainable farming. They are not prone to blight or molds because the hazy white film that covers them acts as a natural antibacterial guard. There are two main blueberry types, high bush and low bush, though nearly all commercial berries, in California and other states, are high bush.

Near Fresno, Mark and Kimberly Sorensen grow four blueberry varieties on a five-acre plot. They call their business Triple Delight Blueberries, after their three daughters, and visitors to the farmers' market often have the chance to meet the girls at the Sorensen family booth.

Season
Late spring through midsummer.

Choosing
Choose firm, plump, uniform berries, keeping in mind that the white dusty exterior is a healthy sign. Check the bottom of the container, too, to make sure there are no juice stains.

Storing
Sort through the berries and remove any hard, squished, or mildewed specimens. Line the bottom of an airtight container with paper towels and arrange the berries on the towels. Cover and store in the refrigerator for 3 to 5 days, depending on ripeness, but eat as soon as possible.

Preparing
Sort through the berries, discarding any bruised, underripe, or damaged berries. Just before using in a recipe or serving, rinse gently with cold water and drain.

Beautiful Blueberry Pie

Serves 6 to 8

Two great bakers are responsible for this gorgeous lattice-topped pie. The pastry dough is a traditional Julia Child recipe and the filling comes from talented dessert cook and author Flo Braker. Serve each slice with some good vanilla ice cream or whipped cream.

FOR THE PASTRY

1³/4 CUPS UNBLEACHED
ALL-PURPOSE FLOUR

1 TEASPOON SALT

¹/2 CUP (¹/4 POUND) PLUS 2
TABLESPOONS CHILLED
UNSALTED BUTTER, CUT INTO
SMALL PIECES

2 TABLESPOONS CHILLED
SOLID VEGETABLE SHORTEN-
ING SUCH AS CRISCO

4 TO 5 TABLESPOONS
ICE WATER

FOR THE FILLING

4 CUPS BLUEBERRIES

3 TABLESPOONS MINUTE
TAPIOCA (SEE NOTE)

¹/8 TEASPOON SALT

¹/4 CUP PACKED LIGHT BROWN
SUGAR

¹/4 CUP GRANULATED SUGAR

2 TEASPOONS FINELY GRATED
LEMON ZEST

3 TABLESPOONS UNSALTED
BUTTER, MELTED

WHOLE MILK FOR BRUSHING
DOUGH

GRANULATED SUGAR FOR
SPRINKLING TOP

To make the pastry dough, sift together the flour and salt into a bowl. Add the butter and shortening and, using a pastry blender, 2 knives, or your fingers, work the fat into the flour until the mixture has the consistency of coarse cornmeal. Alternatively, sift the flour and salt into the work bowl of a food processor and add the butter and shortening. Pulse just until the mixture is the consistency of coarse cornmeal but will hold to-gether if pressed into a ball. Do not overmix. Turn the mixture out into a bowl.

Add the ice water 1 tablespoon at a time, stirring and tossing with a fork until the dough forms a shaggy mass. Turn the mass out onto a floured work surface and knead the dough a few times with the heel of your hand until the clumps of dough come together. Divide the dough into 2 portions, one twice as large as the other. Shape the larger portion into a disk about 4 inches in diameter and wrap tightly in plastic wrap. Shape the remaining portion into a disk about 3 inches in diameter and wrap tightly in plastic wrap. Refrigerate both disks for 1 hour before rolling them out.

Position a rack in the lower third of the oven and preheat to 400°F. Butter a 9-inch pie dish.

Remove the large disk from the refrigerator, unwrap it, place it on a lightly floured work surface, and hit it a few times with a rolling pin, giv-ing it a quarter turn each time you strike it, to soften it slightly. Roll out into a round about 12 inches in diameter and about ¹/4 inch thick. Carefully transfer it to the prepared dish, easing it into the bottom and sides and letting the excess hang over the rim. Refrigerate the pastry-lined dish while you make the filling.

To make the filling, combine the blueberries, tapioca, salt, brown and granulated sugars, lemon zest, and butter in a large bowl. Turn gently with a rubber spatula until evenly mixed. Pour the filling into the pastry-lined pie dish.

continued

On the same lightly floured work surface, roll out the small disk into a round 9 to 10 inches in diameter and about 1/4 inch thick. Cut the round into 6 strips, each 11/2 inches wide. Gently remove the strips from the work surface and arrange them in a lattice design over the blueberry filling. Trim the bottom crust to leave a 1/2-inch overhang. Lightly dampen the rim of the crust with water, and press the ends of the strips against the crust to seal. Fold the edge of the bottom crust under so it is even with the rim, then flute attractively. Brush the fluted edge and the lattice with a little milk and sprinkle the pastry lightly with granulated sugar.

Bake the pie for 30 minutes. Reduce the heat to 375°F and continue to bake until the crust is light golden brown and the filling is bubbling, 20 to 25 minutes longer. Transfer to a wire rack and let cool completely before serving.

Note: After testing the filling with flour, cornstarch, and tapioca, we found that minute tapioca makes the firmest (best-set) and tastiest pie.

Blueberries from Cascade Farms

Blueberry Pancakes

Serves 4

You can use this old-fashioned batter to make pancakes or waffles. But if you like maple syrup with your blueberries, a smooth-topped pancake is no match for the deep grids of a perfectly crisp waffle.

1 CUP UNBLEACHED
ALL-PURPOSE FLOUR OR
CAKE FLOUR

1 TABLESPOON SUGAR

1 TEASPOON BAKING POWDER

1 TEASPOON BAKING SODA

1/2 TEASPOON SALT

3 LARGE EGGS, SEPARATED

1 CUP BUTTERMILK

2 TABLESPOONS UNSALTED
BUTTER, MELTED AND
COOLED, PLUS EXTRA FOR
COOKING AND SERVING

1 1/2 TO 2 CUPS BLUEBERRIES

MAPLE SYRUP FOR SERVING

Sift together the flour, sugar, baking powder, baking soda, and salt into a large bowl. In a small bowl, beat the egg yolks until blended. Add the buttermilk and 2 tablespoons melted butter and beat until mixed.

In a large bowl, using a balloon whisk or an electric mixer, beat the egg whites until stiff peaks form. Add the egg yolk mixture to the flour mixture and stir until just combined. Scoop the whites onto the flour mixture and, using a rubber spatula, fold in just until no white streaks are visible. The batter will be airy.

To make pancakes, place a large nonstick skillet over medium-high heat and add a little butter. (If you don't have a nonstick skillet, place a regular skillet over medium-high heat until hot and coat lightly with butter.) When the skillet is hot, add the batter by heaping tablespoons to form pancakes in whatever diameter you like, being careful not to crowd the pan. Immediately scatter a few blueberries onto each pancake. Cook until bubbles are visible on the surface and the bottoms are lightly browned, about 3 minutes. Flip the pancakes over and cook until the second sides are browned, about 1 minute longer. Transfer to a warmed platter and repeat with the remaining batter and blueberries.

To make waffles, preheat a waffle iron and lightly butter the grid. Ladle in enough batter to cover about three-fourths of the grid and immediately scatter some blueberries over the batter. Close the lid and cook until it opens easily and the waffle is browned, or according to the manufacturer's instructions, usually about 5 minutes. Transfer the waffle to a warmed platter and repeat with the remaining batter and blueberries.

Serve the pancakes or waffles at once with plenty of butter and maple syrup.

Cherries

At his two-hundred-acre diversified organic farm in Escalon, about an hour and a half east of San Francisco, John Lagier raises almonds, grapes, berries, and cherries. Each spring, market shoppers await the arrival of his cherries—fat, deep red Bings, named after a Chinese worker employed by an early American cherry grower, and creamy yellow Rainiers blushed with red, the result of a cross between the Bing and the Van.

The Lagier family has been farming in the San Joaquin Valley for four generations. The earliest members settled there in 1874, to raise cattle, grain, and grapes. John started farming cherries organically in 1979, on eighteen acres.

The cherry season is short, running only three and a half weeks. By the time it ends, John explains, "each tree has had four passes by pickers to make sure all the ripe cherries are found—the ripe clusters are grabbed by the stem and pulled off. Then the cherries are hand sorted from a conveyor belt to eliminate any defects [doubles or spotted cherries]." The irregular cherries go through the pitting machine, destined for jam making. The good ones are exposed briefly to forced air to remove the orchard heat and then sent off to market.

Season
Late spring through early summer.

Choosing
Yellow varieties, such as the Rainier, should have a reddish blush. Ripe Bings should be deep red-black and have a healthy sheen. All cherries should be firm and plump. Since cherries can be chosen by the piece, select carefully, avoiding any with bruises. Bright green stems indicate recent picking. Always taste before buying.

Storing
Eat as soon as possible or store in an open plastic bag in the refrigerator for 1 to 2 days.

Preparing
Just before serving or using in a recipe, rinse with cold water and remove the stems and, if directed, the pits. For the latter task, use a cherry pitter—the simplest hand model pushes a plunger into the fruit, forcing out the pit—or a paring knife.

Cherry Clafouti

Serves 6 to 8

Most commonly described as a flan or a custard, this classic dessert from the Limousin region of France is typically made with unpitted cherries, as it is here. Be sure to warn your guests before they take their first bite. You can use other ripe summer fruits, such as figs (see variation), grapes, or pitted plums, in place of the cherries.

1 TABLESPOON UNSALTED BUTTER

1/2 CUP GRANULATED SUGAR

3 LARGE EGGS

FINELY GRATED ZEST OF 1 LEMON

1 CUP HEAVY CREAM

1 TEASPOON PURE VANILLA EXTRACT OR SPLASH OF KIRSCH

1/2 CUP UNBLEACHED ALL-PURPOSE FLOUR, SIFTED

PINCH OF SALT

3/4 TO 1 POUND RED OR YELLOW CHERRIES, STEMMED

CONFECTIONERS' SUGAR FOR DUSTING

Preheat the oven to 400°F. Butter a shallow 10-inch round baking dish with the butter, and set the dish on a rimmed baking sheet.

In a bowl, whisk together the granulated sugar, eggs, and lemon zest until blended. Add the cream and vanilla or kirsch and whisk again until blended. Then add the flour and salt and whisk until the batter is frothy.

Pour about one-third of the batter into the prepared dish. Scatter the cherries on top in an even layer. Pour the rest of the batter over the cherries, being careful not to dislodge them.

Bake the clafouti until golden and puffed and a knife inserted into the center comes out clean, 35 to 45 minutes. Serve at once, dusted with a little confectioners' sugar, or, if serving later at room temperature, transfer to a wire rack and allow it to cool. Dust with confectioners' sugar just before serving. Remind your guests about the cherry pits before serving.

Variation: You can substitute 1 pound figs, stems trimmed and fruit cut into eighths lengthwise, for the cherries.

(right) Lagier's cherry trees
(far right) Cherries at the Market

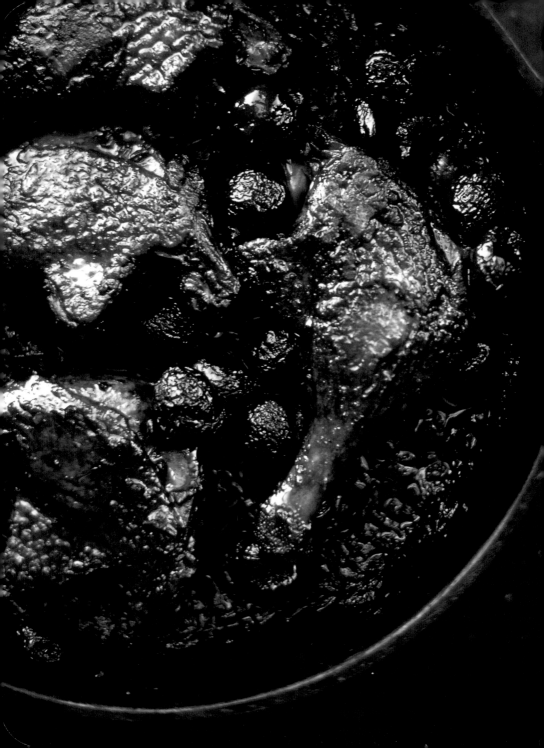

Roasted Duck Legs Smothered with Cherries

Serves 4

This dish was inspired by a recipe for whole duck from Lagier Ranches. The marriage of cherries and duck legs is simple and succulent.

4 WHOLE DUCK LEGS (THIGH
AND DRUMSTICK), TRIMMED
OF EXCESS FAT

SALT AND FRESHLY GROUND
BLACK PEPPER

1 TABLESPOON FRESH THYME,
MINCED, OR 2 TEASPOONS
DRIED THYME

1 LARGE YELLOW ONION,
ROUGHLY CHOPPED

2 CLOVES GARLIC, CHOPPED

3/4 POUND BING CHERRIES,
STEMMED AND PITTED

1 CUP PORT

As soon as you get the duck legs home, rinse them, pat dry, and season generously with salt and pepper and the thyme. Rewrap and refrigerate until ready to cook. This can be done up to a couple of days in advance.

Bring the duck legs to room temperature. Preheat the oven to 400°F.

Heat a large nonstick skillet over medium-high heat until it is very hot. This will take a couple of minutes. Add the duck legs, skin side down, and cook until browned, 3 to 5 minutes. Turn the legs over and brown on the second side, 3 to 5 minutes longer, pouring off the excess fat as you go.

Arrange the onion and garlic in a baking dish large enough to hold the duck legs. When the legs are nicely browned, place them, skin side up, on top of the onion and garlic. Roast, turning the legs once at the midway point, for about 1 1/4 hours. If the fat released during roasting begins to brown and smoke, pour it off. Also, agitate the onion mixture underneath the duck legs every now and again so that it does not stick or blacken.

At the same time you put the duck legs in the oven, combine the cherries and port in a small enameled cast-iron or other nonreactive saucepan, place over medium-low heat, bring to a simmer, and simmer until the cherries are soft and the port has reduced a bit, about 15 minutes. Remove from the heat and set aside.

During the last 15 minutes of roasting the duck legs, pour the cherry mixture evenly over the top. When the duck is done, the meat should fall easily from the bone.

Transfer the duck legs to warmed individual plates or a platter, spoon the cherry-port juices and the onion-garlic mixture over the top, and serve.

Dandelion

Taraxacum officinale and *Chicorium intybus*

Foragers in early March pick wild dandelions from the season's first green growth. Valued for centuries as a nutrient-rich spring tonic, the dandelion has an intensely earthy, bitter flavor that is prized as a culinary sign of the season. Buy wild varieties only in the early spring when the leaves are small. If picked too large or old, they can be tough and unpleasantly strong flavored.

Nancy and Robin Gammon of Four Sisters Farm cultivate and wildcraft beautiful organic greens. Their farm, named after their four daughters, is nestled in the hills between Monterey Bay and the Salinas Valley, and they have been farming organically there, on just five acres, since the 1970s. They cultivate dandelions (actually chicories of the *Chicorium* genus) from organic seeds to sell at the market. Nancy Gammon says, "Our dandelions have saw-toothed, barb-shaped leaves (the name comes from the French *dent-de-lion*, or "lion's tooth") with a milder, more pleasantly bitter taste than their wild cousin. We bring them to the market year-round, but they have the best flavor in early spring." Gammon advises, "Look for tenderness. We always ask our customers to tear off a small piece to taste. If it doesn't taste good, what's the point?"

The classic way to cook "weeds" is to immerse them in a pot of salted boiling water for five minutes, drain, squeeze out any excess water, and serve hot with olive oil and lemon juice. The Gammon family tosses tender dandelion leaves into salads, but their favorite way to eat them is wilted quickly with tender chard in olive oil with garlic and chopped olives. Gammon quips, "They are truly dandy!"

Season
Wild dandelions are gathered in early spring. Cultivated dandelions are found at the market almost year-round, with only a little down time in spring.

Choosing
Choose small, pale green dandelion leaves for salads. Larger, darker green leaves are better for cooking. Avoid wilted or yellowed leaves.

Storing
Remove stems from larger leaves and discard. Then rinse the greens in a large bowl of cold water, lifting the greens to allow any dirt to sink to the bottom. Repeat with fresh batches of cold water until there is no more dirt. Shake off the excess water, wrap the greens in paper towels, and store in a plastic bag in the vegetable bin of the refrigerator. Young, tender leaves will keep for up to 4 days, while larger leaves will last a few days longer.

Preparing

When preparing greens for cooking, if you haven't already done so, use a knife to strip off tough stems and then coarsely chop the leaves. Small, tender leaves can be used whole in salads after rinsing and drying.

Bitter greens and red and white ribbed dandelions greens

Dandelion Salad Lorraine

Serves 4

Use the smallest, most tender dandelion leaves that you can find in the spring market.

4 BACON SLICES, FINELY
CHOPPED

1 SHALLOT, MINCED

SMALL HANDFUL OF FRESH
CHIVES, MINCED

1 TABLESPOON RED WINE
VINEGAR

1/4 CUP WALNUT OIL OR
EXTRA-VIRGIN OLIVE OIL

SALT AND FRESHLY GROUND
BLACK PEPPER

4 LARGE HANDFULS OF
SMALL, YOUNG DANDELION
LEAVES

In a large skillet, cook the bacon over medium-high heat until crisp, about 3 minutes. Using a slotted spoon, remove the bacon to a paper towel to drain.

Put the shallot, chives, vinegar, oil, and a pinch each of salt and pepper in a large salad bowl and mix together with a fork. Add the dandelion leaves and bacon and toss until the leaves are evenly coated. Taste, adjust the seasoning with salt and pepper, and serve.

Fava beans

Fava Beans

Vicia faba

While fava beans, known as broad beans in England, call for considerable preparation, often requiring both shelling and peeling, they are worth it! Thanks to their availability in farmers' markets across America, favas have become a springtime prize for passionate cooks, who scatter them over a fillet of salmon, toss them in a salad with bits of crisp pancetta, or purée them and spread them on toast. Such dishes showcase an ancient staple, and one of the few legumes, along with lentils and possibly chickpeas, native to the Mediterranean.

Pythagoras, the sixth-century B.C. Greek mathematician and philosopher, condemned favas as containing the souls of the dead, while most likely they were just the cause of a rumbling stomach. Oddly, some people of Mediterranean descent suffer from favism, a type of anemia brought on by eating the very bean that is native to their land.

Favas have adapted well to the Mediterranean climate of California. They provide a valuable nitrogen-producing ground cover that reinvigorates the soil, especially during winter when little water is required. At Eatwell Farm near Dixon, Nigel Walker, who grows some of the best fava beans at the market, does what all savvy fava farmers do: he inoculates the seeds with soil bacteria commonly known as *Rhizobium* before planting them, which helps enrich the soil with nitrogen, giving the next crop cultivated in the same ground a good nutrient boost.

Season
Early spring through early summer.

Choosing
Seek firm, bright green, plump, smooth, flexible pods without lots of brown spots. Feel the pods along their length to make sure they are filled with beans. Older beans are bigger and starchier (they are good for puréeing).

1 POUND FAVA BEANS IN THE POD YIELDS ABOUT 1 CUP SHELLED AND PEELED BEANS

Storing
The longer you keep fava beans, the more their sugars turn to starch, so it is best to eat them as soon as possible after purchase. Slip the pods into a plastic bag and keep in the vegetable bin of the refrigerator for no more than a few days.

Fava Beans

Vicia faba

Preparing

Remove the beans from the pod as you do peas from a pod, stripping off the tough string and then prodding the pod open with your thumb. When you've amassed a pile, drop them into a small pot of salted boiling water for 1 minute. Drain and plunge immediately into ice water to stop the cooking and to keep the beans bright green. Drain again and use your fingers to slip the skin off each bean. If the favas are very young, small, and tender, you can skip the peeling.

Fava Bean Crostini

Serves 4

Here's a smart—and delicious—way to use up somewhat mature fava beans. They can't be too big, however, or the purée will taste starchy. This same purée makes a wonderful filling for a buttery omelet.

1 1/2 POUNDS FAVA BEANS IN THE POD, SHELLED AND PEELED (SEE ABOVE)

3 TO 5 TABLESPOONS EXTRA-VIRGIN OLIVE OIL, OR AS NEEDED

2 SHALLOTS, MINCED

12 FRESH ROSEMARY LEAVES, FINELY MINCED (ABOUT 1/4 TEASPOON)

SALT AND FRESHLY GROUND BLACK PEPPER

ABOUT 1/4 CUP WATER

6 THIN SLICES CRUSTY COUNTRY BREAD

1 CLOVE GARLIC

GRATED PECORINO OR PARMESAN CHEESE FOR TOPPING

Set aside about 12 of the smallest peeled beans to use for topping the crostini.

In a skillet, warm 2 tablespoons of the olive oil over medium-low heat. Add the shallots and cook, stirring, until translucent, 2 to 3 minutes. Add the fava beans and rosemary, season with salt and pepper, and cook, stirring often, until the beans are very tender, about 20 minutes, adding the water or additional olive oil gradually as you go to keep the mixture from drying out.

Meanwhile, toast the bread, rub each slice on one side with the garlic clove, and drizzle the garlic-rubbed side with a little olive oil.

When the beans are ready, pour the contents of the skillet into a bowl. Mash with a potato masher or a fork until smooth. Taste and adjust the seasoning, making sure you have added enough salt. Add another splash of olive oil to make the mixture taste rich and delicious.

Spread the purée on the toasted bread, dividing it evenly. Top each toast with a couple of the reserved fava beans and a little cheese. Serve warm or at room temperature.

Springtime Green Pasta   Serves 4 to 6

Favas, peas, and artichokes come back each spring to the market, slowly at first and then in divine abundance. This dish is an ideal way to show off this stunning trio of green. You need to use a substantial pasta, such as orecchiette or penne—one that will hold its own alongside the vegetables. Use your best extra-virgin olive oil for drizzling over the finished pasta.

1/4 CUP EXTRA-VIRGIN OLIVE OIL, PLUS EXTRA FOR DRIZZLING

2 CLOVES GARLIC, MINCED, OR 2 STALKS GREEN GARLIC, WHITE AND TENDER GREEN PARTS ONLY, TRIMMED AND MINCED

1 POUND SMALL ARTICHOKES, TRIMMED (SEE PAGE 179) AND THINLY SLICED LENGTHWISE

1 TEASPOON FRESH THYME LEAVES, MINCED

1/4 CUP DRY WHITE WINE

SALT AND FRESHLY GROUND BLACK PEPPER

3/4 CUP CHICKEN STOCK, PREFERABLY HOMEMADE

1 POUND FAVA BEANS IN THE POD, SHELLED AND PEELED (SEE FACING PAGE)

1 POUND ENGLISH PEAS IN THE POD, SHELLED

1 POUND ORECCHIETTE OR PENNE

1 CUP GRATED PARMIGIANO-REGGIANO OR OTHER GRATING CHEESE

1/4 CUP FRESH MINT LEAVES, CUT INTO A CHIFFONADE (SEE NOTE)

Bring a large pot of water to a boil for cooking the pasta.

In a large skillet, heat the 1/4 cup olive oil over medium-high heat. Add the garlic and sauté until translucent, about 1 minute. Add the artichoke slices and thyme and cook, stirring, until the artichokes start to brown. This should take a few minutes. Add the wine and season with salt and pepper, continuing to stir the contents. Turn the heat down to medium-low.

Once the white wine evaporates, begin adding the stock 1/4 cup at a time, allowing the artichokes to absorb the stock before adding more. When the artichokes are tender, after 7 to 10 minutes, add the fava beans and peas and cook for a minute or so, just until tender.

About 10 minutes before the sauce is ready, add salt to the boiling water and then add the pasta and cook until al dente. Scoop out and reserve 2 ladles of the pasta water and then drain the pasta.

Pour the drained pasta into the skillet with the artichoke, fava, and pea mixture over medium heat. Season again with salt and pepper and turn the mixture gently to combine the sauce and pasta. If the mixture seems a little dry, add some of the reserved pasta water (or stock if you have it).

Transfer the pasta to a warmed serving bowl. Sprinkle a little of the cheese on top along with the mint, and then drizzle with olive oil. Pass the rest of the cheese at the table.

Note: To cut the leaves into a chiffonade, working in batches, stack the mint leaves, roll them up lengthwise, and cut thinly crosswise to create narrow feathery strips.

Fennel

Foeniculum vulgare

Fennel, with its feathery leaves and powdery yellow flowers, is a member of the parsley family. Italians who arrived during the gold rush carried fennel seeds in the hope of planting them in their new country. The local climate proved compatible and soon fennel was being cultivated and growing wild. Not everyone likes the licorice flavor of raw fennel, but its crunchiness in salads and its mild, delicate flavor when long cooked are worth learning to admire.

Cultivated Mediterranean Florence fennel—short and stumpy with onionlike, overlapping, crisp, white stalks; tall stems; and feathery leaves—dates back to the thirteenth century when—as now—the seed was used as a spice and the stalk as a vegetable. The fennel flower produces an edible pollen that can be used to dust fish or pork for a heavenly haunting flavor. Fennel lovers in the Mediterranean, notably in Tuscany, harvest and bottle the fennel pollen. They collect it from the yellow flowers, gathering it as the plant is about to go to seed. The leaves are good in vegetable stocks, for cooking fish, scattered over hot coals when grilling, and as a garnish. Two types of fennel are cultivated, *F. vulgare azoricum*, or Florence fennel, for the bulb, and *F. vulgare dulce* for the seeds, leaves, and pollen.

"In California, Goal fennel is a highly refined variety of Florence fennel, and since Americans seem to love big versions of everything, that is what we offer," explains Andy Griffin of Mariquita Farm, near Gilroy. But his elongated open-pollinated Florence fennel is also available at certain times of the year and is more tender than the slender bulbs sold by some farmers, who are simply marketing tough, fibrous secondary growth.

Season

Spring through fall from the cooler, coastal areas, and spring and fall from the hotter areas.

Choosing

Look for big, round, tight heads with crisp stalks. While it is counterintuitive, the larger bulbs are often more tender than elongated, slender bulbs. Look for bright green, vibrant leaves.

Storing

Do not wash until ready to use. Store in a perforated bag in the vegetable bin of the refrigerator for up to 1 week.

Preparing

Discard any brown-spotted outer stalks. Cut off the green feathery leaves and green, tubular stems. Discard the stems; reserve the leaves for garnish or another use, or discard. Cut out any tough core portion, then cut as directed in individual recipes. If not eating immediately, a little lemon juice squeezed over sliced raw fennel will keep it from discoloring.

Fennel and Parsley Salad with Meyer Lemon Vinaigrette

Serves 4 to 6

Since fennel is a member of the parsley family, it is not surprising that the two ingredients make a good combination. Meyer lemon pulls the flavors together elegantly, but a Eureka lemon works well, too. This recipe was inspired by one that appears in Annie Somerville's *Everyday Greens* cookbook. Serve it as a side dish, a salad, or as a relish for fish.

2 LARGE FENNEL BULBS, STEMS, LEAVES, AND ANY DISCOLORED STALKS TRIMMED

2 CUPS CHOPPED FRESH FLAT-LEAF PARSLEY (ABOUT 1 LARGE BUNCH)

2 TEASPOONS MINCED MEYER LEMON ZEST OR EUREKA

3 TABLESPOONS EXTRA-VIRGIN OLIVE OIL

2 TABLESPOONS FRESH MEYER LEMON JUICE OR EUREKA

SALT AND FRESHLY GROUND BLACK PEPPER

1/4 CUP SHAVED DRY JACK OR OTHER GRATING CHEESE

Cut the fennel bulbs in half lengthwise and cut out and discard any tough core portion. Using a mandoline fitted with the slicing blade, and with the hand guard in place, or using a sharp knife, thinly slice each half lengthwise.

Combine the fennel, parsley, and lemon zest in a salad bowl. Drizzle with the olive oil and lemon juice and toss to combine. Season with salt and pepper, keeping in mind the cheese will add saltiness, and toss again. Scatter the cheese over the top and serve.

Fennel

Tender Braised Fennel

Serves 4

Fennel becomes tender and sweet when it is braised, providing a subtle, sophisticated accompaniment to fish, fowl, or meat. This preparation, which can be made ahead of time and reheated or served at room temperature, is a great way to convert people who contest the delights of fennel.

2 POUNDS LARGE, ROUND FENNEL BULBS, STEMS, LEAVES, AND ANY DISCOLORED STALKS TRIMMED AND SOME LEAVES RESERVED

3 TABLESPOONS EXTRA-VIRGIN OLIVE OIL

8 TO 10 CLOVES GARLIC, UNPEELED

1/3 CUP DRY WHITE WINE, OR AS NEEDED

SALT AND FRESHLY GROUND BLACK PEPPER

Cut the fennel bulbs in half lengthwise, or in quarters if very large, and cut out any tough core portion.

In a large, heavy skillet, heat the olive oil over medium heat. Place the fennel, cut side down, in the oil and cook, shaking the pan or otherwise agitating the fennel so that it does not stick or burn, until the fennel starts to brown, 7 to 10 minutes. Then turn the fennel as needed so that it becomes nicely colored and caramelized on all sides.

Scatter the garlic cloves around the fennel pieces. Splash in the 1/3 cup wine, season generously with salt and pepper, and reduce the heat to medium-low. Cover and cook until the fennel is tender when pierced with a fork, about 45 minutes (or longer). If the liquid starts to evaporate, add more wine or water.

Spoon onto a serving platter and scatter a few of the wispy fennel leaves over the top. Serve hot, warm, or at room temperature.

Fennel bulbs

Cooked and Raw Salad of Assorted Spring Vegetables   Serves 6 to 8

Colman Andrews, editor in chief of *Saveur* magazine, inspired this recipe for a farmers' market salad. Use this ingredients list as a guide, but buy what is fresh and appealing to you. You could add fava beans, thin slices of asparagus, crumbled crisp bacon—whatever you like.

5 TABLESPOONS EXTRA-VIRGIN OLIVE OIL

8 LARGE SHALLOTS, THINLY SLICED

3 CLOVES GARLIC, THINLY SLICED

1/2 POUND GREEN BEANS, TRIMMED AND CUT INTO 2-INCH LENGTHS

2 POUNDS ENGLISH PEAS IN THE POD, SHELLED

1 LARGE FENNEL BULB, STEMS, LEAVES, ANY DISCOLORED STALKS, AND TOUGH CORE PORTION TRIMMED AND BULB FINELY CHOPPED

1 BUNCH WATERCRESS, TOUGH STEMS REMOVED

1 HEAD LITTLE GEM LETTUCE OR 1 ROMAINE HEART, TORN INTO PIECES

PALE, TENDER INNER LEAVES FROM 1 BUNCH CELERY

4 INNER CELERY STALKS, SLICED PAPER-THIN

1 CUP COARSELY CHOPPED FRESH BASIL

1 CUP COARSELY CHOPPED FRESH FLAT-LEAF PARSLEY

4 SCALLIONS, WHITE PART ONLY, FINELY CHOPPED

JUICE OF 1 LEMON

SALT AND FRESHLY GROUND BLACK PEPPER

1/3 CUP PINE NUTS, TOASTED

In a large, heavy skillet, heat 1 tablespoon of the olive oil over medium-high heat. Add the shallots and garlic, and cook, stirring occasionally, until translucent, about 1 minute. Remove the skillet from the heat and set aside.

Bring a saucepan of salted water to a boil over high heat. Add the green beans, reduce the heat to medium, and cook until tender, about 4 minutes. During the last minute of cooking, add the peas. Drain and set aside.

Combine the shallots and garlic, beans and peas, fennel, watercress, lettuce, celery leaves and sliced celery, basil, parsley, and scallions in a large salad bowl. Drizzle with the remaining 4 tablespoons olive oil and the lemon juice and toss to mix. Season with salt and pepper and toss again. Taste to make sure there is a good balance of oil, lemon juice, salt, and pepper and adjust as needed.

Sprinkle the pine nuts on top and serve.

Green Garlic

Green garlic is young garlic, picked when its leaves are green and before cloves have formed. Sometimes called spring garlic, this immature member of the *Allium*, or onion, genus, resembles and grows like its relatives, scallions and leeks, and has a milder, fresher taste than mature garlic.

Garlic is started from cloves, rather than seeds. One clove, planted in early fall, produces one stalk of green garlic. If left in the ground, the clove would eventually become a white, papery multicloved head of garlic. Garlic grows slowly and is labor-intensive, with green garlic taking four to five months before it is ready for market and mature head garlic taking twice that. Once green garlic is harvested, it must be cleaned and trimmed before it's ready for market.

Andy Griffin cultivates organic green garlic on his Mariquita Farm, twelve miles from Gilroy, the Garlic Capital of the World. "But," he says, "very little commercial garlic is still grown there because the practice of monoculture [the repeated growing of a single crop in the same soil] has ruined the soil. Today, most garlic comes from China and Mexico, where labor is cheap. We don't pay our workers cheaply, and we raise something you cannot get from Mexico or China."

Each week during late winter and spring, Griffin sells one hundred bunches of green garlic at the farmers' market, harvested from just one-fifth of an acre. Shoppers know that green garlic is versatile—it can be tossed raw into pastas, salads, or soups or on pizzas; used as a bed under a roasting chicken; or stuffed into a whole fish for grilling—and quickly buy it up. To keep the soil healthy, Griffin rotates crops, with various *Allium* members followed by cabbages and then beets. His consistently bountiful harvest is evidence of his wise stewardship of his farmland.

Season
Winter through spring.

Choosing
Select long, strong, white bases. To distinguish green garlic from spring onions, look for flat, green leaves and a garlicky aroma, rather than tubular leaves and an oniony smell.

Storing
Wrap in moist paper towels, place in a closed plastic bag, and store in the vegetable bin of the refrigerator. It will keep for 4 to 5 days, but tastes best if eaten soon after harvest. Green garlic is milder and more perishable than head, or bulb, garlic.

Preparing

Peel off the strong shaftlike leaves, rinse the remaining pale green tender leaves under cold running water, and then chop off and discard the roots. Use all of the white part and as much of the pale green part as is tender.

Green Garlic Sformatini with
Parmigiano-Reggiano and Fava Bean Salad   Serves 6 to 8

The taste of springtime is steeped in these rich, wobbly custardlike *sformatini* flecked with bits of green garlic. They make a superb lunch with a crisp green salad and toast. Or, serve them with a grilled steak or fish for dinner. The recipe was developed in conversations with chefs Paul Bertolli of Oliveto and Mark Gordon of Rose's Café. The double recipe demonstrates how green garlic can be used both cooked and raw. The salad can also be served on its own, spooned on top of toasted country bread, if desired, as a light starter, or it can be offered as a side dish.

FOR THE CUSTARD

6 TABLESPOONS UNSALTED
BUTTER

4 STALKS GREEN GARLIC,
TRIMMED AND FINELY
CHOPPED

1 QUART WHOLE MILK

1/2 CUP UNBLEACHED
ALL-PURPOSE FLOUR

1 1/4 CUPS GRATED
PARMIGIANO-REGGIANO
CHEESE

SALT AND FRESHLY GROUND
BLACK PEPPER

8 LARGE EGG YOLKS

2 LARGE EGG WHITES

continued

Butter six 1-cup ramekins with 2 tablespoons of the butter.

Position a rack in the upper third of the oven. Select a baking pan large enough to accommodate the ramekins without them touching one another, half fill it with water to create a bain-marie, and place on the oven rack. Preheat the oven to 350°F. The water in the pan will heat along with the oven.

To make the custard, in a small, heavy saucepan, combine the garlic and milk over low heat. Bring to a bare simmer and steep very gently for 15 minutes. If the milk starts to boil, remove it from the heat and let it cool slightly, then put it back on the heat.

In another saucepan, melt the remaining 4 tablespoons butter over medium heat. Whisk in the flour and continue to cook, stirring constantly, until the mixture is smooth and has a glossy sheen, 3 to 4 minutes. Do not allow the roux to color. Slowly whisk in the milk and continue to cook, stirring constantly, until thickened enough to coat the back of a spoon, 5 to 10 minutes. Remove from the heat, whisk in the cheese until melted, and let cool to lukewarm. Season with salt and pepper.

Meanwhile, in a bowl, beat the egg yolks until blended. In another

continued

Green Garlic

1 POUND FAVA BEANS IN
THE POD, THE SMALLER THE
BETTER

1/4 CUP EXTRA-VIRGIN
OLIVE OIL

2 STALKS GREEN GARLIC,
TRIMMED AND MINCED

1/4 CUP GRATED PARMIGIANO-
REGGIANO CHEESE

SALT AND FRESHLY GROUND
BLACK PEPPER

bowl, using a balloon whisk, beat the egg whites until they form stiff peaks.

Stir the egg yolks into the cooled milk mixture, mixing well. Pass the mixture through a fine-mesh sieve held over a bowl, pushing down on the contents of the sieve with the back of a spoon. Discard the contents of the sieve. Using a rubber spatula, fold the egg whites into the strained milk mixture, working gently but thoroughly.

Divide the mixture evenly among the prepared ramekins. Slowly and gently lower the ramekins into the hot-water bath; the water should reach three-fourths of the way up the sides of the ramekins.

Bake the custards for 20 minutes. Rotate the pan 180 degrees and continue to bake until the custards are set, about 20 minutes longer. To test, lightly shake a ramekin; the custard should not wobble in the dish.

To make the salad, while the custards are baking, shell the fava beans, then peel (see page 40). Place in a bowl and add the olive oil, garlic, and cheese and toss to mix. Season with salt and pepper and toss again.

When the custards are ready, remove the baking pan from the oven. Carefully lift the ramekins out of the water bath with tongs and allow them to cool briefly on the counter (a couple of minutes) before you unmold them. Then, one at a time, grasp each ramekin with a thick towel to protect your hand, run a blunt knife blade around the inside edge of the ramekin, invert a plate over the top, and invert the plate and ramekin together. Lift off the ramekin. Scatter the salad evenly over the tops of the *sformatini*. Or, if you prefer, you can serve the *sformatini* in their ramekins and spoon the salad on top. Serve warm.

Green garlic

Lamb

Ovis aries

The five McCormack brothers arrived in California in the 1890s by way of Canada's maritime province of New Brunswick and the Scottish isle of Arran. They worked as farm laborers until they saved money to buy land and raise sheep in the rolling Montezuma Hills on the banks of the Sacramento River. Today, Jeanne McCormack and her husband, Al Medvitz, continue the work of her grandparents and great-grandparents by raising two thousand sheep and growing the wheat, barley, and hay that feed them.

Their flock, which is the result of crossing four breeds, Rambouillet, Dorset, Hampshire, and Suffolk, grazes on the hillsides. "They're mutts really," teases Al. "We have worked on developing the breed and found a good balance of tenderness and great flavor—the best qualities for meat." Their mission is to treat their animals humanely, give them all-natural feed, and allow them to mature naturally. Jeanne and Al operate one of the independent ranches in Northern California and Utah that raise sheep for Niman Ranch, which sells lamb and other meats at the farmers' market.

Historically, sheep were raised for their wool and slaughtered only after their wool-bearing days were over—the meat was gamey, tough, and stringy. Nowadays, lamb, the tender, mild-flavored meat from animals less than one year old, is preferred in America and Europe, while stronger-flavored mutton, from older sheep, is a favorite meat of Middle Easterners and North Africans. Domestic grass-fed and organic grain–finished lamb, like those Jeanne and Al produce, tends to be richly marbled, meatier, and milder tasting than the imported grass-fed frozen lamb from Australia and New Zealand.

Season
Available year-round (frozen).

Choosing
Select lamb with bright pink meat, pink bones, and white fat. Dark red bones and meat indicate older meat (mutton). Most lamb is tender because it comes from a young animal, but each cut requires its own method of cooking. If you are looking forward to lamb stew or roast leg of lamb, you will need to choose the correct cut.

Shoulder and shank: These flavorful cuts need long, slow cooking, such as braising or stewing. The best stew meat comes from the shoulder and neck.

Leg: You can buy whole or half legs with or without the shank, or you can buy a boneless leg, which can be cooked as is or cut into cubes for kebabs. Grill or roast this cut.

Lamb

Loin: The most tender cut of all, the loin is usually divided into "classic" lamb chops. It is best panfried or grilled.

Ribs: These are sold two ways, as a rack or as individual chops. Chops are ideally panfried or grilled, while racks can be seared on the stove top and then transferred to a 350°F oven to finish cooking.

Storing

When you get the lamb home, remove the original packaging and wrap tightly with plastic wrap and then slip into a zippered plastic bag. Keep in the refrigerator for up to 4 days and in the freezer for up to 6 months.

Preparing

Remove large cuts of lamb, such as a leg, from the refrigerator an hour or so before cooking, to bring them to room temperature. This will help ensure even cooking, especially for cuts that will be cooked by a dry-heat method, such as roasting or grilling. The fell (the thin, parchmentlike membrane that covers some lamb cuts) can cause smaller cuts to curl during cooking. To remove it, slip a flexible, thin-bladed knife between the fell and the meat and carefully trim it away.

A great way to bone a leg of lamb is to remove the hip bone, then tunnel out and remove the center bone without splitting the leg. Leave the shank bone in place for shape and ease of carving. Tie the boned portion of the lamb with kitchen string so it keeps its shape.

Guide to Roasting Lamb

Use an instant-read thermometer to test for doneness, inserting it into the thickest part of the meat away from the bone. Always allow a roast to rest for 15 minutes before carving so that the meat can reabsorb some of the juices. The meat will continue to cook and the temperature will rise another 5°F to 10°F, depending on the size of the cut. Meat is cooked rare, or deep pink, at 125°F; medium-rare, or pink, at 130°F; and medium, or grayish pink, at 140°F.

The San Francisco Ferry Plaza Farmers' Market Cookbook / *Spring*

HIGHLAND LAMB

- LOIN CHOPS
- 1/2 LEG of LAMB
- RACK of LAMB
- CNTR CUT LEG STEAKS

Selling lamb at the Market

Lamb

"Let's Have the Chops"

Jeanne and Al are partial to this simple but precise no-name family recipe. Sear loin or shoulder chops, 1 inch thick, in a seasoned cast-iron skillet over high heat for 4 minutes on the first side, 3 minutes on the second side, 2 minutes on the fatty edge, and then back on the 3-minute side for 1 more minute. Remove the skillet from the heat, transfer the chops to a platter, and add to the skillet, still off the heat, "a lot of butter and chopped garlic." Swirl them around and then pour the garlic butter over the chops.

Lamb Stew with Artichokes

Serves 4 to 6

Romans often cook their lamb and artichokes with mint, garlic, olive oil, and white wine, as is done in this hearty springtime stew.

24 BABY ARTICHOKES

1 LEMON, HALVED

2 POUNDS BONELESS LAMB SHOULDER, CUT INTO 2-INCH PIECES

SALT AND FRESHLY GROUND BLACK PEPPER

3 TO 5 TABLESPOONS EXTRA-VIRGIN OLIVE OIL

3 CLOVES GARLIC, MINCED

2 CUPS CHOPPED FRESH MINT LEAVES

3 CUPS DRY WHITE WINE

MINCED FRESH CHIVES FOR GARNISH

Preheat the oven to 350°F.

Trim the artichokes (see page 179), rubbing them with the lemon halves as you work, but leave whole. Set the artichokes and lemon halves aside. Liberally season the lamb pieces with salt and pepper.

In a large, heavy enameled cast-iron or nonreactive pot, heat about 3 tablespoons olive oil over medium-high heat. Add half of the lamb and cook, turning as needed, until browned on all sides, about 10 minutes. Using a slotted spoon, transfer to a plate. Repeat with the remaining lamb, adding more oil to the pot if necessary to prevent scorching.

When the second batch of lamb is ready, return the first batch to the pot and add the garlic and mint and stir to distribute evenly. Tuck the artichokes in and around the meat, add the lemon halves, and pour in the wine. Cover tightly, place in the oven, and cook until the lamb and artichokes are tender when pierced with a fork, about 1 hour.

Remove from the oven, garnish with the chives, and serve.

Lamb Shanks with Olives   Serves 4

Lamb shanks benefit from long, slow cooking, as in this braise where they are paired with olives. If you can't find anchovy-stuffed green olives, add 3 anchovy fillets, mashed, along with the onions, and use any kind of olives you like.

4 LAMB SHANKS

SALT AND FRESHLY GROUND
BLACK PEPPER

1/4 CUP EXTRA-VIRGIN
OLIVE OIL

2 YELLOW ONIONS, SLICED

2 CLOVES GARLIC, CHOPPED

1 CUP CHOPPED FRESH OR
CANNED PLUM TOMATOES

1 1/2 CUPS DRY RED WINE

2 BAY LEAVES

1 CUP ANCHOVY-STUFFED
GREEN OLIVES

CHOPPED FRESH PARSLEY
FOR GARNISH

Preheat the oven to 325°F. Liberally season the lamb shanks all over with salt and pepper.

In a large, heavy enameled cast-iron or other nonreactive pot, heat the olive oil over medium-high heat. Working in batches to prevent crowding, add the lamb shanks and cook, turning them as needed, until browned all over, about 10 minutes. Using tongs, remove the shanks from the pot and set aside.

Add the onions and garlic to the oil remaining in the pot and cook over medium-high heat, stirring, until soft, about 5 minutes. Add the tomatoes, wine, and bay leaves, raise the heat to high, and boil until the liquid is reduced by half, 5 to 10 minutes.

Return the lamb shanks to the pot and add the olives. Cover, place in the oven, and cook until the lamb is nearly falling off the bones, 2 to 3 hours.

Remove the bay leaves, then taste the sauce and adjust the seasoning. Transfer to a warmed serving platter or individual plates. Garnish with the parsley and serve.

Lamb

Fran's Leg of Lamb

Serves 6 to 8

Fran Humphreys, Christopher's mother, was a third-generation San Franciscan. She grew up in a big family who loved food, including her Irish aunt's roasted leg of lamb, her Italian uncle's *abaccio* at Easter, and her grandmother's simple Irish stew. After traveling the world, she found herself preparing her own versions of the national lamb dishes of other countries, including this French-inspired dish that includes rosemary, parsley, garlic, and Dijon mustard.

1 LEG OF LAMB, 7 TO
8 POUNDS, AT ROOM
TEMPERATURE

1 CUP FINE FRESH BREAD
CRUMBS

4 CLOVES GARLIC, MINCED

1/4 CUP MINCED FRESH
PARSLEY

2 TABLESPOONS MINCED
FRESH ROSEMARY

4 TABLESPOONS EXTRA-VIRGIN
OLIVE OIL

SALT AND FRESHLY GROUND
BLACK PEPPER

2 TABLESPOONS DIJON
MUSTARD

Preheat the oven to 450°F.

If your butcher hasn't already done so, remove all but a thin layer of fat from the lamb. Use the tip of a paring knife to make about 10 evenly spaced incisions, each 1 inch deep, all over the lamb. In a small bowl, stir together the bread crumbs, garlic, parsley, rosemary, 1 tablespoon of the olive oil, and salt and pepper to taste, mixing well. Divide about 1/2 cup of the bread-crumb mixture evenly among the incisions, using your fingers to stuff it into them. Rub the lamb all over with the remaining 3 tablespoons olive oil and then with the mustard. Sprinkle the remaining bread-crumb mixture over the lamb and pat down to form a thick, even coating.

Place the lamb, fat side up, in a roasting pan. Put in the oven and roast for 15 minutes. Reduce the oven temperature to 300°F and continue to roast until an instant-read thermometer inserted into the thickest part of the meat away from bone registers 130°F, about 1 hour longer. Remove from the oven and let rest for 20 minutes before carving.

Carve the lamb and arrange on a warmed platter to serve.

Variation: For curried leg of lamb, omit the seasoned bread crumbs, mustard, and olive oil. Instead, rub jarred curry paste all over the lamb and then roast as directed.

Peas

Pisum sativum

Everyone loves peas, even kids who are usually afraid of most green things. English peas were the first vegetable to be canned (maybe not such a good idea) and the first to be frozen (a pretty good idea). But a bowl of steamed and buttered fresh peas with a sprinkle of salt and a few grinds of white pepper tastes sweet, earthy, and green—the perfect vegetable.

Peas are legumes, plants that produce pods with fleshy seeds. Like all seeds, they are storehouses of nutrition and an excellent source of low-fat protein—one cup of peas has more protein than an egg. Such typical dried peas as chickpeas and split peas have been found in Bronze Age ruins and in Egyptian tombs. But Europeans did not begin eating fresh immature peas until the sixteenth century, when Italian gardeners developed new varieties. One of those, *piselli* or *petits pois*, was grown in the kitchen gardens of Versailles and quickly became a rage with the ladies in the court of Louis XIV, who secretly devoured peas in their boudoirs just before bed.

Over the centuries, the popularity of peas has not diminished. Every Saturday morning at the farmers' market, people line up at the Iacopi Farm booth to buy their peas. Farmer Louis Iacopi has grown English peas on the cool "coast" side of his Half Moon Bay farm for forty-two years. Rondo and Utrillo are his favorite varieties, both good tasting and with a long growing season. "I love walking out into the fields and picking peas," Iacopi says. And when asked his favorite pea recipe, he smiles and says, "I just shell 'em and eat 'em."

Season

English peas, which thrive in cool weather, are generally a spring and early summer crop, April through June. But in coastal Northern California, where cool, moist air off the Pacific creates an ideal microclimate, peas can be found in the market from April until the end of December.

Choosing

For the sweetest and most tender English, or garden, peas, choose small, medium green, plump pods that are velvety to the touch. The peas should fill the pods and not rattle inside, a sign of immaturity. Before buying, always open a pod and taste the peas to be sure they are sweet. Snow peas, which are eaten pod and all, should have unblemished flat, translucent pods. Sugar peas, a cross between English peas and snow peas developed in the 1970s and also eaten pod and all, should be small, bright green, and plump and deliver a crisp "snap" when you break them in half.

1 POUND ENGLISH PEAS IN THE POD YIELDS ABOUT 1 CUP SHELLED PEAS

1 POUND SUGAR SNAP PEAS OR SNOW PEAS YIELDS 4 SERVINGS

Peas

Pisum sativum

Storing

Store all peas unwashed, and unshelled in the case of English peas, in a perforated plastic bag in the vegetable bin of the refrigerator for up to 2 or 3 days. Or, store them in brown paper bags to keep the peas from "sweating." Their natural sugars quickly turn to starch even under refrigeration, so cook and eat them as soon as possible after purchase.

Preparing

To shuck English peas, pinch off the stem and pull the string down the side of the pod, pushing out the peas with your thumb as you go. Discard the pods or add them to stock to add a "green" flavor to a soup. To prepare sugar snap peas, remove the stems and any strings that run up the side of the pod. Most young, tender snow peas need only the stem removed.

All these peas can be eaten raw, or they can be steamed or parboiled briefly to preserve their delicate sweetness and bright color.

English peas

Risi e Bisi

Serves 4

This spring classic, from Mara Martin at Da Fiore, one of the best restaurants in Venice, was featured in *Saveur* magazine. A traditional dish of the Veneto, it is slightly soupier than a typical risotto.

2 POUNDS ENGLISH PEAS IN THE POD

8 CUPS WATER

SALT

4 TABLESPOONS UNSALTED BUTTER

2 OUNCES PANCETTA, MINCED

1 SMALL YELLOW ONION, MINCED

2 TABLESPOONS EXTRA-VIRGIN OLIVE OIL

1 1/3 CUPS CARNAROLI OR OTHER ITALIAN RICE FOR MAKING RISOTTO

FRESHLY GROUND BLACK PEPPER

LEAVES FROM 1/2 BUNCH FRESH FLAT-LEAF PARSLEY, MINCED

1/2 CUP GRATED PARMIGIANO-REGGIANO CHEESE

Shell the peas, reserving the pods. Place the pods in a saucepan with the water and salt the water lightly. Bring to a boil over medium heat, reduce the heat to low, cover, and simmer for 1 hour. Strain through a fine-mesh sieve, pressing on the pods with the back of a spoon. Discard the pods and pour the broth back into the pan. Keep warm over the lowest heat setting.

In a large, heavy pot, melt 2 tablespoons of the butter over medium heat. Add the pancetta and onion and cook, stirring often, until the onion is golden, about 10 minutes. Add the peas and 1/2 cup of the warm broth, cover, and cook until the peas are tender, 5 to 10 minutes.

Uncover, raise the heat to high, and cook off the liquid. Add the olive oil, and when the oil is hot, add the rice and stir to coat well. Add about 3/4 cup of the broth and cook, stirring often, until most of the broth is absorbed. Add another 3/4 cup broth and again cook, stirring often, until most of it is absorbed. Continue adding the broth, 3/4 cup at a time, always waiting until each batch is nearly absorbed before adding the next batch. The dish is ready when the rice is tender and creamy but the center of each kernel is still firm to the bite. This should take about 20 minutes total, and you should have about 1 cup broth remaining.

Remove the pan from the heat and season to taste with salt and pepper. Stir in 1 more cup broth, the remaining 2 tablespoons butter, the parsley, and 1/4 cup of the cheese. Cover and allow to rest for a few minutes before serving. Pass the remaining cheese at the table.

Fresh Pea Soup

Serves 4

This spring soup couldn't be simpler to prepare, which is exactly what you want so that all that grassy green pea flavor comes through.

4 CUPS CHICKEN STOCK

1 RUSSET POTATO, PEELED
AND CHOPPED

6 SCALLIONS, WHITE PART
ONLY, CHOPPED

2 POUNDS ENGLISH PEAS IN
THE POD, SHELLED (ABOUT
2 CUPS SHELLED)

SALT AND FRESHLY GROUND
WHITE PEPPER

MINCED FRESH CHIVES FOR
GARNISH

In a saucepan, combine the stock, potato, and scallions, place over medium heat, and bring to a simmer. Cover and cook until the potato is tender, about 15 minutes. Add the peas, re-cover, and cook until the peas are tender, 5 to 10 minutes longer.

Remove from the heat and let cool slightly. Purée the soup in a blender or food processor. Strain through a fine-mesh sieve into a clean saucepan, if serving hot, or into a bowl, if serving cold.

To serve hot, reheat gently, season to taste with salt and pepper, ladle into warmed bowls, and garnish with the chives. To serve cold, let cool, cover, and refrigerate until well chilled. Season to taste with salt and pepper, ladle into chilled bowls, and garnish with the chives.

Peas and Morels

Serves 4

Peas and morels arrive in the market at the same time. The earthy mushroom flavor of morels is the perfect match for the fresh, green flavor of the peas. Use any fresh mushrooms if morels aren't available.

2 TABLESPOONS SALTED BUTTER

1/4 POUND FRESH MORELS,
SOAKED BRIEFLY IN COOL WATER
TO CLEAN, DRAINED, PATTED DRY,
AND SLICED LENGTHWISE

2 POUNDS ENGLISH PEAS IN
THE POD, SHELLED (ABOUT
2 CUPS SHELLED)

1/4 CUP CHOPPED FRESH CHIVES

SALT AND FRESHLY GROUND
WHITE PEPPER

1/4 CUP HEAVY CREAM

In a heavy saucepan, melt the butter over medium-low heat. Add the morels, peas, and chives and season with salt and pepper. Cover and simmer until the peas are soft but not mushy and still have their bright green color, about 10 minutes. Uncover, increase the heat to medium-high, add the cream, and cook just until the cream comes to a simmer.

Remove from the heat, spoon into a serving dish, and serve.

Peas and Lettuce Serves 4

The French are credited with being the first to mix peas and lettuce, a culinary combination that demonstrates their legendary finesse in the kitchen.

2 POUNDS ENGLISH PEAS IN THE POD, SHELLED (ABOUT 2 CUPS SHELLED)

1 HEAD BIBB LETTUCE, LEAVES SLICED INTO RIBBONS

3 SCALLIONS, INCLUDING TENDER GREEN TOPS, CHOPPED

1/4 CUP MINCED BOILED HAM (OPTIONAL)

2 TABLESPOONS BUTTER, PLUS EXTRA FOR SERVING (OPTIONAL)

1 TEASPOON SUGAR

2 TABLESPOONS WATER

SALT AND FRESHLY GROUND WHITE PEPPER

1/4 CUP CHOPPED FRESH MINT

In a saucepan, combine the peas, lettuce, scallions, ham (if using), the 2 tablespoons butter, sugar, water, and a pinch of salt. Place over medium heat, bring to a simmer, cover, and cook until the peas are soft but not mushy and are still bright green, about 10 minutes.

Season to taste with salt and pepper, and a little more butter if you like. Then add the mint, toss to combine, spoon into a warmed serving dish, and serve.

Iacopi's peas at the Market

Potatoes

Solanum tuberosum

"A potato is a living thing," farmer David Little says passionately. "Even after it's pulled out of the ground, it's evolving into its next growing cycle. Nothing wrong with a potato with a little sprout or one that is a bit soft—it's just doing its thing. Some people like a newer potato flavor and others like an older one. I just like potatoes."

Much of Little's acreage is made up of small leased parcels in the rolling hills of Tomales, northwest Marin, and southwest Sonoma counties. His operation is called Little Organic Farm, and he plants and harvests March through November. He stores his potatoes through the winter in his barn, where it is cool, dry, and dark. His goal is to extend the season to year-round.

Potatoes, a tuber in the nightshade family, have been feeding people for centuries. In the sixteenth century, Spanish conquistadors brought them back from South America to Spain; eventually potatoes spread throughout Europe, gaining great popularity in Ireland and Scotland. It was the Scotch Irish who began cultivating them in North America in the mid-eighteenth century, launching America's love affair with the potato. Today, along with such familiar favorites as russets, news, and golds, markets abound with heirloom varieties—white, yellow, purple, red, and even striped.

"The produce industry is looking for the silver bullet, a perfect potato, one that boils, bakes, mashes, and hashes with a rich, nutty, buttery, earthy flavor," says Little. "But, in fact, dry-fleshed potatoes are better for baking, mashing, and frying, while waxy do best steamed, boiled, or roasted." David Little favors two types—the medium-starch Katahdin, a Maine potato with white flesh and good potato flavor, and the Carola, a yellow-fleshed German with a rich, buttery taste. "First and foremost," Little stresses, "is flavor, because flavor equals nutrition."

Season

Because potatoes are planted in rotation from March through July and store well through the winter, you'll find potatoes at the market year-round.

Choosing

Select potatoes according to how you plan to cook them. New potatoes, freshly dug immature potatoes with papery tender skins and waxy flesh, are low in starch and have never been stored. Many varieties exist, but all are best suited to boiling, steaming, or roasting. Russets are relatively dry fleshed, high in starch, and low in sugar. Use these potatoes to make gratins, classic baked potatoes, fluffy mashed potatoes, and the best French fries. Long whites are a medium-starch, all-purpose potato. Round white, or "boiling," potatoes should be boiled or steamed. They are moist and develop a sticky texture when baked.

So many unfamiliar potato varieties—most of them heirloom, that is varieties that were popular years ago—are appearing in farmers' markets across the country that it's impossible to describe and name them all. Many of the best heirlooms are small or unusually colored, such as little Peruvian potatoes, and are often genetically closer to the original wild varieties from South America. What's old is new again.

Any potato you buy should be firm. It should not have sprouting eyes, a sign of a flabby interior; soft black spots, which indicate rot; or green areas, which taste bitter and can be mildly toxic. Little quotes Joe Carcione, the "Green Grocer" (a Bay Area television produce guru of the 1970s), when giving advice on picking potatoes: "Choose for looks. If it looks good, it probably is!"

2 MEDIUM-SIZED RUSSETS WEIGH ABOUT 1 POUND

10 TO 12 NEW POTATOES, EACH 1 TO 1^1/$_2$ INCHES IN DIAMETER, WEIGH ABOUT 1 POUND

Storing

David Little keeps his potatoes in doubled brown paper bags under his kitchen table. Store potatoes unwashed (excess moisture encourages decay) in a cool, dark, ventilated place. They develop an unpleasant sweetness under refrigeration, and if exposed to bright light, turn green. Potatoes, with the exception of new potatoes, will keep well up to 2 months, or longer if stored at 50°F.

Preparing

Use a swivel-bladed vegtable peeler to peel skins from russets, and immediately submerge the peeled potatoes in cold water to prevent them from turning black. Thin-skinned potatoes don't usually need peeling, but if you want them peeled, the skins will slip off easily after the potatoes are cooked. If you notice a green patch on any potato, just cut it away and use the rest of the potato. Always start with cold water when boiling potatoes. That way, the whole potato heats up and cooks evenly, rather than from the outside in. When making a gratin or scalloped potatoes, be sure that you coat the potatoes with butter, oil, milk, or cream to keep them from drying out and turning dark in the oven.

The Ultimate Scalloped Potatoes

Serves 4

Sister Mildred, one of the last remaining Shakers from Maine's Sabbathday Lake Community, shared her deliciously simple recipe (pictured opposite) with us.

3 LARGE RUSSET POTATOES, PEELED AND CUT INTO 1/2-INCH CUBES

SALT

4 TABLESPOONS BUTTER, MELTED

1 CUP HALF-AND-HALF, OR AS NEEDED

FRESHLY GROUND WHITE PEPPER

FINELY CHOPPED FRESH CHIVES AND/OR PARSLEY FOR GARNISH

Preheat the oven to 350°F.

In a saucepan, combine the potatoes with cold water to cover and a large pinch of salt. Bring to a boil over high heat, reduce the heat to medium, and simmer until the potatoes are tender when pierced with a knife, about 5 minutes. Drain the potatoes and transfer to a baking dish. Pour the butter and then the 1 cup half-and-half evenly over the potatoes and season with salt and pepper. Add a little more half-and-half if needed to cover the potatoes completely.

Place the potatoes in the oven and bake until most of the liquid has been absorbed, about 30 minutes. Remove from the oven, sprinkle with the chives and/or parsley, and serve.

Patatas con Chorizo

Serves 4

Maria Millan, a wonderful cook from the beautiful Spanish city of San Sebastián, never uses a recipe for this classic dish. She uses one potato and one chorizo per person. When more guests show up for dinner, she just throws in a couple more potatoes to stretch the stew. Sometimes she adds green bell peppers along with the onions.

3 TO 4 TABLESPOONS EXTRA-VIRGIN OLIVE OIL

3 CLOVES GARLIC, SLICED

1 YELLOW ONION, HALVED AND THINLY SLICED

4 THIN-SKINNED POTATOES, PEELED AND CUT INTO 2-INCH CUBES

4 CHORIZOS, CUT INTO 1-INCH PIECES

SALT

In a heavy 9-inch skillet, heat the olive oil over medium-high heat. Add the garlic and onion and cook, stirring often, until soft, about 10 minutes. Add the potatoes, chorizos, and water just to cover. Bring to a simmer, reduce the heat to medium, and cook, uncovered, until the potatoes are very soft and the broth has thickened slightly, about 20 minutes.

Season to taste with salt and serve.

Mashed Potatoes, Three Ways

Serves 4

Mashed potatoes are the ultimate comfort food. Here, we offer the classic preparation, plus two variations, one lighter and one richer.

1¹/₂ POUNDS RUSSET
POTATOES, PEELED AND CUT
INTO QUARTERS

SALT

2 TABLESPOONS BUTTER

FRESHLY GROUND WHITE
PEPPER

³/₄ CUP WHOLE MILK, HEATED

In a saucepan, combine the potatoes with water to cover and add a large pinch of salt. Bring to a boil over high heat, reduce the heat to medium, and simmer, uncovered, until the potatoes are tender when pierced with a knife, about 20 minutes.

Drain the potatoes and return them to the pan. Add the butter and season with salt and pepper. Using a potato masher, mash together the potatoes and butter until there are no lumps. Whisk in the milk a little at a time, until the potatoes are the consistency that you like. Taste and adjust the seasoning, then serve.

Variations: For lighter potatoes, reserve ³/₄ cup of the potato cooking water to use instead of the milk, and use olive or walnut oil in place of the butter. For classic puréed potatoes, substitute heavy cream or half-and-half for the milk, and use an electric mixer to beat the warm cream into the potatoes.

(right) Katahdin potatoes
(far right) David Little

Rhubarb

Rheum rhabarbarum

Walk behind farmer David Winsberg's house in the middle of East Palo Alto, just a half mile off Highway 101, and you'll step into a surprising two-acre agrarian paradise, Happy Quail Farms. A state-of-the-art greenhouse covers a half acre of ground where peppers and cucumbers are grown year-round. The rest of the property is a series of small garden plots separated by old wooden fences and rickety gates to keep the chickens in their henhouse, out of the gardens and off the road.

In the farthest plot, about three hundred rhubarb plants, arranged in five rows, fill most of the field. Every plant, with its big heart-shaped, crinkled leaves atop an eighteen- to twenty-inch-long succulent stalk, will produce up to ten pounds of "fruit" each season. Even though Winsberg points out that "rhubarb's kind of finicky for California; it's just not cold enough here," his field-grown, green-stemmed Victoria variety seems to have adapted well to the Northern California climate.

In 1980, when Winsberg started farming here, he planted five rhubarb plants. It was one of his first crops. "I like to grow unusual things . . . but I only grow what sells," he says. Today, Happy Quail Farms sells about one ton of rhubarb annually.

This popular market item, a member of the buckwheat family, has an earthy, sour flavor. It is one of the first edible plants up in the early spring garden, and historically it was used as a spring tonic or botanical purgative. Clifford Faust, in *Rhubarb: The Wondrous Drug*, writes of "its immense worth in a world in need of mild dependable relief from its ever recurrent constipation." Even today, the pulverized roots and rhizomes of *Rheum palmatum*, the Chinese species, are prized as a cathartic remedy for intestinal ailments.

Although rhubarb is botanically classified as a vegetable (a stem or leaf), it is most often prepared as a fruit. In 1947, the U.S. Customs court proclaimed it a fruit, since that is the way it is eaten. But never eat rhubarb leaves, cooked or raw, because they contain a high concentration of oxalic acid, which, if eaten in large quantities, can be lethal. Even the stalks contain a small amount of oxalic acid (as do spinach and chard). So, remember rhubarb's purgative power and eat moderately.

Season

Though generally thought of as a spring crop, Happy Quail Farms harvests from mid-March through mid-August.

Choosing

Look for thick, sturdy, solid stalks with bright color and cut ends showing a solid interior with no pithiness. Sometimes stalks will wilt if left in the sun, but they will regain their crispness when chilled. The red varieties grown in hothouses and found in supermarkets year-round are milder than the larger and robustly tart red and green varieties of field-grown rhubarb.

1 POUND RHUBARB (ABOUT 5 STALKS) YIELDS ABOUT 1 CUP COOKED FRUIT

Storing

Cut off and discard any leaves from the stalks, and store stalks in the refrigerator unwashed and wrapped in a damp paper or cloth towel inside a plastic bag. Rhubarb will keep in the coldest part of the refrigerator for up to 3 weeks.

Preparing

If you are preparing stalks immediately after purchase, trim off and discard the leaves as you would for storing. Rinse the stalks well, then cut them into 1- to 2-inch pieces. Peeling rhubarb is unnecessary, and if using a red variety, doing so will remove some of the color.

Rhubarb, which can be cooked into a sauce to be served over ice cream, encased in pies and tarts, layered into summer puddings, cooked down to conserves, and even made into wine, requires sweetening to minimize its extreme tartness.

Freezing

Trim, rinse, and cut into 1-inch pieces. Blanch in boiling water for 1 minute, drain, and then refresh in ice water until cool. Pat dry with paper towels and put in zippered plastic freezer bags, carefully forcing out all the air before sealing. Freeze for up to 1 year.

Rhubarb growing at Happy Quail Farms

Rustic Rhubarb Scone Cake

Serves 6 to 8

Quicker to make and easier to handle than pastry dough, this rustic Irish cake soaks up the delicious rhubarb juices.

FOR THE DOUGH

3 CUPS UNBLEACHED
ALL-PURPOSE FLOUR

1 TEASPOON BAKING POWDER

1/4 CUP SUGAR

PINCH OF SALT

1/2 CUP (1/4 POUND) CHILLED
UNSALTED BUTTER, CUT INTO
SMALL PIECES

3/4 CUP BUTTERMILK

FOR THE FILLING

1 POUND RHUBARB (ABOUT
5 STALKS), CHOPPED

GRATED ZEST OF 1 ORANGE

1/2 CUP SUGAR

1 EGG WHITE, LIGHTLY
WHISKED WITH A LITTLE
WATER

SUGAR FOR SPRINKLING
ON TOP

Preheat the oven to 350°F. Butter a 10-inch deep-dish pie dish and set aside.

To make the scone dough, sift together the flour, baking powder, sugar, and salt into a large bowl. Add the butter and, using a pastry blender, 2 knives, or your fingers, work the butter into the flour mixture until the mixture has the consistency of coarse cornmeal. Gradually add the buttermilk, folding the wet and dry ingredients together until a soft, shaggy dough forms. Turn out onto a floured work surface and knead lightly just until the dough comes together. Don't work the dough too much, or it will be tough. Divide the dough into 2 equal portions.

To make the filling, combine the rhubarb, orange zest, and sugar in a bowl and stir to mix well.

Roll out half of the dough into a 12-inch round on the floured work surface and transfer it to the prepared pie dish. If it falls apart, don't worry. Just gently pat it back into place. Fill the dough-lined dish with the rhubarb mixture. Roll out the remaining dough into a 12-inch round to form a pastry lid. Brush the rim of the bottom crust with water and put on the lid. Press the top crust to the bottom crust to seal.

Brush the whisked egg white evenly over the top crust and then sprinkle lightly and evenly with sugar. Make 3 or 4 steam slits in the lid. Bake until the crust is golden brown and looks dry and the fruit is soft when tested with a knife tip through a slit, about 1 hour.

Serve warm or at room temperature.

Rhubarb with Vanilla and Crème de Cassis   Makes 2 to 3 cups

This simple recipe is perfect eaten on its own, used as a filling for a free-form tart, or folded into whipped cream for a rhubarb fool—a lovely spring dessert.

2 POUNDS PLUMP RHUBARB
STALKS (8 TO 10 STALKS), CUT
INTO 1-INCH PIECES

1/3 CUP SUGAR

1/3 CUP CRÈME DE CASSIS

1/2 VANILLA BEAN, SPLIT
LENGTHWISE

Preheat the oven to 350°F.

In a large baking dish, stir together the rhubarb, sugar, crème de cassis, and vanilla bean. Place in the oven and bake until the rhubarb has released its juices and is tender when pierced with a knife, about 30 minutes. Avoid stirring the rhubarb as it bakes—you don't want the pieces to break up.

Remove the dish from the oven. Pick out the vanilla bean and, using the tip of a knife, scrape the tiny seeds into the rhubarb and stir gently to mix. Serve warm, or let cool and store in an airtight container in the refrigerator for up to 2 weeks.

Variation: To assemble a rhubarb fool, fill stemmed glasses with alternating layers of the cooled baked rhubarb and freshly whipped cream, ending with the cream. This dessert can be made several hours ahead, covered with plastic wrap, and refrigerated until serving.

(right) David Winsberg
(far right) picking rhubarb

Sorrel

Nancy and Robin Gammon of Four Sisters Farm (see page 36) devote two acres of their five-acre organic farm to growing greens. Although they allow and encourage many wild greens to grow that they then harvest, they cultivate many others, including common or garden sorrel, sometimes known as sour grass.

This slender plant, with juicy stems and long, spear-shaped leaves, has an acidic green apple–lemon taste that can be an intense tart counterpoint to rich or creamy flavors. It is most often cooked to tame its tartness, but a few small, young uncooked leaves can brighten the flavor of a green salad. When sorrel's vibrant green leaves are cooked, they change to a drab olive green and melt into a delicious purée.

Season

In Northern California, the growing season is almost year-round for this perennial. Although it may disappear from the market in midwinter, it will return again in early spring.

Choosing

Select bright green, crisp leaves with no sign of yellow. Limpness can be a sign of age or improper handling. Remember that a large bunch of sorrel will cook down to a small flavorful purée, so be sure to buy enough.

Storing

Wrap the unwashed greens in a paper towel, slip into a perforated plastic bag, and store in the vegetable bin of the refrigerator. They will keep for up to 1 week.

Preparing

Just before using, rinse the greens in a large bowl of cold water, lifting them to allow any dirt to sink to the bottom. Repeat with fresh batches of cold water until no more dirt is visible. Shake off the excess water and allow the greens to air dry on paper towels. Strip and discard the stems from the leaves. Use a stainless-steel knife to chop the leaves. A carbon-steel knife will react with the oxalic acid present in the leaves, causing them to discolor.

Sorrel

Sorrel Soup

Serves 4

This simple soup lets the tart taste of sorrel shine through. Top each serving with a spoonful of crème fraîche or sour cream, if you like.

2 TABLESPOONS BUTTER

3 OR 4 LEEKS, WHITE PART ONLY, CHOPPED

SALT AND FRESHLY GROUND WHITE PEPPER

1 LARGE RUSSET POTATO, PEELED AND CHOPPED

4 CUPS CHICKEN STOCK, OR AS NEEDED

2 BUNCHES SORREL, STEMMED AND CHOPPED

CHOPPED FRESH CHIVES FOR GARNISH

In a saucepan, melt the butter over medium heat. Add the leeks, season with salt and pepper, and cook, stirring often, until soft, about 10 minutes. Add the potato and 4 cups stock, reduce the heat to low, cover, and simmer until the potato is very soft, about 20 minutes.

Add the sorrel and cook for a minute or so. Taste and adjust the seasoning with salt and pepper, ladle into warmed bowls, garnish with the chives, and serve hot.

Or, after adding the sorrel and cooking for a minute or so, let the soup cool slightly and, working in batches if necessary, purée in a blender or food processor until smooth. If serving hot, pour the puréed soup into a clean pan and reheat until piping hot, adding stock if needed to achieve a good consistency. Taste and adjust the seasoning with salt and pepper, ladle into warmed bowls, and garnish with the chives. To serve chilled, pour the puréed soup into a bowl, thin with a little stock if needed to achieve a good consistency, let cool completely, cover, and refrigerate until well chilled. Taste and adjust the seasoning with salt and pepper, ladle into chilled bowls, and garnish with the chives.

Sorrel Sauce

Makes about 1 cup

Renowned cookbook editor Judith Jones, who championed Julia Child's *Mastering the Art of French Cooking*, among many other classic titles, makes this classic French sauce from the sorrel that she grows in her Vermont garden. For a richer flavor, stir in a big spoonful of demi-glace as the sorrel cooks. This is the perfect sauce to serve with grilled fish.

1 TABLESPOON BUTTER

1 LARGE SHALLOT, MINCED

5 CUPS STEMMED AND FINELY CHOPPED SORREL

1/2 CUP HEAVY CREAM

In an enameled cast-iron or other nonreactive skillet, melt the butter over medium-low heat. Add the shallot and cook, stirring often, until soft, about 5 minutes. Add the sorrel and cook, stirring often, until the leaves are wilted and have melted into a purée, 5 to 10 minutes.

SALT AND FRESHLY GROUND
WHITE PEPPER

Pour in the cream and bring to a simmer. Season to taste with salt and pepper. Remove from the heat and serve warm or at room temperature.

Sorrel-and-Rice Meatballs

Serves 4 to 6

Meatballs seem to be out of fashion these days, but what could be more delicious and homey? Serve them over wide egg noodles or rice, with lots of the lemony-tasting creamy sauce.

$1^1/_2$ TABLESPOONS BUTTER

1 YELLOW ONION, FINELY
CHOPPED

$1/_2$ POUND SWEET ITALIAN
SAUSAGES, CASINGS REMOVED

1 POUND GROUND VEAL

1 POUND GROUND PORK

3 CUPS STEMMED AND FINELY
CHOPPED SORREL

1 CUP COOLED COOKED RICE

1 LARGE EGG, LIGHTLY
BEATEN

1 CUP HEAVY CREAM

SALT AND FRESHLY GROUND
BLACK PEPPER

1 CUP CHICKEN STOCK

Preheat the oven to 375°F.

In a skillet, melt the butter over medium heat. Add the onion and cook, stirring often, until soft, about 15 minutes. Remove from the heat and let cool.

Meanwhile, in a large glass or stainless-steel bowl, combine the sausage meat, veal, pork, sorrel, rice, egg, and $1/_2$ cup of the cream. Season generously with salt and pepper and mix gently. Add the cooled onion and mix again to distribute evenly. Avoid handling the mixture too much, or the meatballs will be tough; just mix until the ingredients are fairly well incorporated. Shape into walnut-sized balls and arrange in a large baking pan. Pour the stock around the meatballs.

Bake the meatballs until cooked through, about 30 minutes. Remove from the oven and, using a slotted spoon, transfer the meatballs to a warmed serving platter. Cover to keep warm.

Place the pan with the juices on the stove top over medium-high heat. Add the remaining $1/2$ cup cream and bring to a simmer. Cook, stirring constantly, until the sauce has thickened slightly, about 3 minutes. Pour the sauce over the meatballs and serve.

Stinging Nettles

Urtica dioica

Stinging nettles sprout up naturally in weed patches along the creek and in the planting beds at Four Sisters Farm (see page 36). "We just cut them as they volunteer, working carefully with gloves because they really sting," says Nancy Gammon.

Native to Europe and Asia, stinging nettles are rich in vitamins A and C, high in protein, and loaded with chlorophyll. The hardy perennials usually die back in late fall and begin to grow again in early spring. The heart-shaped leaves are distinguished by saw-toothed edges. The leaves have tiny hairs that, if broken or rubbed, secrete formic acid, which causes a stinging skin rash, thus the plant's name. If itchy spots appear on the skin, apply a soothing paste of baking soda mixed with water.

The stinging feature of the leaves is quickly mitigated with heat, either by a plunge in boiling water or in olive oil in a hot pan. Cooks love the dense green color and earthy flavor of nettles in soups, braises, or pastas. Eat young shoots early in the season and go for the leaves, discarding the stems.

Nettles have long been used as a home health remedy for allergy sufferers, for brightening the hair and skin, and for aiding digestion. If you want to try its curative properties, boil the leaves and drink the resulting tea.

Season
Typically early spring, but some farms bring them to market throughout the year.

Choosing
Look for bright green, crisp stems with vibrant tips.

Storing
Wrap in paper towels, place in a plastic bag, and store in the vegetable bin of the refrigerator for no more than a few days.

Preparing
Nettles won't hurt if you take the proper precautions. Using tongs or gloves to hold the raw nettles, separate the tips from the stems by cutting them off with scissors or a knife. Discard the stems, place the tips in a colander, and rinse with cold water. Then all you need to do to rid the tips of the formic acid that causes the stinging skin rash is plunge them into boiling water.

Stinging nettles

Stinging Nettles Buried with Ravioli

Serves 4

The few precautions that you must take to render stinging nettles edible are definitely worth it. Their rich green flavor is remarkable. Buy or make fresh ravioli. At the Ferry Plaza Farmers' Market, the Pasta Shop booth carries an assortment of top-notch fresh ravioli and other stuffed pastas, and its lemon-ricotta ravioli are particularly good with stinging nettles. Then all you need to do is make a broth out of the nettles and float the ravioli in it.

SALT

1/2 POUND STINGING NET-
TLES, STEMMED

2 CUPS CHICKEN STOCK,
PREFERABLY HOMEMADE

SALT AND FRESHLY GROUND
BLACK PEPPER

EXTRA-VIRGIN OLIVE OIL
FOR DRIZZLING

20 FRESH RAVIOLI,
PURCHASED OR HOMEMADE

GRATED PARMIGIANO-
REGGIANO CHEESE FOR
SERVING

Bring a large pot of water to a boil over high heat and then salt the water. The water will be used twice, first for blanching the nettles and then for cooking the ravioli.

Plunge the nettles into the boiling water and cook for 3 minutes. Pull the nettles out with tongs or a flat strainer, drain, and set aside. Leave the water in the pot.

Pour the stock into a saucepan and bring to a boil over medium-high heat. Add the nettles and a little salt and pepper and braise until the stock has reduced by about one-fourth, about 5 minutes. Remove from the heat, drizzle the nettles with olive oil, and keep warm.

Just before the nettles are ready, return the water in the large pot to a boil, add the ravioli, and cook until al dente. Drain carefully to avoid breaking the skins.

Divide the soupy nettles among 4 warmed individual soup plates and nestle 5 ravioli in each bowl. Drizzle with olive oil and sprinkle with grated cheese.

**(right) Stinging Nettles Buried
with Ravioli
(far right) Annabelle Lenderink
with nettles at Star Route Farms**

Strawberries

Fragaria spp.

Wild strawberries are indigenous to both the Old World and the New. The first cultivated strawberry, called the Hudson, was hybridized in the United States in 1780, and thus began the commercial farming of America's most beloved berry. Strawberries were first grown in California in 1900, where today a billion pounds are harvested each year. But that big number refers primarily to a commercial harvest that retains more dangerous chemicals per pound than any other agricultural commodity. Strawberries are fragile, so many farmers believe that they are difficult to grow successfully without toxic chemicals.

But the state's organic strawberry growers are a renegade lot, dismissing the opinion of conventional thinkers. Thanks to the stewardship and intuition of Jim Cochran, whose Swanton Berry Farm, on the central coast, was the first organic strawberry farm in the state, and to the inventiveness and hard work of other farmers, such as Ben Lucero and Apolinar Yerena, a tastier, juicier, more healthful berry is now widely available at farmers' markets locally.

Apolinar Yerena's transition to farming organic strawberries is the definitive farmers' market story. He brought conventional strawberries to the market early on, but soon, at his customers' request, he converted acreage near Watsonville for organic strawberries. He had nothing to lose because he was fetching, some thirty years later, the same price for a pallet of conventional strawberries he had received in 1970. Given the steady rise in the standard of living, conventional strawberry farming was making it unrealistic for his growing family to continue as "sharecroppers" for industrial distributors. And so, following his decision to farm organically, his business has flourished. He is now able to provide work for fifteen family members, who farm five varieties of organic strawberries and other berries. The family farm sells directly at farmers' markets in and around the Bay Area.

Born into a family of farmworkers, Ben Lucero, of Lucero's Organic Farms, in Lodi, also struggled before the farmers' market movement provided him with a steady customer base for his organic harvests. Lucero's strawberries have a particularly intense, old-fashioned taste, the result of taking the unusual step of leaving the plants in the ground for a second year, thereby diminishing output but increasing flavor.

Berries from these farmers and others, such as Ella Bella Farm (page 139), are picked at optimum ripeness and sweetness to sell the next day. Large-scale commercial operations, in contrast, grow berries more for looks and uniform size than for taste, and harvest them for transport in refrigerator trucks that carry them for long distances at temperatures so low that their flavor is sapped out by the chill. It is safe to say that anyone who has tasted the berries at the Ferry Plaza market will never be satisfied with their conventional supermarket counterparts again.

Strawberries

Fragaria spp.

Season
Early spring through summer.

Choosing
One of many advantages of shopping at farmers' markets is that you can taste before you buy. Look for firm, bright red, shiny berries without white shoulders or bruises. The green attachment should appear fresh, and the berries should not be bleeding juice.

Another advantage, of course, is the availability of organic berries, which is particularly important to every shopper's future good health. The soil in which nonorganic strawberries are grown is typically treated with methyl bromide, a fumigant that cannot be washed off the berries. According to organic farmer Andy Griffin, "The ozone-depleting chemical fumigant methyl bromide is a colorless, odorless biocide that is injected into the soil before planting occurs. It kills everything from gophers and bacteria to weed seeds, bugs, slugs, and worms. It renders a field sterile or dead. An alternative to gassing fields with methyl bromide is to rotate strawberries with other crops such as broccoli or onions, thereby ameliorating the pest problems that develop under monoculture cropping systems."

Storing
Ideally, ripe strawberries are eaten as soon as possible after purchase, making the question of storage moot. Failing that, do not rinse the berries until you are ready to eat them, as water will cause them to break down, promoting rot. Remove and discard any bruised berries, then leave the berries on a tray on a kitchen counter for no more than a day or two. The chill of a refrigerator will sap their sugars. If you must keep them longer, store them in a sealed plastic container with a dry paper towel in the lowest part of the refrigerator for no more than a few days.

Preparing
Gently rinse strawberries in cool water, being careful not to bruise them. Cut off the stem and any white shoulders with a small, sharp knife.

Strawberry Sorbet with Infusion of Rose Geranium

Serves 6

You can make this simple frozen dessert with or without the infusion. Scented geraniums, including rose geraniums, are prized for the subtle flavor of their leaves rather than for their flowers. The leaves of lemon verbena, favored primarily for making a tea that benefits digestion, have a clean, bright taste. This refreshing dessert is a lovely finish to a rich meal, delivering a light, fragrant taste and cleansing the palate at the same time.

4 TO 5 PINTS STRAWBERRIES, HULLED

5 LARGE FRESH ROSE GERANIUM LEAVES OR 1 SMALL FRESH LEMON VERBENA SPRIG (OPTIONAL)

1/2 CUP SUGAR

1 CUP SPRING WATER

2 TABLESPOONS FRESH LEMON JUICE

Place the strawberries in a food processor or blender and purée until smooth. Strain the pulp through a fine-mesh sieve into a large bowl, pressing on the solids with the back of a spoon. Cover the strained pulp and refrigerate.

In a small, heavy pot, combine the rose geranium leaves or lemon verbena (if using), sugar, and water over medium heat. Bring to a simmer, stirring until the sugar dissolves. Remove from the heat, let cool to room temperature, and, if you have used the leaves, remove and discard them.

Add the cooled sugar syrup and lemon juice to the puréed berries and stir well. Cover and chill well.

Pour the strawberry mixture into an ice cream maker and freeze according to the manufacturer's instructions. Serve at once, or store for up to 2 days in a sealed container in the freezer. Remove from the freezer about 10 minutes before serving to soften slightly.

Quick Strawberry Jam

Makes about 5 cups

The success of this jam is in the deliciousness of the strawberries. Tim Savinar, market shopper and husband of food writer Patricia Unterman, makes this freezer jam annually, as soon as strawberries are plentiful at the market. Follow the recipe exactly and you will have the best jam ever. He uses Sure-Jell brand powdered pectin, but other brands can be used. The jam improves after about three weeks in the freezer.

2 PINTS STRAWBERRIES, HULLED

4 CUPS SUGAR

Have ready 2 sterilized pint jars and 1 sterilized half-pint jar (or whatever combination you have that will accommodate about 5 cups jam).

1 BOX SURE-JELL POWDERED
PECTIN

3/4 CUP WATER

Place the strawberries in a large heat-proof bowl and crush them with a potato masher or the bottom of a clean wine bottle. Stir in the sugar, mixing well. Allow to stand for 10 minutes, stirring occasionally.

In a small saucepan, combine the pectin and water over high heat and bring to a boil, stirring constantly for 1 minute until the pectin is smoothly incorporated. It may start out being lumpy. Remove from the heat.

Pour the pectin mixture into the strawberry mixture and stir vigorously until the sugar is completely dissolved and no longer grainy. This will take at least 3 minutes.

Pour the mixture into the jars, leaving about 1/2 inch headspace to allow for expansion during freezing. Cover with tight-fitting lids and let stand at room temperature for 24 hours until set, and then place in the freezer.

The jam will keep for a few months. Thaw overnight in the refrigerator when you are ready to use it.

Strawberries with Aged Balsamic on Greek Yogurt   Serves 4

Here is a great idea on how to deal with dead-ripe strawberries. Fragrant, syrupy aged balsamic vinegar, at least three years old, helps to intensify the flavor of the strawberries, while yogurt imported from Greece is thicker, richer, and more luscious than most commercial yogurts, making it a perfect partner for the equally luscious berries. In its absence, a locally made Greek-style yogurt or first-rate ice cream can be substituted.

2 PINTS STRAWBERRIES,
HULLED AND SLICED
LENGTHWISE

SPLASH OF AGED BALSAMIC
VINEGAR

2 TABLESPOONS PACKED DARK
BROWN SUGAR

1 PINT IMPORTED GREEK
PLAIN YOGURT OR HIGH-
QUALITY VANILLA ICE CREAM

In a bowl, combine the strawberries, vinegar, and sugar. Toss briefly to coat evenly and let sit for a few minutes to draw out some of the juices.

Place a big scoop of yogurt or ice cream into 4 individual bowls. Top with the strawberry mixture and serve.

SUMMER

(opposite) Tomatoes

Beets

Beta vulgaris

Beets can be traced back to a wild seashore plant, the sea beet, that grows throughout southern Europe and North Africa and, along with their close relatives, spinach and Swiss chard, have been consumed since prehistoric times. They are a signature deep red, which comes from a combination of a purple pigment, betacyanin, and a yellow pigment, betaxanthin, and stain everything they touch.

Today, common red beets are facing fierce competition from other colorfully vivid varieties, such as the candy-striped Chioggia (bright pink and white), golden beets, and even white beets. While high in carbohydrates due to their concentration of natural sugars, all beets are low in calories.

Farm manager Liz Milazzo explains that Green Gulch Farm, which is operated by the San Francisco Zen Center and is located north of San Francisco, on the coast near Muir Beach, provides the ideal environment—ample moisture and cool weather—for raising some of the best beets at the farmers' market. The soil has been amended by some thirty-odd years of dedicated organic composting, and, Milazzo explains, "since we do not crowd the beets, they have a chance to grow into the best beetlike shapes with vibrant green tops."

Beets flourish when they are planted from seed and are allowed to grow quickly, with harvest set after just fifty to sixty days. The farm, tended by residents of the Buddhist center, supplies most of the food for the famed Greens vegetarian restaurant in San Francisco's Fort Mason. There, chef Annie Somerville loves to work with the farm's Chiogga and red beets, and is particularly taken with the variety dubbed Bull's Blood, for its renegade name and bright flavor. She advises always adding red beets to a dish at the last moment so they won't bleed onto the other ingredients.

Season
Summer through winter.

Choosing
If the stems of the beets are crisp, colorful, and vibrant, chances are that the beets will be fresh. And it is usually only at farmers' markets that you find beets with their greens attached, which should always be bright looking. Avoid beets with soft, shriveled skin or very large beets, which tend to have woody cores. Keep in mind that beet leaves tend to wilt before the beets do.

Storing
Cut the greens off and store separately. They will last in the refrigerator, in a perforated bag, for a couple of days. The beets will keep, also in a perforated bag in the vegetable bin, for

about a week; their sugars will turn to starch if kept too long. Remove any brown or tender spots with a sharp knife before storing, but do not rinse until ready to prepare.

Preparing

The best method for urging the earthiness out of beets is to wrap them individually in foil, then roast them in a hot oven until tender. Boiling is fine (an old-fashioned approach), but beets tend to lose nutrients and flavor along the way. If you decide to boil beets, leave a bit of the stem intact and don't cut into the skin, or the beets will bleed into the water. Rinse the beets well in both cases, but do not peel. After cooking, peel away the skins with your fingers or a small, sharp knife. Remove the tough stems from beet greens; both the leaves and tender stems are edible.

Beets with Blue Cheese and Candied Walnuts
Serves 6

Here is a delightful Ferry Plaza Farmers' Market salad. The beets come from Green Gulch Farm, the candied walnuts are from Sally Oliver's stand (page 166), the cheese is Point Reyes Blue (page 285), the apple balsamic vinegar is made by The Apple Farm (page 170), and the Ascolano extra-virgin olive oil is pressed by the Sciabica family (page 290).

6 TO 8 MEDIUM-SIZED BEETS, GREEN TOPS REMOVED

1 SHALLOT, MINCED

2 TABLESPOONS APPLE CIDER BALSAMIC OR RED WINE VINEGAR

SALT AND FRESHLY GROUND BLACK PEPPER

1/3 CUP EXTRA-VIRGIN OLIVE OIL, PREFERABLY PRESSED FROM ASCOLANO OLIVES

1/4 CUP CRUMBLED BLUE CHEESE

1/4 CUP CANDIED WALNUTS, ROUGHLY CHOPPED (RECIPE FOLLOWS)

A FEW HANDFULS OF TORN ARUGULA LEAVES

Preheat the oven to 400°F.

Wrap the beets individually in aluminum foil, twisting the ends, and place them on a baking sheet. Bake until a fork easily pierces the flesh, about an hour, depending on their size. (You'll need to unwrap a beet to test for doneness.)

Meanwhile, in a small bowl, combine the shallot, vinegar, and a little salt and pepper. Let stand for at least 5 minutes or up to a few hours, then whisk in the olive oil to make a vinaigrette.

When the beets are ready, remove them from the oven and unwrap them. When they are cool enough to handle, peel off the skin with your fingers or a small, sharp knife. Slice the beets into wedges or rounds 1/3 inch thick and place them in a serving bowl. Add the vinaigrette and toss to coat evenly.

Sprinkle on the cheese and walnuts and scatter the arugula leaves over the top, then serve.

continued

Candied Walnuts

Makes about 1 pound

Leo Wong, a San Francisco graphic designer, helps Sally Oliver at her farmers' market stand, which is outfitted at the rear with a big banner that reads www.experienceanut.com. Here is his recipe for the nuts sold at the stand.

1/2 CUP FIRMLY PACKED BROWN SUGAR

1/2 CUP WATER

1 POUND WALNUT HALVES

2 TABLESPOONS UNSALTED BUTTER

PINCH OF SALT

Preheat the oven to 250°F. In a large, heavy skillet, combine the sugar and water over medium-high heat and cook, stirring continuously with a wooden spoon, until the sugar dissolves and the syrupy mixture comes to a boil. Add the walnuts, butter, and salt and turn the walnuts continuously with the spoon until the syrup thickens. When almost no liquid remains and the walnuts are "goopy" and well coated, spread them out on a rimmed baking sheet in a single layer. Place in the oven and toast for 15 to 20 minutes. To test for doneness, remove 1 walnut, cool it briefly in the freezer, and then taste it. If it's good and crunchy, remove the pan from the oven and let the walnuts cool completely on the pan on a wire rack. Store in a jar with a tight-fitting lid or in a zippered bag for up to 2 weeks.

Beets

Beta vulgaris

Braised Beet Greens

Serves 2

Don't throw away the bonus of buying beets at the farmers' market: beet greens. They make a good side dish or can be swirled into pasta with a little olive oil and grated cheese. They are also great stirred into a bowl of soupy white cannellini beans and then drizzled with a first-rate extra-virgin olive oil. For an extra layer of flavor, add 2 olive oil–packed anchovy fillets after you have cooked the onion and garlic and heat for a minute or two so they melt into the oil.

TOPS FROM 1 OR 2 BUNCHES BEETS

3 TABLESPOONS EXTRA-VIRGIN OLIVE OIL, PLUS EXTRA FOR DRIZZLING

1 SMALL YELLOW ONION, FINELY CHOPPED

1 CLOVE GARLIC, FINELY CHOPPED

SALT AND FRESHLY GROUND BLACK PEPPER

Remove the tough parts of the stems, and then cut the leaves and tender stems into 2-inch pieces.

In a large skillet, heat the 3 tablespoons olive oil over medium heat. Add the onion and garlic and cook, stirring, for just a minute or two. Add the stems and a splash of water, cover, reduce the heat to low, and cook slowly for about 10 minutes. Uncover, add the leaves, and continue to cook until the stems and leaves are tender, 15 to 20 minutes longer. If the pan becomes dry while the greens are cooking, add a few more splashes of water.

Season the greens with salt and pepper. Transfer to a serving dish and drizzle a little olive oil over the top. Serve warm.

Red (left) and Golden (right) Beets

Blackberries

Rubus fruticosus

In San Francisco, blackberries grow wild, their thorny vines loaded with pretty flowers and dark fruits sprouting up in vacant lots and in wooded patches. At the farmers' market, however, it is a trio of blackberry hybrids, rather than blackberries themselves, that are most commonly sold.

The deep red to purple boysenberry, a cross between a blackberry and a loganberry or a raspberry, is slightly wild tasting. Large and sweet, the berries freeze well and are good for baking and for eating out of hand. Dark red loganberries, a blackberry and raspberry mix named after a late-nineteenth-century Santa Cruz judge who discovered them growing wild in his garden, resemble elongated raspberries. They are best suited for jams and sorbets. Tart-sweet olallieberries, in contrast, are a cross between a loganberry and a youngberry, both of which have the blackberry in their family trees. They are excellent candidates for jams, syrups, and baked goods.

The best blackberries ripen on the vine, providing a balance of sweetness and tartness. They are uniformly high in vitamin C, fiber, and antioxidants, delivering good health along with good flavor.

Season
June through September.

Choosing
Look for plump, deep-colored berries that are neither oozing juice nor show signs of bruising. If you are thinking about making jam, syrup, or a frozen dessert, overripe berries with no evident mold are fine.

Storing
Check through the berries and discard any that are overripe or underripe, but do not rinse. Spread the berries out on a baking sheet or a pretty plate lined with paper towels and keep on the countertop if using within a day. Otherwise, cover with a paper towel and store in the refrigerator, but use as quickly as possible.

Preparing
Rinse gently with cool water, but never soak them in water for any length of time, or they will become soft and mushy.

Blackberries

Blackberry and Nectarine Crisp   Serves 6

Here, the natural sweetness of the nectarines and the inherent acidity of the berries create a pleasant balance of flavors. The fruits' tenderness is a good counterpoint to the crunch of the crisp topping. The recipe was inspired by a crisp served at Foreign Cinema, a popular restaurant in San Francisco's Mission District. The topping is so good that we suggest you double the recipe for it, slip the extra batch into a zippered plastic bag, label and date it, and then freeze it. Then, when you bring home summer fruit, you are just a few tosses away from an easy, delicious summer dessert. Any of the blackberry hybrids will work with the nectarines.

FOR THE TOPPING

3/4 CUP UNBLEACHED ALL-PURPOSE FLOUR

1/3 CUP PACKED DARK BROWN SUGAR

1 TABLESPOON GRANULATED SUGAR

PINCH OF SALT

PINCH OF GROUND CINNAMON

1/2 CUP CHOPPED TOASTED NUTS SUCH AS ALMONDS, PECANS, OR WALNUTS

6 TABLESPOONS CHILLED UNSALTED BUTTER, CUT INTO 1-INCH PIECES

FOR THE FILLING

1 PINT BLACKBERRIES

4 OR 5 NECTARINES, DEPENDING ON SIZE, PITTED AND SLICED

2 TABLESPOONS UNBLEACHED ALL-PURPOSE FLOUR

3 TABLESPOONS PACKED DARK BROWN SUGAR

FEW DROPS AGED BALSAMIC VINEGAR OR SQUEEZE OF FRESH LEMON JUICE

VANILLA ICE CREAM OR CRÈME FRAÎCHE FOR SERVING

Preheat the oven to 375°F.

To make the topping, in a bowl, stir together the flour, brown and granulated sugars, salt, cinnamon, and nuts. Add the butter to the flour mixture and, using your fingers, work in the butter until a crumbly mixture forms. Alternatively, combine the dry ingredients in a food processor, process briefly to mix, add the butter, and pulse until a crumbly mixture forms.

To make the filling, in a large bowl, combine the berries, nectarines, flour, brown sugar, and vinegar or lemon juice and toss to coat evenly. Transfer the mixture to a gratin dish or earthenware baking dish just large enough to hold the fruit in a double layer. Sprinkle evenly with the topping.

Place the baking dish on a rimmed baking sheet. Bake the crisp, rotating the dish 180 degrees once or twice during baking to ensure even cooking, until the topping is golden brown and the fruit is bubbling, 45 minutes to 1 hour.

Remove the crisp from the oven and serve hot, or let cool on a wire rack and serve warm or at room temperature. Serve with ice cream or crème fraîche.

Corn

Zea mays

From April to October, Glenn Stonebarger eats corn every morning. Sunrise finds him out in his fields walking between the cornstalks. To tell how the corn is progressing, he breaks off an ear, pulls back the husk, and takes a bite or two. It's part of quality control at G & S Farms in Brentwood, fifty miles east of San Francisco. He wants his harvest to have a sweet "corn" taste and skins so tender that they melt in your mouth.

Stonebarger has been farming since 1974. In fact, his father was the first farmer to grow corn commercially in the area. G & S plants six hundred of its seven hundred acres in corn every year, harvesting twelve million ears from June through October. Stonebarger credits the area's unique microclimate, with its warm days, cool nights, and exceptional soil, for what he calls "the best corn around."

Originally from Central America, corn, like sorghum and millet, belongs to the grass family. It has the largest seed heads (cobs) of all the grasses, and they mature relatively quickly (seventy-four days). Every cob always has an even number of rows (eight to thirty-two) and anywhere from six hundred to twelve hundred kernels. Corn itself has changed a lot. It has a longer shelf life and is sweeter and more tender—no more corn stuck in your teeth when you take a bite.

Farming has its challenges—weather, market prices, and rising land values, with housing developments pushing at the fields' edges—but Stonebarger is committed. "I love the springtime when the corn is just coming up from the ground and the days start to warm up—it feels great." He pauses, then says, "I just love to see corn grow."

Season

June through October, with the peak season June and July.

Choosing

Ideally, corn has been picked the same morning you buy it, and at the market it should be kept cool in the shade or on ice, as warmth converts the sugars to starch. If you know you're off to buy corn, throw a cooler in your car with a few ice packs for the ride home.

One of the best ways to judge whether an ear of corn is fresh is to look at the stem. If the stem is moist and pale green, the corn has just been picked. After 24 hours, the stems turn dry and chalky and eventually become woody and brown. The husks should be tightly closed, bright green, look full and fat, and have lots of dry golden brown corn silk coming out of the top. The ear should feel plump through the husk. If the farm stand permits, pull back enough of the husk to expose the kernels. They should be small, plump, and in evenly spaced rows from stem to tip. Milky juice should spurt out of a kernel when "popped" with

White corn

your fingernail. Stonebarger says that today there is really no difference, other than color, between his yellow, white, and bicolor corn.

5 LARGE EARS YIELD ABOUT 2 CUPS KERNELS

Storing

Refrigerate corn still in the husk in plastic bags in the coldest part of the refrigerator. The husks will keep it moist. Keep it for no more than a day—or two if you must. If the ears are already fully or partially husked, refrigerate them in a perforated plastic bag. New corn varieties are bred to retain their natural sugars, so they stay sweeter and keep longer. Ask the vendors what type of corn they are selling.

Preparing

Cook corn as soon as you can after it is picked. Unless you are grilling or roasting it in its husk, shuck corn by pulling off the husk and as much of the silk as comes with it. Snap off the stems. Use a dry vegetable brush to remove any strands of silk caught between the rows.

To cut whole kernels from the cob, hold an ear vertically, with the stem end resting in a bowl to catch the kernels. Run a sharp knife down the length of the cob to slice off the kernels, rotate the ear and repeat until all the kernels are removed. For cream-style corn, slit each row of kernels with a sharp knife, then run the back of the knife down the length of the cob to squeeze out the pulp and juice, leaving the skins of the kernels on the cob.

Boiling: There are opinions on the best way to boil corn on the cob, but two basic rules apply in all cases. First, don't add salt to the cooking water, as it toughens the kernels. Second, cook the corn until just tender—a matter of minutes. Drop shucked corn into a large pot of boiling water over high heat and cook until tender but still a little crisp, 4 to 7 minutes.

Roasting: To roast corn in the husk, pull back the husks, remove the silk, and then pull the husks up around the ears. Dampen the corn with cold water, then bury the ears in the hot coals of a grill fire for 10 to 15 minutes, or place them on the grill rack and cook, turning occasionally, for 15 to 20 minutes. To roast corn in an oven, place the ears in a preheated 375°F oven for 20 to 30 minutes.

Glen Stonebarger doesn't bother removing the silk when he roasts corn directly in hot coals. He just pulls the silk off with the husks. He likes the flavor of roasted corn so much he says it doesn't even need butter.

Corn Cooked in Milk

Makes 12 ears

Evan Jones found this old Mississippi recipe for cooking corn and shared it in *American Food*, his culinary history. The sweeter, more tender varieties now available have reduced the cooking time once necessary.

2 QUARTS WHOLE MILK

2 QUARTS WATER

1 CUP (1/2 POUND) UNSALTED BUTTER

12 EARS CORN, SHUCKED

In a large pot, combine the milk, water, and butter and bring to a boil over high heat. Add the corn and boil just until tender, 8 to 10 minutes, depending on how fresh the corn is.

Remove the pot from the heat. The corn can stay in the pot for up to an hour before serving and still taste freshly cooked.

Niloufer's Chile Butter for Grilled Corn

Makes about 1/2 cup

Food scholar and cookbook author Niloufer Ichaporia King slathers this delicious chile butter on grilled corn.

2 OR 3 DRIED RED CHILES, INCLUDING 1 CHIPOTLE CHILE

1 TEASPOON CUMIN SEEDS, CRUSHED

2 CLOVES GARLIC, CHOPPED

1/2 CUP (1/4 POUND) BUTTER, AT ROOM TEMPERATURE

Put the chiles in a small pot, add water to cover, and bring to a boil over high heat. Reduce the heat to medium-low and simmer for 5 minutes. Remove from the heat and set aside until the chiles are very soft, about 10 minutes. Drain and remove and discard the stems.

In a mortar, combine the chiles, cumin, and garlic and mash with a pestle until a smooth paste forms. In a small bowl, whisk the butter until light and fluffy. Stir in the chile paste with a wooden spoon until evenly distributed. If not using right away, or cover and refrigerate until needed. Bring to room temperature before serving.

Cucumbers

Cucumis spp.

Davis farmer Nick Atallah escaped war in his homeland, Lebanon, in 1976 and ended up at the University of California at Davis, where he earned a master's degree and a PhD in water-resources engineering. After putting those degrees to work in Saudi Arabia, "turning deserts into Gardens of Eden," Atallah explains, "I returned to the United States to educate my two children and retire." But the energetic Atallah didn't take well to retirement and instead, in 1987, set up ten greenhouses in Madison, near Davis, putting to use a technique he had learned in the Middle East. On his farm, Madison Growers, he raises delectable, smooth, thin-skinned, seedless, "burpless" Mediterranean cucumbers (*Cucumis sativus*) that never exceed five inches in length and one inch in diameter.

"All over the eastern Mediterranean, these same sweet Beit Alpha cucumbers are named after the country where they are cultivated—Persian, Turkish, Greek," explains Atallah. Ever the diplomat, Atallah has decided to call them simply Mediterranean cucumbers.

No matter what name his cucumbers are called by others, Nick Atallah has figured out a way to grow some forty thousand pounds of them every year from March through Thanksgiving. "They need lots of daylight to flourish and do not do well when the days are short," he says. In the greenhouses at Madison Growers, cucumbers are planted in plastic bags in a mix of ground pine bark, ground volcanic sand (for a balanced pH), and fine minerals such as vermiculite (for permeability). He uses no pesticides, controlling pests with beneficial insects instead. Shoppers at the farmers' market wait patiently all winter for the return of Atallah's cucumbers, having grown intolerant of bitter, seedy conventional versions that are waxed to maintain moisture and weight at most mainstream markets.

Atallah is following in the footsteps of a longstanding tradition. Thought to be native to southern India, cucumbers are one of the oldest cultivated vegetables. They were brought to the West by Columbus in the late fifteenth century, and by the time the Pilgrims arrived, they were being grown by the Iroquois.

The Mediterranean cucumbers that Atallah grows are all-purpose—good for salads, sandwiches, soups, pickles, and any other way you normally prepare cucumbers. Shoppers will also encounter gherkins (*C. anguria*), sometimes called pickling cucumbers, which are typically short and small, perfect for fitting whole into jars with various spices that usually include dill. Also popular are lemon cucumbers (*C. sativus*), which are small, round, and yellow—just like a lemon. They tend to be a bit sweeter and milder than other varieties and can be substituted in most recipes.

Season

March through November, with the peak from late summer through early fall.

Choosing

Crisp, mild-flavored cucumbers are 96 percent water and must be eaten soon after purchase, before they lose moisture. Choose small cucumbers that feel firm, are a vivid green, and have thin, smooth skin. Lemon cucumbers should be the size of a baseball, have light yellow skin, and white flesh. Generally, the smaller the cucumber, the smaller the seed.

Storing

Since cucumbers are filled with water, they should not be given a chance to dry out. Store them in a plastic bag in the vegetable bin of the refrigerator for no more than a few days.

Preparing

Atallah's Mediterranean cucumbers typically need no peeling or seeding. Do not slice cucumbers until just before serving. The slices release too much water if allowed to sit. If you are using a relatively large slicing cucumber from a conventional source, trim the ends, peel the cucumber, and then check the seeds visible from the ends. If they appear big and tough, slice the cucumber in half lengthwise, scoop out the seeds with a sharp teaspoon, and then slice by hand or on a mandoline. Sliced cucumbers taste great with just a splash of rice wine vinegar and a little salt and pepper.

Bread-and-Butter Pickles

Makes 6 pints

Dorothy Kalins, former editor in chief and one of the founders of *Saveur* magazine, makes these delicious pickles every summer. They are the best. Atallah's Mediterranean cucumbers are ideal for this use. Serve with meats, burgers, or by themselves.

4 POUNDS SMALL, GREEN
CUCUMBERS, EACH 4 TO
6 INCHES LONG, CUT INTO
1/4-INCH-THICK SLICES
(ABOUT 12 CUPS)

3 SMALL WHITE ONIONS,
THINLY SLICED

3/4 CUP KOSHER SALT

3 CUPS SUGAR

1 TABLESPOON GROUND
TURMERIC

2 TABLESPOONS YELLOW
MUSTARD SEEDS

4 CUPS CIDER VINEGAR

In a large, wide enameled cast-iron or other nonreactive pot, layer 4 cups of the cucumber slices with one-third of the onion slices. Sprinkle 1/4 cup of the salt over the mixture. Repeat the layering twice until all the cucumbers, onions, and salt are used up. Place a plate on top of the mixture, and place a heavy weight, such as a brick or a large can of tomatoes, on the plate. Set aside overnight to macerate.

Have ready 6 sterilized pint jars (or whatever combination of jars you have that will accommodate about 12 cups of pickles). Transfer the contents of the pot to a colander to drain off the liquid. Add the sugar, turmeric, mustard seeds, and vinegar to the pot, place over medium heat, and bring to a simmer, stirring to dissolve the sugar, about 3 minutes. Add the drained cucumbers to the sugar-vinegar mixture and cook uncovered, stirring occasionally, until the cucumbers look and taste like pickles, about 20 minutes.

Using a slotted spoon, transfer the pickles to the sterilized jars. Ladle the hot liquid over them, immersing them fully. Allow the pickles and their liquid to cool before screwing on the lids. Store in the refrigerator for up to 2 months to be safe, but they will probably keep longer.

Cool Cucumber Salad with Capers, Anchovies, and Marjoram — Serves 6

Here's a cooling salad for a hot summer's day, inspired by one served at Berkeley's Chez Panisse restaurant. You can use long, slender slicing cucumbers, called English cucumbers, or smaller Mediterranean cucumbers.

1 CLOVE GARLIC, PEELED
BUT WHOLE

GENEROUS PINCH OF SEA SALT

3 SALT-PACKED ANCHOVIES,
FILLETED AND RINSED, OR 6
OLIVE OIL–PACKED ANCHOVY
FILLETS

2 TABLESPOONS CAPERS,
PREFERABLY SALT PACKED,
RINSED

2 TABLESPOONS FRESH
LEMON JUICE OR RED WINE
VINEGAR

FRESHLY GROUND BLACK
PEPPER

1/2 CUP EXTRA-VIRGIN
OLIVE OIL

2 LONG, SLENDER CUCUM-
BERS OR 4 SMALLER
CUCUMBERS (SEE NOTE)

2 TABLESPOONS FRESH
MARJORAM OR OREGANO
LEAVES, CHOPPED

In a mortar, combine the garlic and salt and pound with the pestle until a paste forms. Then add the anchovies and pound the mixture to combine. Add the capers and pound again until the anchovies and capers are well integrated but still chunky. Add the lemon juice or vinegar and pepper to taste and pound and mix with the pestle until incorporated. Finally, add the olive oil and mix well. Allow the flavors to mingle as you cut the cucumbers.

Cut the cucumbers on the diagonal into thin slices by hand or with a mandoline and place in a bowl. Add the dressing and toss to coat evenly. Taste and adjust the seasoning.

Pour the cucumber mixture onto a white serving platter. Scatter the marjoram or oregano over the top, taste for seasoning, and serve.

Note: If you can find only waxed cucumbers, large or small, peel them, halve lengthwise, and scoop out the seeds before slicing.

Choosing cucumbers
at the Market

Eggplants

Solanum spp.

There is something mysterious and a little dangerous about the eggplant. In fact, over the centuries, eating it has been associated with madness, leprosy, cancer, and even bad breath. Its Italian name is *melanzana*, from the Latin *mala insana*, or "apple of madness." The eggplant is related to the tomato, potato, and some sweet and hot peppers and all belong to the controversial nightshade family. Even today, practitioners of holistic medicine advise arthritis sufferers to avoid the nightshades, believing that the alkaloids they contain may adversely affect joint function. To add to the intrigue, this "vegetable" is a fruit, and to put a fine point on it, it is actually a berry.

In sixteenth-century England, the eggplant was grown as an ornamental plant that bore white egg-shaped fruits, hence the name. Today, in the United States, beautiful purple globe-shaped eggplants are most familiar, but they actually come in a variety of colors—deep purple, pale lavender, jade green, orange, yellow-white—sizes, and shapes.

Slice open an eggplant and you will expose a flavorless, greenish white flesh. But cooking transforms this bland interior, turning it supple, meaty, rich, unctuous, and silky. Eggplants figure prominently in the cooking of South Asia, southern Italy, and in the Middle East, where cooks claim to know a thousand ways to prepare them.

Season

Eggplants are at their peak from July through October.

Choosing

Select eggplants that are firm and heavy for their size. The stems and caps should be bright green. The skin of a just-picked eggplant will be firm and shiny and its flesh will spring back when squeezed. Eggplants should be free of discoloration, scars, and bruises, all possible signs that the flesh is damaged and maybe decayed. When selecting globe eggplants, choose young, small to medium specimens no larger than 6 inches in diameter. Overlarge eggplants can be tough, spongy, full of seeds, and bitter.

Long, lavender Chinese eggplants are thin skinned, sweet, and mild and have few seeds. Gently curving, dark purple Japanese eggplants have tender flesh with few seeds. The common European globe eggplant, with its thicker skin and creamy flesh, is at its best early in the season. When it is young, there is less chance of it having too many seeds and an unpleasant bitter flavor. Green, white, and multicolored eggplants, some no larger than a grape, are prized in Asia for their mildly bitter flavor and crunchy texture.

A 1-POUND EGGPLANT YIELDS ABOUT 3 CUPS DICED FLESH

Eggplants

Solanum spp.

Slip eggplants into a plastic bag with a wet paper towel to provide humidity and store in a cool place, neither too hot nor too cold (50°F is ideal). Don't put them in the refrigerator. It's too cold and their flesh can quickly turn spongy and bitter. Handle carefully, as bruised or punctured flesh will spoil quickly. Try to use eggplants within 3 days of purchase.

Preparing

Cut off the stem and cap and then the blossom end with a stainless-steel knife. Carbon steel alone will make the flesh turn black. After cutting an eggplant into pieces of whatever size and shape you want, put the pieces in a colander, generously sprinkle with salt, and set aside to drain for at least 30 minutes or up to 1 hour. Topping the eggplant pieces with a plate and a heavy can or other weight will speed the process. Salting rids the eggplant of excess water and condenses the flesh so that it will absorb less oil when you cook it. You can also freeze the eggplant pieces to remove water. Arrange the pieces on a plate and put the plate in the freezer for about 4 hours. When the pieces thaw, you can press out the water with your hand.

An eggplant may be cooked and eaten with or without its skin. The skin of smaller, younger eggplants is typically more tender, so there is no need to peel it. Use a swivel-bladed vegetable peeler to remove the tough skin of older, larger eggplants.

Eggplants can be grilled, fried, sautéed, baked, roasted, or steamed. If baking whole, pierce the eggplant several times with a fork to make small holes for the steam to escape, then place in a preheated 350°F oven for 15 to 25 minutes, depending on size. You can test for its readiness by gently inserting a knife or fork to see if it passes through easily. Halve the baked eggplant and scoop out the flesh.

Assorted eggplants

Eggplants

Caponata

Serves 6

Authentic Sicilian *caponata,* like this one from *Saveur Cooks Authentic Italian,* is a vibrant balance of sweet and sour flavors that reflect its Italian-Arabic heritage.

4 SMALL GLOBE-SHAPED EGG-
PLANTS, TRIMMED AND CUT
INTO 1-INCH CUBES

ABOUT 3 TABLESPOONS
COARSE SALT

6 CELERY STALKS, TRIMMED
AND CUT INTO 1-INCH PIECES

FOR THE TOMATO SAUCE

3 TABLESPOONS EXTRA-VIRGIN
OLIVE OIL

2 CLOVES GARLIC MINCED

8 RIPE PLUM TOMATOES,
PREFERABLY SAN MARZANO,
PEELED AND CHOPPED WITH
JUICE RESERVED

SALT AND FRESHLY GROUND
BLACK PEPPER

3 FRESH BASIL LEAVES,
MINCED

1 1/2 CUPS EXTRA-VIRGIN
OLIVE OIL

1 YELLOW ONION, CHOPPED

1 CUP PITTED GREEN OLIVES

1/2 CUP SALT-PACKED CAPERS,
RINSED AND DRAINED

1/2 CUP WHITE WINE VINEGAR

2 TABLESPOONS SUGAR

Put the eggplant cubes in a colander, sprinkle with the coarse salt, and toss to coat well. Place a plate on the eggplant and top the plate with a heavy can. Let drain for 1 hour.

Meanwhile, bring a saucepan filled with water to a boil, add the celery, and blanch for 1 minute. Drain and set aside to cool.

To make the tomato sauce, in an enameled cast-iron or other non-reactive saucepan, heat the olive oil over medium heat. Add the garlic and cook, stirring frequently, until golden, about 3 minutes. Add the tomatoes and their juice and season with salt and pepper. Raise the heat to high, bring the sauce to a boil, and cook to reduce the liquid, about 5 minutes. Reduce the heat to medium-low and simmer, stirring occasionally, until the sauce thickens, about 30 minutes. Add the basil during the last 5 minutes of cooking. Remove from the heat. You should have about 2 cups sauce.

Quickly rinse the eggplant cubes in cold water and pat dry with paper towels.

In a large, heavy skillet, heat 1 cup of the olive oil over high heat until hot but not smoking. Fry the eggplant, in batches, until golden brown on all sides, about 5 minutes per batch. Using a slotted spoon, transfer the eggplant to paper towels to drain.

Pour off and discard the oil remaining in the skillet and add the remaining 1/2 cup oil. Place over medium heat, add the onion, and sauté, stirring with a wooden spoon, until it begins to brown, about 5 minutes. Add the blanched celery and cook for 1 minute longer. Add the tomato sauce, olives, capers, vinegar, and sugar and simmer for 5 minutes to blend the flavors. Add the eggplant, reduce the heat to medium-low, and cook for 10 minutes longer.

Remove from the heat and let cool. Transfer to a container with a tight-fitting lid and refrigerate for 24 hours before serving to mellow the flavors. It will keep for up to 1 week. Bring to room temperature before serving.

Pickled Eggplants with Walnut Sauce

Makes 6 eggplants

This Charles Perry recipe appeared in one of the first issues of *Saveur* magazine. It is a perfect first course or makes a good addition to an assortment of antipasti.

6 SMALL JAPANESE
EGGPLANTS

2 TEASPOONS SALT

2 TABLESPOONS GROUND
WALNUTS

1/2 TEASPOON CAYENNE
PEPPER

EXTRA-VIRGIN OLIVE OIL AS
NEEDED

Bring a large pot of water to a gentle boil. Add the eggplants and poach until slightly soft, 5 to 10 minutes. Drain and slit each eggplant lengthwise from the blossom end to the stem end, stopping just short of the stem end so that the eggplant splays into 4 "fingers" attached to the stem end.

In a mortar, combine the salt, walnuts, and cayenne and grind to a paste with a pestle. Rub the paste evenly on the cut sides of the eggplant flesh. Reassemble the eggplants and place, stem end up, in a sterilized tall jar with a lid. Cover and set aside at room temperature for 12 hours.

Uncover and pour off any liquid at the bottom of the jar. Pour olive oil into the jar to cover the eggplants completely. Place a ball of aluminum foil on top of them to keep them submerged. Cover the jar and store in the refrigerator for up to 2 weeks.

Small globe eggplant

Figs

Ficus carica

High in fiber, iron, and calcium, figs are not conventional fruits, but rather inverted flowers with a thousand seeds. In prehistoric times, they made their way from western Asia to the Mediterranean. Father Junipero Serra planted California's first figs at the mission in San Diego in 1769, but it wasn't until 1900 that they became a commercial crop unique to California, which produces 100 percent of the U.S. crop (and is the third largest world producer, behind Turkey and Greece and just ahead of Spain and Portugal). Because ripe figs do not travel well, some thirty million pounds of the California harvest are turned into dried figs every year.

Rick and Kristie Knoll, who operate Tairwa Knoll Farm in Brentwood, began growing figs nearly a quarter century ago. They employ every sort of traditional organic farming method, from harvesting by hand to planting cover crops to introducing beneficial birds and insects, and have nearly perfected the process of producing exquisite figs. But because they are critical of the big industrial food companies that have stretched the definition of organic beyond what purist organic farmers like themselves feel is healthy and acceptable, they have eschewed the old label, and their farm is no longer certified organic. They have created in its place the term *tairwa*, phonetic for the French *terroir*, "the essence of place," to indicate a new standard for farming practices that respect both the earth and the customer. While placing their figs in some retail outlets has proven difficult because of the decision to forgo certification, top-restaurant chefs and discerning home cooks continue to scuffle over the Knolls' luxurious, oozing selection of fruits. They harvest two crops each year, one in early summer and a second smaller crop from August until November. Simply put, business has never been better.

The Knolls' fig offerings at the market regularly include four or five varieties, along with fig wood for perfuming grilled meats and fig leaves for lining cheese platters and wrapping fish for the grill.

Season

Two seasons, June through July and August through November.

Choosing

Immature figs do not ripen once they are picked, so you must always buy figs that are ready to eat. Split skins and droplets of sugar water are good indicators of ripeness, as is softness. Mission figs shrivel when ripe.

Figs

Figs

Ficus carica

Storing

Always treat figs tenderly. Store in a cool, dark spot on a plate shielded with a wire-mesh cover to allow air to circulate, and eat as soon as possible. If you have extremely ripe figs and must store them, place in a paper (not plastic) bag in the refrigerator

Preparing

For the best taste, peel figs with tough skins. Cut off the hard stems before eating or using for cooking.

Varieties

A number of different fig varieties can found at the market. The most familiar is the Black Mission, which has purple-black skin and strawberry red flesh and is wonderful eaten out of hand. Brown Turkey figs are fat, with thin, reddish brown skin and a pale pink interior. Juicy and good for baking, their sugars caramelize nicely in the heat of the oven. Adriatic figs have thin, green skin with a raspberry tinge, strawberry-colored flesh, and a high sugar content. Kadotas, in contrast, have thick, green skin and a salmon-colored interior. They are good candidates for preserving and are excellent with prosciutto.

Sunset - Simple plates for 1st course each:
Layer:
3-4 slice prosc.
2 stems arugula
basil +/or mint slivers
2 figs cut in ¼
1 Tb olive oil

Fig ¼ts + chevre on oven toasted, olive oil + garlic-rubbed pitas. Drizzle w/ honey + thyme s+p.

Roast w/ pork tenderloin (1 lb).
- Brown meat 1st in oil in cast iron (4 mins). → Add figs ¼ + thyme → 400° oven ~ 20-25 min
Reduce pan juices w/ 1 c red wine + 1 Tb honey + 1 Bf orange peel.

Crostini of Figs and Prosciutto

Serves 4

Grilling figs caramelizes their sugars and enhances their sweetness. This pairing of salty prosciutto and sweet figs makes a stunning combination. Kadotas are a good choice here, but any ripe, flavorful fig will do.

4 RIPE FIGS, STEMS REMOVED AND FRUIT CUT IN HALF LENGTHWISE

4 SLICES COUNTRY BREAD, CUT ON THE DIAGONAL 1 INCH THICK

EXTRA-VIRGIN OLIVE OIL FOR DRIZZLING

4 THIN SLICES PROSCIUTTO

FRESHLY GROUND BLACK PEPPER

HANDFUL OF ARUGULA LEAVES

Prepare a medium-hot fire in a grill, or preheat a skillet over medium-high heat.

Place the fig halves, cut side down, on the grill or in the skillet and cook until the underside begins to caramelize, just a few minutes. At the same time, grill or toast the bread on both sides and drizzle one side with a little olive oil.

Place 2 fig halves on the oil-drizzled side of each bread slice. Lay a slice of prosciutto over the figs, grind on a little pepper, scatter a few arugula leaves on top, and serve.

Fig Galette with Gorgonzola Custard

Serves 8 to 10

There is a wonderful late-summer earthiness about a flaky, buttery pastry crust enclosing a stash of ripe figs drizzled with a creamy custard of blue cheese. You can make the pastry a day or two in advance, saving you time on the day you plan to serve it.

FOR THE PASTRY

2 CUPS UNBLEACHED ALL-PURPOSE FLOUR

1 CUP (1/2 POUND) CHILLED BUTTER, CUT INTO 1/2 -INCH CUBES

1 LARGE EGG YOLK

1 TABLESPOON SUGAR

1/4 TEASPOON SALT

1/4 CUP SPARKLING WATER, WELL CHILLED

To make the pastry, combine the flour, butter, egg yolk, sugar, and salt in a bowl and rub together with your fingers until the mixture looks like coarse meal. This will take about 5 minutes. Alternatively, combine all the ingredients in a food processor and pulse just until the mixture looks like coarse meal. In both cases, the butter should not be completely mixed in but still be visible in tiny pieces. Add the cold water in small amounts, continuing to mix with your fingers or to pulse in the processor just until the dough starts to hold together. Do not overwork the dough, or you will end up with a tough crust.

Pat the dough into a ball and then flatten it into a disk with smooth edges (pat away any cracks on the periphery, or it will have cracks and gaping holes when it is rolled out). Wrap the disk in plastic wrap and refrigerate for at least 1 hour or up to 2 days before rolling it out.

continued

Figs

FOR THE FILLING

1/2 CUP HEAVY CREAM

PINCH OF SALT

2 TABLESPOONS HONEY

1/2 CUP CRUMBLED
GORGONZOLA OR OTHER BLUE
CHEESE

1 LARGE EGG YOLK

2 TO 3 POUNDS KADOTA OR
BROWN TURKEY FIGS

1 LARGE EGG WHITE,
LIGHTLY BEATEN WITH A
SPLASH OF WATER

SUGAR FOR SPRINKLING

Position a rack in the upper half of the oven and preheat to 425°F. Have ready a nonstick rimmed baking sheet or line a regular-finish baking sheet with parchment paper.

To make the filling, in a small saucepan, combine the cream, salt, and honey. Place over medium-low heat and cook, stirring constantly, until reduced to a thick, creamy consistency, about 8 minutes. Add the cheese and mix well. The mixture will be lumpy.

In a small bowl, stir the yolk with a fork until blended. Add a tablespoon or so of the hot cream mixture and mix again. Then add the egg-cream mixture to the remaining cream mixture and mix well. Set aside.

On a lightly floured work surface, roll out the dough into a round about 15 inches in diameter and 1/4 inch thick. Cut away any ragged edges and save the dough for patching. Carefully transfer the pastry round to the baking sheet, laying it out flat. Patch any holes that develop in the move with the pastry scraps.

Trim the stems from the figs and cut the fruit lengthwise into halves if small or quarters if large. Mound the figs evenly on the pastry round, leaving a 3 inch border uncovered around the edge. Fold the uncovered edge over, partially covering the fig filling. Be careful not to create any holes in the pastry, or the juices will run out during baking (if necessary, patch holes with dough scraps as you go, moistening them with water and pressing them in place). The edges of the dough will overlap in some places, creating small pleats that lend a pleasing rustic appearance. Pour the blue cheese custard evenly over the visible figs at the center of the galette. It will be slightly runny but will thicken as it bakes. Brush the pastry border with the diluted egg white and then sprinkle the border with sugar.

Bake the galette until the crust is browned and the figs are bubbling, 40 to 45 minutes. Transfer to a wire rack and let cool on the pan for at least a few minutes. Slide onto a flat serving plate and serve warm or at room temperature.

Garlic

Allium sativum

"In looking for a crop to complement my potato crop, to give the soil a rest, and to confuse the pests, I decided to plant garlic," says Wally Condon, who cultivates a variety of culinary necessities on his Lodi farm (page 124). He also appreciated the fact that garlic has high value and a good shelf life. He grows stiff-necked garlics because of their complexity and their sweet, spicy taste, and a single soft-necked type, all of them heirloom varieties.

Rocambole, one of his stiff-necked crops, yields heads with five to ten easy-to-peel cloves. Like most garlic, rocambole is at its tastiest from late spring into fall, but also has a good shelf life. Before the heads come to market in their papery stage, they send off scapes, soft, green shoots that emanate from the neck and have elflike tips. Persian Star of Samarkand, a purplish red garlic, is another of Condon's stiff-necked harvest.

Inchelium Red, which was discovered on a Native American reservation, has a good soft neck that braids easily and, to Condon's mind, has the best flavor in the soft-neck kingdom, far superior to its soft-necked Gilroy cousins.

Season

Garlic is at its flavor peak in the summer. As the season progresses, it slowly loses its fresh taste.

Choosing

Look for firm, hard, compact cloves. During the fall, garlic begins to sprout and the cloves become smaller and dry. Check heads carefully to avoid purchasing sprouted cloves.

Storing

Keep in a cool, dry spot where air circulates freely.

Preparing

The volatile oils present in garlic that are responsible for its unique flavor are released once garlic is crushed or cut, so never peel it in advance. Instead, prepare it as you go. To ease peeling, crush a clove gently with the side of a knife blade to loosen the skin. The green sprout that sometimes develops at the center of a clove is bitter, so if a sprout is visible, cut the clove in half lengthwise and pull out and discard it. When cooking garlic, you typically want to keep it from browning, which turns it bitter. If you are concerned that the garlic you have may be too pungent, taste it before adding it to a dish and adjust the amount accordingly.

Head of garlic

Aioli

Makes about 1 cup

This simple mayonnaise for raw vegetables, steamed asparagus, or grilled or poached fish or shellfish is rich and yellow. You can add some finely chopped parsley or other herbs to make it more colorful and give it a fresh flavor. It will keep in an airtight container for a few days in the refrigerator.

1 CLOVE GARLIC

PINCH OF SALT

2 TEASPOONS DIJON MUSTARD

DASH OF FRESHLY GROUND
WHITE PEPPER

1 LARGE EGG

1 CUP MILD EXTRA-VIRGIN
OLIVE OIL

2 TABLESPOONS FRESH
LEMON JUICE

2 TABLESPOONS FINELY
CHOPPED FRESH FLAT-LEAF
PARSLEY (OPTIONAL)

To make by hand, mince the garlic and place in a glass bowl with the salt, mustard, pepper, and egg. Place the bowl on a folded towel on the countertop (to keep it from sliding) and whisk vigorously until smooth. While whisking constantly, start to add the olive oil a few drops at a time until the mixture emulsifies and begins to thicken. At this point, you can begin adding the remaining oil in a thin, slow, steady stream. Continue to whisk until all the oil is incorporated. Then gradually whisk in the lemon juice until combined. Stir in the parsley, if using.

To make in a food processor, mince the garlic and place in the work bowl of the processor with the salt, mustard, and pepper. Pulse until blended, then add the egg and pulse until creamy. With the motor running, begin adding the olive oil a few drops at a time until the mixture emulsifies and begins to thicken. At this point, you can begin adding the remaining oil in a thin, slow, steady stream. Add the lemon juice and pulse to incorporate.

Add the parsley, if using, and pulse again.

Transfer to a small bowl and serve, or cover and refrigerate until serving.

Cheesy Garlic Soup

Serves 4

Here is a great last-minute soup for when garlic is irresistible or you are feeling a little under the weather. Simmering the garlic in the stock reduces any "bite" while retaining the aroma. Do not reheat the soup, as the eggs can curdle.

2 HEADS GARLIC, SEPARATED INTO CLOVES AND PEELED

4 CUPS HOMEMADE CHICKEN STOCK OR REDUCED-SODIUM CHICKEN BROTH

1 TEASPOON CHOPPED FRESH THYME OR 1/2 TEASPOON DRIED THYME

4 THIN SLICES FRENCH BREAD

EXTRA-VIRGIN OLIVE OIL FOR DRIZZLING

2 LARGE EGGS, AT ROOM TEMPERATURE

1/3 CUP GRATED PARMIGIANO-REGGIANO CHEESE

SALT AND FRESHLY GROUND BLACK PEPPER

Set aside 1 garlic clove to use for rubbing on the toasts. In a saucepan, combine the remaining garlic cloves, the chicken stock, and the thyme. Place over medium heat, bring to a simmer, and cook until the garlic can be easily pierced with a fork, 12 to 15 minutes.

Just before the soup is ready, toast the bread slices, rub them with the reserved garlic clove, and drizzle on a little olive oil. Keep warm.

Remove the soup from the heat and strain through a fine-mesh sieve, discarding the garlic and thyme. In a small bowl, whisk together the eggs and a few tablespoons of the hot soup. Then pour the egg mixture into the hot soup (off the heat) while stirring constantly. Be sure not to halt your stirring until the eggs are fully incorporated or they can curdle. Add the cheese and stir to integrate, then season to taste with salt and pepper.

Ladle the soup into warmed bowls. Serve the toasts alongside.

(right) Wally Condon of
Small Potatoes
(far right) Shallots and garlic

Herbs

In a flower-studded hat, Joseph Minocchi of White Crane Springs Ranch, near Healdsburg, presides over a stunning shady stall splashed with color. There, he is as widely known for his unusual flowers as he is for his small, pristine bundles of herbs and greens, including miner's lettuce, parsley, sage, bay, burnet, purslane, borage, watercress, and other seasonal herbs that any good cook recognizes as culinary gold. Minocchi graciously dispenses advice on herbal remedies, insisting that dark, leafy greens are a superior source of calcium.

His eighty-three-acre biodynamic ranch is distinguished by a series of double-dug beds of healthy enriched soil, cool artesian wells, and a simple composting system. "I dig deep holes, line them with cardboard or newspaper, fill them with compost, and plant," Minocchi explains. The paper lining keeps the composted soil moist while discouraging bugs. Nothing is haphazard at White Crane Springs Ranch. Rambling beds of thyme are painstakingly trimmed to keep them renewed and fit. And Minocchi insists that the irresistibility of his produce is due in large part to the well water from the aquifer connected to Mount Shasta.

Cooks who appreciate Minocchi's extraordinary herbs also respond to his beautiful blooms, and they often stop by his stand before shopping elsewhere to reserve unusual flowers and dramatic flowering branches—dahlias, David Austin Floribunda roses, peonies (from his grandmother's cuttings), drought-resistant bearded irises, bronze fennel blossoms, colorful tulips, branches of crab apple, dogwood, and long-lasting beech—for retrieving when they have finished their market rounds. "It's like having access to a hillside of flowering trees," one devotee explains.

Season
Spring through fall.

Choosing
Herbs should be scented and glowing green. The tips should be vibrant and the ends not shriveled.

Storing
The woody herbs—thyme, rosemary, and oregano—can be dried and the leaves pulled from the stems and stored in a jar. Or, the sprigs can be kept in a glass, without water, and the leaves pulled of as they dry. If you want to use the woody herbs while they are still fresh, slip them into a plastic bag and keep in the vegetable bin of the refrigerator for up to 1 week. Put more fragile herbs, such as tarragon, parsley, and cilantro, in a plastic bag in the vegetable bin of the refrigerator for up to 1 week. Stand lemon verbena in a glass of water, cover the tips with damp paper towels, and place in the refrigerator for a few days.

Herbs

None of Joseph Minocchi's organic herbs needs rinsing before use. Never rinse other fresh herbs until you plan to use them, and, in most cases, add them near the end of cooking to retain their fresh flavor. When using dried herbs, crush them between your fingers to release their flavor before adding them to a dish.

White Crane Springs Ranch herbs

Green Goddess Dressing

Makes about 1¹/₄ cups

You will not find a truer San Francisco salad dressing than this one. It was created by the chef of the Palace Hotel in the early 1920s in honor of the British actor George Arliss, who stayed at the hotel during his run in William Archer's play *The Green Goddess*. Serve it over chilled romaine or Little Gem lettuce leaves.

1 CUP MAYONNAISE, HOME-
MADE OR BEST FOODS
(HELLMANN'S)

3 SCALLIONS, WHITE PART
AND 2 INCHES OF THE GREEN,
CHOPPED

¹/₄ CUP CHOPPED FRESH
FLAT-LEAF PARSLEY

2 TABLESPOONS CHOPPED
FRESH CHIVES

3 OLIVE OIL–PACKED ANCHOVY
FILLETS, CHOPPED

8 FRESH TARRAGON LEAVES,
CHOPPED

1 TABLESPOON RED WINE
VINEGAR

FRESHLY GROUND BLACK
PEPPER

In a blender or food processor, combine the mayonnaise, scallions, parsley, chives, anchovies, tarragon, and vinegar and process until well mixed. Scoop into a bowl and season to taste with the pepper. Cover and chill well before using.

Herbs

Gremolata Potatoes

Serves 4

Here's a lively way to prepare potatoes that borrows from the traditional mixture of parsley, garlic, and lemon zest that is traditionally sprinkled on osso buco just before serving. The potatoes are attractively flecked with green and have a bright, assertive flavor.

1 1/2 POUNDS YUKON GOLD POTATOES OR OTHER WAXY POTATO, UNPEELED

3/4 CUP EXTRA-VIRGIN OLIVE OIL

1/2 CUP CHOPPED FRESH FLAT-LEAF PARSLEY

1 TEASPOON MINCED FRESH ROSEMARY

1 TABLESPOON MINCED FRESH THYME

FINELY GRATED LEMON ZEST OF 2 LEMONS, PREFERABLY MEYER

GENEROUS PINCH OF RED PEPPER FLAKES

1 LARGE CLOVE GARLIC, MINCED

SALT AND FRESHLY GROUND BLACK PEPPER

Cut each potato into small, uniform wedges. Depending on the size of the potatoes, you will get 4 to 6 wedges from each potato. In a large, heavy skillet, heat 1/4 cup of the olive oil over high heat. When it sizzles, add the potatoes and cook, shaking the pan gently as they begin to brown so they don't stick to the bottom, until they are a nice golden brown. Reduce the heat to medium-high and continue to cook, stirring occasionally, until the potatoes are tender when pierced with a fork and browned on all sides, 25 to 30 minutes.

While the potatoes are cooking, in a bowl large enough to accommodate the potatoes, whisk together the remaining 1/2 cup olive oil, the parsley, rosemary, thyme, lemon zest, pepper flakes, and garlic until well combined. Set aside.

When the potatoes are ready, remove them from the heat, add them to the herb mixture, and toss to coat the potatoes evenly. Season to taste with salt and pepper. Transfer to a warmed serving bowl or small platter and serve.

Salsa Verde

Makes about 1 cup

This vibrant salsa verde is deliciously piquant. Use it on chicken, white beans, seafood, or roasted beets. You can add other herbs if you like, such as sage, basil, or marjoram, or a combination. Don't be put off by the anchovies, even if you are not fond of them. They add a level of flavor that makes the sauce exceptional.

2 CLOVES GARLIC

PINCH OF SALT

3 OLIVE OIL–PACKED ANCHOVY FILLETS, RINSED AND CHOPPED

1/4 CUP CAPERS, PREFERABLY SALT PACKED, RINSED

3 CUPS FRESH FLAT-LEAF PARSLEY LEAVES

GRATED ZEST OF 1 LEMON

3 TABLESPOONS FRESH LEMON JUICE

1/3 TO 1/2 CUP EXTRA-VIRGIN OLIVE OIL

SALT AND FRESHLY GROUND BLACK PEPPER

In a mortar, combine the garlic and salt and crush together with the pestle. Add the anchovies and capers and pound until a paste forms. Add the parsley, in batches, pounding the leaves with each addition to incorporate. Transfer to a bowl, add the lemon zest and juice, and mix with a fork. Add 1/3 cup olive oil and mix again. Taste for balance. If it is too tart, add a little more olive oil. Season to taste with salt and pepper. Use immediately, or float a little olive oil on top to preserve the color. It can be left at room temperature for a few hours if treated this way.

Star Route Farms' herbs

Melons and Watermelons

Cucumis melo and *Citrullus lanatus*

Melons, squashes, and cucumbers are members of the Cucurbitaceae, or gourd, family and all grow on vines. It is a little hard to make sense of this big family beyond that single characteristic, however, though there are some general rules. Melons and squashes have thick flesh, with a central seed-filled cavity. Watermelons and cucumbers have seeds throughout their flesh. Squashes are used as vegetables and melons as fruits.

There are three melon categories: cantaloupe, muskmelon, and winter melon. Cantaloupes are fragrant, small, and round, with a rough surface divided into segments. The famed French Cavaillon melon is a good example. Muskmelons have a light netted pattern on the surface, usually orange flesh, and include the misnamed American "cantaloupe." Winter melons (not to be confused with winter melon squashes, a favorite of Chinese cooks) ripen slowly, taking about 120 days. They are slightly elongated and their skin is finely ribbed, like the Crenshaw. White- and green-fleshed melons have very little aroma, but are higher in sugar and have more flavor. Salmon-, orange-, and red-fleshed melons have a lot of aroma (their perfume is part of their flavor) but are not quite as sweet.

"I've been on the melon trail a long time and melons are still a mystery to me," muses Dave Fredericks of Genuine Exotic Melons (page 240), in Yolo County. "It started early. When I was a kid, I saved up $1.59 from my paper route to buy a Crenshaw. I guess I recognized these gifts of nature." Today, Fredericks has been growing melons for thirty-plus years, and everyone at his farm is proud of the care they take judging and hand choosing melons in the field. Fredericks's aim is to grow fruit that can live up to people's memories of melons they ate with their grandparents. "We love our customers at the Ferry Plaza Farmers' Market," Fredericks says. "A guy came back the other day to tell me that he had bought a watermelon from us and it was so good it made him cry."

Season

Melons and watermelons are available mid-July through October.

Choosing

Since melons have no starch reserves to convert to sugar, they won't continue to ripen once they have been harvested. They should have bright color, be regularly shaped (symmetrically round, oval, or oblong), and be free of cracks, soft spots, or dark bruises. Ripe melons should be firm (not too hard, not too soft) with a fresh, light, sweet smell. If you can hear the seeds when you shake the melon, it is overripe. Hold a watermelon to your chest and thump it with the flat of your hand; it should sound like a jug of water.

American "cantalope"

Storing

Keep melons in a cool place in your kitchen. While they won't get any sweeter, their flesh will soften and become juicier. Once ripened (or cut), refrigerate a melon (with plastic wrap pressed against the flesh if cut) in a plastic bag and use within 2 or 3 days. Ripe melons are very fragrant and the aroma of a cut melon can penetrate other foods.

An uncut watermelon can, if necessary, be stored at room temperature for up to 1 week, but in summer, as temperatures soar, the fruit should be kept in a cool place or refrigerated. It takes 8 to 12 hours to chill a whole watermelon thoroughly. Cut watermelon should be tightly wrapped in plastic wrap and refrigerated for no more than 4 days.

Preparing

With the exception of watermelon, the preparation is the same for all melons. Simply cut the melon open and remove the seeds and strings. The simplest, least messy way to eat water-melon is to halve it lengthwise and then cut it crosswise into wedges. Slide a knife between the rind and flesh to remove the rind; leave the wedges whole or cut each one into bite-sized pieces. Seed melon chunks, wedges, or balls with the tip of a knife.

Varieties

The well-known American cantaloupe has cream-colored netting over a yellowish green rind, pale orange flesh, and is extremely juicy and sweet. Crenshaws are slow-ripening, large mel-ons with big flavor. Their sweet, juicy salmon-colored flesh has a spicy aroma. The interior of the Casaba is white and sweet with very little aroma and flesh so tender you almost don't have to chew—just swallow. A little larger than a softball and slightly oval, the French Cavaillon has sweet, mildly crisp, gorgeously perfumed deep orange flesh. Honeydew lives up to its name, with sweet, pale green flesh and melt-in-your-mouth texture. The heavily per-fumed Persian melon, which looks like a big cantaloupe, has very fine netting and sweet, rich, salmon-colored flesh that is a good match for thin prosciutto slices. Sharlyn, with net-ted, greenish orange skin and white flesh, tastes like a cross between a cantaloupe and a honeydew.

Melon with Wild Strawberries and Port

Serves 4

In her classic book *Summer Cooking*, the late culinary writer Elizabeth David advised not to put melons in the refrigerator. Their scent penetrates everything, especially butter. The perfumed flesh of a melon is at full flavor at room temperature.

2 SMALL CAVAILLON MELONS, HALVED THROUGH THE STEM AND SEEDS AND STRINGS DISCARDED

1 TO 2 CUPS WILD STRAWBERRIES

1/2 CUP PORT

Scoop out the flesh from the melon halves with a melon baller, taking care to keep the rinds intact. Gently mix the strawberries, melon balls, and port together in a bowl. Fill the melon halves with the fruit and serve.

Agua de Sandia

Makes about 1 gallon

Niloufer Ichaporia King, food scholar and historian, makes this refreshing watermelon punch. Use your own taste, she advises, to make it sweeter or tarter, depending on the flavor of the watermelon.

1 YELLOW OR RED WATERMELON, 8 TO 10 POUNDS, HALVED LENGTHWISE, CUT INTO CHUNKS, AND PIECES SEEDED

3 TO 5 LIMES

1/4 TO 1/2 CUP SUGAR

6 TO 8 CUPS WATER

ICE CUBES

WHITE RUM (OPTIONAL)

In a blender or food processor, working in batches, purée the watermelon pulp. Strain the juice through a fine-mesh sieve into a 2-gallon wide-mouthed jug. Juice and then quarter 3 limes and add the lime juice and lime quarters along with 1/4 cup sugar to the watermelon juice and stir well. Add 6 cups water, stir again, and then taste and add up to 2 additional cups water and more lime juice and lime quarters and sugar to taste.

Add plenty of ice to the jug and then ladle the juice into glasses. Add a splash of rum to each glass, if you like.

Onions

Wally and Nancy Condon grow one type of onion on their three-and-a-half-acre farm, Small Potatoes, in Lodi: the Stockton Sweet Red. When Wally Condon retired from teaching about fifteen years ago, he decided to farm, he explains, "with the intent of leaving the land better than I found it." There, in soil amended with compost, leaves, and cover crops, he grows potatoes, French gray shallots, garlic, fava beans (*the* great cover crop), and the special red-skinned onions of the region.

"Brought by the Italians after the gold rush," says Condon, "Stockton Reds have been grown locally ever since and are a superior sweet onion—with a little more heat than the Vidalia or the Walla Walla." They have bright red skins but snowy white flesh.

Onions can be harvested at different stages. In early spring, they are scallions; later in the same season they are spring bulb onions, purple or white, and used in the same way you use more mature onions, although their flavor is typically fresher, sweeter, and never as strong. By summertime, onions have fully matured and formed protective papery, dry skins, which makes them good keepers. In addition to Condon's Stockton Sweet Reds, football-shaped, purple-red torpedo onions are a market favorite, as are cipollini, small, flat yellow or purple onions. Both are sold by Mariquita Farm (page 182).

Season

Depending on the type, onions are available year-round at the market, with scallions and spring bulb onions in spring, Stockton Sweet Reds in summer, and cipollini and torpedoes from late summer through early fall.

Choosing

In the case of scallions and spring bulb onions, look for white ends and bright green shoots. Mature onions should feel firm and have smooth skins without any breaks. When picking out cipollini, keep in mind that the flatter the bulb, the better the taste. Also remember, the bigger the better for sweet onions.

Storing

Store scallions and spring bulb onions in perforated plastic bags in the vegetable bin of the refrigerator for up to a week. Onions with papery skins are still alive in storage, so keep them where air can circulate and the temperature is dry and consistent—not in the refrigerator. And don't store them near potatoes or other vegetables, which can hasten spoilage. The torpedoes do not store well, so eat them while they are fresh

Deep-fried Onion Rings Serves 4 to 6

Follow these few tips and your onion rings will be sensational: Use firm, large onions for the best texture and flavor and use peanut oil. Clip a deep-frying thermometer to the side of the pan to make sure that the oil is at 365°F before you add the onions. Do not crowd the rings in the hot oil, or the temperature will drop and the batter will absorb the oil. When you remove a batch, remove any stray bits of batter at the same time with a wire skimmer. Finally, always make sure the oil returns to 365°F before adding the next batch.

2 LARGE ONIONS, SUCH AS
STOCKTON SWEET RED, SLICED
ABOUT 1/4 INCH THICK

11/2 CUPS BUTTERMILK OR
WHOLE MILK

PEANUT OIL FOR DEEP-FRYING

11/2 CUPS UNBLEACHED
ALL-PURPOSE FLOUR

2 CUPS FINE-GRIND YELLOW
CORNMEAL

SEA SALT, KOSHER SALT, OR
REGULAR TABLE SALT

In a bowl, combine the onion slices and buttermilk or milk and let soak for about 1 hour. Lift out the slices, drain on paper towels, and separate into rings. Discard the liquid.

Select a deep, heavy pan wide enough to accommodate 3 or 4 onion rings at a time. Pour the peanut oil to a depth of 2 to 3 inches into the pan, place over medium-high heat, and heat to 365°F on a deep-frying thermometer. While the oil is heating, in a shallow bowl, stir together the flour and cornmeal until well mixed. One at a time, dip the onion rings into the mixture, coating the rings evenly and tapping them against the side of the bowl to release the excess. Set aside on a platter.

When the oil is ready, add 3 or 4 onion rings and deep-fry, turning as needed, until golden brown, about 3 minutes. Remove with tongs or a wire skimmer, drain briefly on paper towels, and sprinkle with salt. Repeat with the remaining onion rings. Serve piping hot as they come off the stove—don't wait until all of them are cooked.

Stockton red onions

Onions

Cipollini in Agrodolce

Serves 4

This typical southern Italian dish of sweet-and-sour onions makes an appealing accompaniment to fowl or meat dishes, but around Rome it is usually served as an antipasto. The sweetness comes from the onions and the sour from the vinegar, which together create a pleasing balance. Some recipes also add sugar, but here, small, flat cipollini provide enough sweetness to offset the acidity of the vinegar.

12 TO 15 CIPOLLINI ONIONS

3 TABLESPOONS EXTRA-VIRGIN OLIVE OIL

SALT AND FRESHLY GROUND BLACK PEPPER

1/2 CUP RED WINE VINEGAR

2 TABLESPOONS AGED BALSAMIC VINEGAR

Preheat the oven to 400°F.

Place the onions in a bowl of cold water to cover for a few minutes, to loosen their skins. Drain and peel with a small, sharp knife.

In a small, ovenproof skillet, heat the olive oil over medium-high heat. Delicately add the onions so that the oil does not spatter, and cook for a few minutes on each side until golden brown. Sprinkle with salt and pepper, pour in the red wine vinegar, and cook for a few minutes until it reduces slightly, just a few minutes longer. Turn the onions over and drizzle the balsamic vinegar over them.

Place the pan in the oven and roast the onions until their exteriors caramelize and they are tender at the center when pierced with a knife tip, 45 minutes to 1 hour. Remove from the oven and serve at room temperature.

Pasta with Crumbled Bacon and Melting Onions

Serves 4

This is one of those astonishingly good dishes that you can make any time you have four basic ingredients on hand: great onions such as Stockton Sweet Reds, bacon, pasta, and Parmesan. During the spring or summer, you can throw in a cup of English peas just before you toss the sauce with the noodles. Or, you can add a sprinkle of red pepper flakes, a handful of chopped flat-leaf parsley, or even some minced sage at the end.

1 POUND SLICED BACON

2 LARGE WHITE OR RED
ONIONS, MINCED

SALT

3/4 POUND SPAGHETTI

1/4 TO 1/3 POUND
PARMIGIANO-REGGIANO
CHEESE, GRATED

FRESHLY GROUND BLACK
PEPPER

HANDFUL OF CHOPPED FRESH
FLAT-LEAF PARSLEY

Place a large, heavy skillet over medium-low heat and add the bacon. Fry the bacon, making sure that the rendered fat does not begin to smoke or burn, until the bacon is almost crisp but not dark, 5 to 10 minutes. Using a fork or tongs, transfer the bacon to paper towels to drain. When cool enough to handle, crumble into a small bowl and set aside.

Pour off one-half of the bacon drippings and return the pan to medium-low heat. Add the onions and cook very slowly, stirring often, until they melt into the bacon fat. This will take about 30 minutes. The onions should be a caramel brown; do not allow them to blacken.

Meanwhile, bring a large pot of salted water to a boil. When the onions are almost ready, add the pasta and cook until al dente. Scoop out and reserve about 1/2 cup of the pasta water and then drain the pasta.

Add the drained pasta to the onions in the skillet and toss over medium-low heat, add the reserved pasta water as needed to moisten, until the pasta is evenly coated with the sauce.

Transfer to a warmed serving bowl, sprinkle with half of the crumbled bacon and half of the cheese, and toss to mix. Season with salt and pepper and toss again. Scatter the parsley and the rest of the crumbled bacon over the top and serve. Pass the rest of the cheese at the table.

Peaches

Amygdalus persica

"Everyone is always squeezing my peaches at the market . . . and I just let 'em," jokes the engaging and energetic Al Courchesne. The soil and the climate at his Frog Hollow Farm in Brentwood, an hour east of San Francisco in the lush Sacramento River Delta, are perfect for growing peaches. He sells his fruits to the best local restaurants, at his shop in the Ferry Building, and at a booth at the market. This guy is the rock star of stone-fruit farmers.

Courchesne allows his peaches to ripen on the tree longer than most farmers would dare. He takes a risk leaving them so long, but they're so exquisitely sweet that they sell out at the market. "The best possible peach," he explains, "is the peach that is allowed to ripen until it is just about to drop off the tree, and then harvested and allowed to ripen for three more days."

At Frog Hollow Farm, Courchesne gives a chemistry lesson using an instrument called a refractometer that gauges the Brix, or sugar content, of a peach. Most commercial peaches Brix out at 8, while his peaches Brix out at an astounding 12 to 18—and 18 is the maximum on the scale. "They don't call me Mr. Brix for nothing," he jokes.

Season

May almost through October.

Choosing

The velvet-skinned peach is typically bred to be a dominant rosy red, the color associated with ripe, juicy peaches. But the true indicator of maturity is a dominant golden yellow background. Softness does not necessarily mean that a peach is ripe. It should be firm, with a bit of give. Immature peaches that are hard with a green undertone will never ripen properly.

All of Al Courchesne's peaches are freestone, meaning that the flesh comes away from the pit freely. (In contrast, the flesh of cling, or clingstone, peaches adheres to the pit, making the peaches more suitable for canning.) He features a different peach variety every week or two from June until mid-September.

Some peach farmers sell seconds—peaches that are too ripe or whose shape is too oddball to be sold for eating out of hand. Often half the price of their prettier sisters, they are perfect for making jams or desserts such as crisps, sorbets, and ice creams.

Storing

If the peaches are not yet ripe, arrange them in a single layer on a platter and allow them to ripen at room temperature (55° to 78°F, but not over 80°F). Never refrigerate peaches until they are absolutely ripe. Refrigerated peaches quickly lose their flavor. And don't throw away overripe fruits. Instead, transform them into a fresh-fruit conserve.

Peaches

Preparing

To peel a peach, run the blunt side of the blade of a small, sharp paring knife over the peach skin, loosening it. Then peel with the sharp side of the blade, holding the peach over a bowl to capture all of the juices. For peeling lots of peaches, blanch them for 30 seconds in a pot of rapidly boiling water. Be certain that the peaches are completely submerged. Remove with a slotted spoon and drain on a kitchen towel. When the peaches are cool enough to handle, slip off the skins.

To pit a peach, cut it in half lengthwise, working your way around the pit, and then gently twist the halves in opposite directions and pull them apart. Remove and discard pit.

White Peaches in Sauternes

Serves 4

This elegant recipe enhances the delicate peach flavor without overpowering it. The peaches macerate, rather than poach, in the light wine syrup, preserving their floral sweetness.

1 BOTTLE (325 ML/1³/4 CUPS) SAUTERNES OR BARSAC

2 CUPS WATER, PREFERABLY SPRING WATER

1 CUP SUGAR

4 LARGE WHITE PEACHES

In a deep saucepan, combine the wine, water, and sugar and bring to a simmer over medium heat, stirring to dissolve the sugar. Lower the peaches into the simmering liquid until the skins loosen, about 2 minutes. Using a slotted spoon, remove the peaches and, when cool enough to handle, carefully peel the peaches and set them aside in a large, deep bowl. Continue to simmer the poaching liquid until it has thickened slightly to a light syrup and has reduced by about half, about 30 minutes.

Remove the syrup from the heat and let cool for 15 minutes. Pour the syrup over the peaches and macerate for 2 to 4 hours, turning the peaches occasionally in the syrup.

Serve the peaches in shallow bowls with a generous spoonful of syrup.

Peach Ice Cream

Serves 4 to 6

Make the peach mixture before you sit down for dinner. Pour it into an ice-cream maker just before you serve your main course, and let it freeze while you finish your meal. Or, you can make it earlier in the day, store it in a plastic container in the freezer, and then let it sit for several minutes before serving so that it softens a bit.

4 LARGE, VERY RIPE PEACHES, PEELED AND PITTED

ABOUT ³/4 CUP PACKED DARK BROWN SUGAR

1 CUP WHOLE MILK

1 CUP HEAVY CREAM

Place the peaches in a large bowl. Add the sugar, using a little less or a little more depending on how sweet the peaches are. Mash the peaches and sugar together with your hands until evenly combined. Add the milk and cream and mix well.

Pour the peach mixture into an ice-cream maker and freeze according to the manufacturer's instructions.

Peaches

Peach Bruschetta with Blue Cheese

Serves 4

Becky Smith, Al Courchesne's partner in life and business, worked as a pastry chef at the celebrated Oliveto restaurant in Oakland. Now she makes marvelous pastries and legendary preserves for Frog Hollow Farm. Al and Becky eat these peach-topped toasts (pictured opposite) every morning for breakfast in the summer. They make a great appetizer, too. The recipe also works with nectarines.

4 SLICES COUNTRY BREAD

2 PEACHES

EXTRA-VIRGIN OLIVE OIL FOR
BRUSHING

1/4 POUND POINT REYES BLUE
(PAGE 285), GORGONZOLA, OR
BLUE CASTELLO CHEESE

Preheat the broiler. Arrange the bread slices on a rimmed baking sheet, slip under the broiler, and toast, turning once, until golden brown on both sides. This should take only a few minutes.

While the bread is toasting, halve the peaches lengthwise, pit them, and then peel each half. Cut each half lengthwise into 1/4-inch-thick slices, keeping the shape of each half intact.

When the bread is ready, remove from the broiler and brush each slice on both sides with olive oil. Spread one-fourth of the cheese on each slice of warm bread, place a sliced peach half on top, and serve.

Bellini

Serves 2

Invented at Harry's Bar in Venice, this peachy drink was inspired by the rosy glow in a painting by the famous fifteenth-century Venetian painter Giovanni Bellini. It's traditionally made with white peach purée, but feel free to use any ripe peach.

1 VERY RIPE PEACH

WELL-CHILLED PROSECCO OR
CHAMPAGNE

Peel the peach over a blender container to capture the juice and discard the peel and pit. Slice the peach, allowing the slices to drop into the blender. Purée until smooth.

Divide the purée evenly between 2 Champagne flutes, then fill the glasses with sparkling wine.

Perfect Peach Jam

Makes 6 half pints

These peach preserves, tucked away in your pantry, are like money in the bank. A spoonful on buttered toast brings back the warmth of summer.

12 LARGE PEACHES
JUICE OF 1 LEMON
3 CUPS SUGAR

Blanch and peel the peaches, then working directly over a large, heavy enameled cast-iron or other nonreactive pot, cut half of the peaches lengthwise into 1/2 -inch-thick slices, letting the slices drop into the pot. Discard the pits. Sprinkle the peach slices with half of the lemon juice and toss gently with your hands to coat the fruit evenly to prevent discoloration. Evenly sprinkle half of the sugar over the peaches. Repeat with the remaining peaches, lemon juice, and sugar. Set the pot aside to allow the peaches to release their juices and the sugar to melt, 1 to 3 hours.

Place the pot over medium-high heat and bring the peaches to a gentle boil. Cook, without stirring, until the liquid has reduced by half, the peaches are translucent, and the temperature registers 220°F on a candy thermometer, about 1 hour.

While the jam cooks, sterilize 6 half-pint canning jars with their lids and rings, and keep them in hot water until you are ready to use them. Just before you are ready to fill the jars, drain them and arrange them together for easy filling. At the same time, fill a pot large enough to hold the jars, not touching and in a single layer, with enough water to cover them by 4 inches once they are added. A canning kettle with a rack is ideal, but a deep pot lined with a folded kitchen towel works fine. (The towel keeps the jars from banging around too much.)

When the jam is ready, ladle it into a glass measuring cup and pour about 1 cup of the jam into each of the jars, leaving about 1/4 inch headspace. Wipe any spills from the mouth of each jar with a damp towel to ensure a good seal. Top each jar with a lid and then screw on a ring.

Arrange the jars in the pot of water, bring to a rolling boil over medium-high heat, and boil for 10 minutes. Using jar tongs, transfer the jars to a tray lined with a kitchen towel. Let the jars cool undisturbed for 12 hours.

If the jars have sealed properly, the lids will be slightly indented and not springy to the touch. If they haven't, you can repeat the water bath, or you can refrigerate the jars and use the jam within 2 months. Store jars with a good seal in a cool, dark place for up to 6 months.

Plums

Prunus domestica

"I adore plums," exclaims June Taylor, who makes and sells exquisite handmade fruit products under her name. "In 1987, I made my first conserve from Santa Rosa plums. They are insanely fruity, with beautiful red color, great acidity, very deep flavor, and the perfect tart-sweet balance. The Santa Rosa," Taylor quips, "is a very plum plum." Taylor buys some of her fruit from farmer Steve Kashiwase, who grows plums and other stone fruits ten miles north of Merced, up against the Sierra foothills, where the climate is particularly fine for fruit farming. Warm summer days encourage growth, but cool evening breezes off the nearby delta slow the process down, allowing more color and rich sugar flavors to develop.

The United States is home to three main plum types: European, Asian, and American. European plums, such as the Damson, are small and firm and particularly good for making jams. Some varieties, like the Argen, are grown specifically for drying into prunes. Asian plums, like the Santa Rosa, introduced to California by horticulturist Luther Burbank in 1885, are bigger and juicier than their European counterparts. American plums are wild varieties, like beach plums and sloes. They are always cooked.

Kashiwase also grows Pluots, a hybrid that is much more plum than apricot. These juicy beauties have purple skins and scarlet flesh. Their sugar content is the same as that of a plum, but the skin of a Pluot is only mildly tart. "There is very little difference between the two," he says. "I like the new plum varieties, but I still grow my old favorite, the Santa Rosa."

Season

Mid-May though mid-October.

Choosing

The best sign that plums are ready to eat is a rich, well-developed color. Some plums may have a slight whitish bloom. It just means that they haven't been overhandled. Depending on the variety, some ripe plums are firm while others are slightly soft. A very soft plum is always overripe.

Storing

Tree-ripened plums will continue to ripen after they have been picked. At home, arrange them in a single layer on a platter and allow them to ripen at room temperature. Refrigerate ripe plums in a perforated plastic or paper bag for up to 4 days. Allow the fruits to come to room temperature before eating.

Plums

Prunus domestica

Preparing

There is no need to peel plums. The tartness in their skins makes their flesh taste even sweeter. To pit freestone plums, cut them in half lengthwise, rotate the halves in opposite directions to separate them, and then remove and discard the pit. To remove the flesh of clingstone plums, using a sharp paring knife, cut toward the pit and remove the flesh in segments.

Plum Galette

Serves 8 to 10

This summery dessert (pictured opposite) was inspired by an unforgettable galette that Deborah Madison, a well-known chef and author and a great advocate of farmers' markets, made many years ago for a dinner before a performance by the Sante Fe Opera.

FOR THE PASTRY

1 3/4 CUPS UNBLEACHED
ALL-PURPOSE FLOUR

1 TEASPOON SALT

1/2 CUP (1/4 POUND) PLUS
2 TABLESPOONS CHILLED
UNSALTED BUTTER, CUT INTO
SMALL PIECES

2 TABLESPOONS CHILLED
SOLID VEGETABLE SHORTENING

4 TO 5 TABLESPOONS
ICE WATER

FOR THE FILLING

1 1/2 POUNDS PLUMS

3 TABLESPOONS SUGAR

1/2 VANILLA BEAN, SPLIT
LENGTHWISE

2 TABLESPOONS WHOLE MILK
OR HALF-AND-HALF

To make the pastry dough, sift together the flour and salt into a bowl. Add the butter and shortening and, using a pastry blender, 2 knives, or your fingers, work the fat into the flour until the mixture has the consistency of coarse cornmeal.

Add the ice water 1 tablespoon at a time, stirring and tossing with a fork until the dough forms a shaggy mass. Turn the mass out onto a floured work surface and knead the dough a few times with the heel of your hand until the clumps of dough come together. Shape into a disk, wrap tightly in plastic wrap, and refrigerate for 1 hour before rolling out.

To make the filling, while the dough rests, working over a large bowl, cut the plums into quarters, discarding the pits. Sprinkle with the sugar. Using the tip of a knife, scrape the seeds from the vanilla bean into the bowl. Stir to mix everything together.

Preheat the oven to 375°F. Place a pizza stone near the work surface where you will be rolling out the dough.

Remove the dough from the refrigerator. Hit the dough a few times with the rolling pin, giving it a quarter turn each time you strike it, to soften it slightly. On a lightly floured work surface, roll out the dough into a 15-inch round. Cut away the ragged edges. Wrap the dough over the rolling pin and carefully transfer the pastry round to the pizza stone, laying it out flat. Arrange the plums, cut side up, on the center of the round in an overlapping spiral 10 inches in diameter. Loosely gather the dough and arrange over the edge of the fruit. Make sure there are no holes in the pastry (pat away any cracks) or the juices will run out. Brush the dough with the milk or half-and-half.

Bake the galette until the crust is golden brown and the filling is bubbling, about 1 hour. Carefully remove the pizza stone from the oven and allow the tart to rest on the stone for 30 minutes. Use the removable bottom of a tart pan to transfer the cooled tart to a flat serving plate. Serve warm or at room temperature.

Plums

Plum Candy

Makes 36 candies

Here is a homemade version of the elegant *pâte de fruits* sold in Hédiard, one of the great food shops of Paris, and in other specialty-foods stores across France. It can also be made with quinces, pippin apples, or fresh currants. If you like, dip the candies in sugar or melted bittersweet chocolate before storing.

4 POUNDS PLUMS, PITTED AND CHOPPED

2 TABLESPOONS WATER

JUICE OF 1/2 LEMON

ABOUT 4 CUPS SUGAR

In a large, heavy enameled cast-iron or other nonreactive pot, combine the plums, water, and lemon juice. Place over low heat and cook until the fruit is very soft, about 20 minutes.

Remove from the heat. Purée the plum mixture by forcing it through a fine-mesh sieve or a food mill fitted with a fine screen held over a bowl. Measure the purée, return it to the pan, and stir in an equal amount of sugar. Cook over low heat, stirring constantly, until the fruit reduces and thickens and begins to hold together as a mass, 20 to 30 minutes.

Line a 9-by-12-inch rimmed baking sheet with plastic wrap overlapping the edges. Pour the plum paste onto the lined pan and spread into an even sheet with a rubber spatula. Let cool, cover, and allow to stand at room temperature for 48 hours. The paste will become firm.

Invert the pan onto a cutting board, peel off the plastic wrap, and cut the paste into about 36 small squares. Arrange in layers on waxed paper and store in an airtight plastic container at room temperature.

Plums

Raspberries

Rubus spp.

Raspberries, indigenous to Asia Minor and North America, are aggregate fruits composed of numerous tiny, hairy drupelets that adhere to one another. They are no longer untouchably expensive, aromatic jewels of summer. If bought at peak season, everyone can afford them. Forgo expensive underripe versions, shipped in all year from South America and New Zealand; they cannot touch the raspberries of Apolinar Yerena (page 77) or Brandon Ross of Ella Bella Farm, in Watsonville. These farmers grow bush berries in the perfect coastal climate.

Ross has farming in his blood. His paternal grandfather was a founding member of the United Farm Workers Union, while his maternal grandfather was a grape grower who was boycotted by the union during the Great Grape Boycott of 1965. Today, Ross is dedicated to both ecological sustainability and farmworkers' rights.

He runs Ella Bella with his wife, Michelle, and the sixteen-acre operation is named after her daughter. Through cover cropping, crop rotation, and organic fertilizers, the soil has been carefully rebuilt and today Ross plants four acres of red and golden raspberries and five acres of blackberries, along with a variety of vegetables, including tomatoes.

Season
Summer.

Choosing
Look for plump, velvety, dark pink berries without any mold or bleeding juices that stain the bottom of the box. Taste before buying and avoid watery, large, bland berries. Golden raspberries, whose color is determined by a single recessive gene, taste similar.

Storing
You don't need to wash organic raspberries, and they are too delicate anyway. Spread them out on a tray or platter lined with paper towels, sorting through them carefully and discarding any bruised or moldy ones. Eat as soon as possible. Avoid refrigerating them, as the cold robs them of flavor.

Freezing
Of course, freezing berries is never our first choice. If you end up with a huge amount of berries, it is better to make jam, as a frozen berry never equals the divine quality of the in-season juicy ripe original. But if you have no time to make jam, spread the raspberries (or any other berries) out on a baking sheet and place in the freezer. Once they are hard, transfer them to zippered plastic bags, label with weight and date, and place back in the freezer. They will keep for a couple months.

Raspberries at Yerena Farm

Christopher's Raspberry Jam   Makes 3 half pints

Make this jam in small batches all summer long and you will end up with a well-stocked pantry of jam that your family and friends can use on toast all winter long. To adjust the recipe to the amount of berries you have, use the ratio of a quart of berries to a cup of sugar for each half pint of jam.

3 QUARTS RED RASPBERRIES

3 CUPS SUGAR

Place the raspberries in a large, deep, heavy pot. Place over the lowest heat setting until the berries have released their juices and have collapsed on themselves, about 3 hours.

To eliminate most of the raspberry seeds, push the berries and their juices through a fine-mesh sieve placed over a bowl. Return the contents of the bowl to the pot and add the sugar. Place over high heat and bring to a rolling boil, stirring to dissolve the sugar. Then boil, skimming off any foam that forms on the surface, until the temperature registers 220°F on a candy thermometer. The timing will depend on how juicy the berries were. Stir occasionally to prevent sticking.

Meanwhile, sterilize 3 half-pint canning jars with their lids and rings, and keep them in hot water until you are ready to use them. Just before you are ready to fill the jars, drain them and arrange them together for easy filling. At the same time, fill a pot large enough to hold the jars, not touching and in a single layer, with enough water to cover them by 4 inches once they are added. A canning kettle with a rack is ideal, but a deep pot lined with a folded kitchen towel works fine. (The towel keeps the jars from banging around too much.)

When the jam is ready, ladle it into a glass measuring cup or a pitcher and then pour about 1 cup of the jam into each of the jars, leaving about 1/4-inch headspace. Wipe any spills from the mouth of each jar with a damp towel to ensure a good seal. Top each jar with a lid and then screw on a ring.

Arrange the jars in the pot of water, bring to a rolling boil over medium-high heat, and boil for 15 minutes. Using jar tongs, transfer the jars to a tray lined with a kitchen towel. Set the tray out of the way and let the jars cool undisturbed for 12 hours.

If the jars have sealed properly, the lids will be slightly indented and not springy to the touch. If they haven't, you can repeat the water bath,

continued

or you can refrigerate the jars and use the jam within a month or two. Store jars with a good seal in a cool, dark place for up to a few months. If any mold is visible on the top of the jam when you open a sealed jar, discard the jam.

Raspberry-Studded Lemon Tart

Serves 8

During the 1960s and 1970s, this was a popular dessert, only to be forgotten in the decades that followed. Let's bring it back—it is a true beauty! Meyer, Lisbon, or Eureka lemons can be used.

FOR THE CRUST

1 CUP (1/2 POUND) UNSALTED BUTTER, AT ROOM TEMPERATURE

1 CUP UNBLEACHED ALL-PURPOSE FLOUR

1/4 CUP CONFECTIONERS' SUGAR

FOR THE FILLING

2 LARGE EGGS, WELL BEATEN

1 CUP GRANULATED SUGAR

GRATED ZEST OF 1 LEMON

1/4 CUP FRESH LEMON JUICE

2 TABLESPOONS UNBLEACHED ALL-PURPOSE FLOUR

1/2 TEASPOON BAKING POWDER

2 CUPS PLUMP RED OR GOLDEN RASPBERRIES

CONFECTIONERS' SUGAR FOR DUSTING

Preheat the oven to 350°F.

To make the crust, combine the butter, flour, and confectioners' sugar in a bowl. Using an electric mixer, beat until the ingredients come together. The mixture will be slightly dry and crumbly. Turn the mixture into a 9-inch square pan and, using your fingertips, press to form an even layer in the bottom of the pan.

Bake the crust until very lightly browned, about 15 minutes. Transfer to a wire rack and let cool completely. Leave the oven set at 350°F.

To make the filling, combine the eggs, granulated sugar, lemon zest and juice, flour, and baking powder in a bowl. Using an electric mixer or an egg beater, beat until slightly frothy. Pour into the cooled crust.

Bake the tart until set, about 20 minutes. It may be a little bubbly but it should not be browned on the top. Transfer to a wire rack and let cool completely.

Starting at the edge of the cooled tart, arrange the raspberries over the top, fitting them so snugly that the lemon filling is not visible. Sift a light dusting of confectioners' sugar over the berries. Cut into squares to serve.

Salmon

Salmonidae oncorhynchus

Every week, May through October, fisherman Larry Miyamura steers his forty-foot troller, the *Shogun*, under the Golden Gate Bridge and into the rich fishing grounds of the Pacific. Alone on the boat, Miyamura will stay out for up to three days at a time. He trolls as far north as Fort Bragg and as far south as Santa Cruz until he's caught all the wild salmon, halibut, and albacore that he thinks he and his wife, Roz, can sell. His catch is kept in refrigerated seawater on his boat to ensure the freshest fish possible for his customers.

Miyamura fishes and sells halibut and California albacore, but it is Chinook salmon that makes his heart beat a little faster. There are eight species of salmon worldwide, and five of them live in the coastal waters of the northern Pacific. But the Chinook is the rightly named "king" of the species. It runs about three feet long, weighs around twenty-two pounds, and has firm, deep red, fatty flesh. "These wild salmon have rich, natural flavor, like a full-bodied wine," say Miyamura. "They feed on anchovies, herring, krill, and shrimp, which give them their natural salmon color." Whenever possible, choose wild over farm raised, asking the vendor if you are not sure. Bland-tasting farmed fish are fed mainly on soy-based pellets and are given dye to add color.

"For me," says Miyamura, "the ideal fish is a sixteen-pound Chinook caught in August. That's when the fish are storing their fat reserves for their migration. Roz and I love salmon and use every part except the tail. It's bad karma to waste fish."

But wild salmon doesn't only taste good. It is good for you, too. It is low in calories and saturated fat, yet high in protein and in health-promoting omega-3 fatty acids. Some studies show that eating salmon or other cold-water, oily fish high in omega-3 fatty acids only once a week may significantly lower the risk of Alzheimer's disease, heart disease, stroke, rheumatoid arthritis, arrhythmia, diabetes, ovarian cancer, depression, and even your hostility level.

Season

May through October.

Choosing

Use your nose; smell is a good indicator of freshness. Fresh salmon should smell sweet, and not the least bit unpleasantly fishy. Avoid prepackaged fish, since off odors cannot be detected through plastic. Fresh salmon is sold whole, in fillets, or in steaks. The flesh should be firm, translucent, and moist, with no liquid pooling around it. Ask if the fish has been frozen and thawed, so you will know if you can freeze it at home. If you know you're off to buy fish, throw a cooler in your car with a few ice packs to keep the fish cold on the ride home.

Salmon

Salmonidae oncorhynchus

Storing

Fresh fish must be kept very cold until it is cooked. Whole fish will keep better than steaks or fillets. Home refrigerators are not cold enough for storing fish (fishmongers store fish at 40°F). As soon as you get salmon home, rinse it with cold water, pat dry and wrap it in plastic wrap, put it in a clean plastic bag, and store on the bottom shelf of the refrigerator with an ice pack or two on top. Very fresh fish will last 3 to 5 days if handled correctly.

Preparing

Run your fingers over the surface of fish fillets to feel for pin bones. Use needle-nosed pliers to remove any bones you find, pulling them out with the grain of the flesh to keep from tearing it. Wait to remove skin until after cooking, when it will slip right off.

Freezing

Make sure the fish that you purchase has not been frozen and thawed, as fish should never be refrozen. Cut large pieces (2 pounds or more) into steaks or fillets so they will freeze quickly. Rinse in cold water and pat dry with paper towels, then wrap in thick plastic wrap and put in a zippered plastic freezer bag (ideally fish is vacuum-packed). In most home freezers, frozen salmon keeps for about 1 month. Thaw in the refrigerator overnight.

Salmon with Aunt Mae's Miso Sauce

Serves 4

Larry and Roz Miyamura's Aunt Mae shared this delicious method for preparing salmon. Any type of miso can be used.

FOR THE MISO SAUCE

1/2 CUP MISO

2 TABLESPOONS PEELED AND GRATED FRESH GINGER

2 TABLESPOONS SUGAR

1/2 CUP WATER

FOR THE SALMON

4 WILD SALMON FILLETS, 6 TO 8 OUNCES EACH

SALT AND FRESHLY GROUND BLACK PEPPER

1/2 TEASPOON BUTTER

To make the miso sauce, in a small bowl, stir together the miso, ginger, sugar, and water until well combined. Set aside. (This sauce can be covered and refrigerated for up to 2 weeks before using. It thickens a little on standing; thin as needed with water.)

Check the salmon fillets for pin bones and remove any you find. Season the fillets on both sides with salt and pepper, taking care not to oversalt, as the miso can be salty. In a large nonstick skillet, melt the butter over medium heat. Add the salmon, cover, and cook, turning once, about 2 minutes on each side. Transfer to a warmed platter.

Bring the skillet to medium-high heat and add the miso sauce. Stirring constantly, bring to a boil, about 1 minute. Spoon the sauce evenly over the salmon and serve.

Salmon with Lavender-Fennel Salt   Serves 4

Chef Shannon Kelly, who cooks for Knickerbockers' Catering in St. Helena, in California's wine country, makes this recipe all summer when lavender is blooming.

2 TEASPOONS BLACK
PEPPERCORNS

2 TEASPOONS COARSE SEA
SALT OR KOSHER SALT

2 TEASPOONS FENNEL SEEDS

2 TEASPOONS CHOPPED
FRESH LAVENDER BLOSSOMS

4 SKIN-ON WILD SALMON
FILLETS, 6 OUNCES EACH

2 TABLESPOONS EXTRA-VIRGIN
OLIVE OIL

Preheat the oven to 300°F. Line a baking pan large enough to accommodate the salmon fillets in a single layer with heavy-duty aluminum foil.

In a mortar, combine the peppercorns, salt, and fennel seeds and crush and grind with the pestle to release the flavors. Add the lavender blossoms and crush again. Alternatively, use a small food processor or coffee grinder, grinding the peppercorns, salt, and fennel seeds by pulsing a few times, and then adding the lavender and pulsing once or twice to combine.

Check the salmon fillets for pin bones and remove any you find. Brush a little olive oil on both sides of each fillet, then liberally season the flesh side only with the lavender-fennel mixture, pressing it firmly into the salmon. Arrange the fillets, skin side down, on the prepared pan.

Bake until an instant-read thermometer inserted into the thickest part of a fillet registers 140°F, about 30 minutes. Serve warm or at room temperature.

Gravlaks

Serves 8

This recipe comes from a small island off the west coast of Norway, in the North Sea. The locals salt the salmon and then bury it in the cold ground (in Norwegian, *gravlaks* means "buried salmon").

1 SKIN-ON, CENTER-CUT WILD SALMON FILLET, ABOUT 2 1/4 POUNDS

2 TABLESPOONS COARSE SALT

1 TABLESPOON SUGAR

1 TABLESPOON PLUS 1 TEASPOON FRESHLY GROUND WHITE PEPPER

2 TABLESPOONS AQUAVIT, EAU-DE-VIE, OR COGNAC

1 LARGE BUNCH FRESH DILL

FOR THE MUSTARD SAUCE

1/4 CUP DIJON MUSTARD

1/4 CUP HONEY MUSTARD

1 TABLESPOON EXTRA-VIRGIN OLIVE OIL

JUICE OF 1/2 LEMON

1 TABLESPOON CHOPPED FRESH DILL

SALT AND FRESHLY GROUND WHITE PEPPER

Check the salmon fillets for pin bones and remove any you find. In a small bowl, stir together the salt, sugar, and pepper. Use your hands to rub the mixture into the flesh side of the salmon. Place the fish, skin side down, on a large piece of plastic wrap. Sprinkle the aquavit or other spirit over the fish. Reserve some of the dill for garnish, and place the remainder on top of the salmon. Wrap up the fish in the plastic wrap, and put it in a ceramic or glass dish. Place a small tray about the same size as the salmon directly on the salmon, and top it with a couple of heavy cans to weight the fish. Refrigerate for 2 to 3 days.

Remove the fish from the refrigerator, unwrap it, remove and discard the dill, and rinse off the salt mixture with cold water. Pat dry with paper towels.

To make the mustard sauce, in a bowl, stir together the Dijon and honey mustards, olive oil, lemon juice, and chopped dill. Season to taste with salt and pepper.

Using a sharp knife, cut the salmon into very thin slices on the diagonal and arrange the slices on a platter. Chop the reserved dill and garnish the salmon. Serve with the mustard sauce.

Shogun Salmon Cakes with Corn and Tomato Salsa   Serves 2 to 4

Sometimes the Miyamuras make these cakes bite sized and serve them as hors d'oeuvres. The colorful salsa, delicious at midsummer when both corn and tomatoes are at their seasonal peak, is the ideal accompaniment.

FOR THE SALMON CAKES

1 POUND WILD SALMON
FILLET, SKINNED, PIN BONES
REMOVED, AND COARSELY
CHOPPED

1/2 CUP CHOPPED FRESH
CILANTRO

1/4 CUP CHOPPED SCALLIONS

1/4 CUP FRESH BREAD
CRUMBS

2 TABLESPOONS DIJON
MUSTARD

SALT AND FRESHLY GROUND
BLACK PEPPER

EXTRA-VIRGIN OLIVE OIL FOR
FRYING

FOR THE CORN AND TOMATO
SALSA

EXTRA-VIRGIN OLIVE OIL FOR
SAUTÉING

1 SMALL YELLOW ONION,
MINCED

2 CUPS CORN KERNELS

2 TOMATOES, DICED

1/4 CUP CHOPPED FRESH BASIL

SALT AND FRESHLY GROUND
BLACK PEPPER

To make the salmon cakes, combine the salmon, cilantro, scallions, bread crumbs, and mustard in a large bowl and mix well. Season the mixture with salt and pepper. Divide into 4 equal portions and shape into patties.

Film the bottom of a skillet with a little olive oil and heat over medium heat until hot but not smoking. Put the patties in the skillet and fry, turning once, until lightly browned on both sides and cooked through, about 5 minutes per side.

To make the salsa, while the salmon is cooking, film the bottom of a second skillet with a little olive oil and heat over medium-high heat. Add the onion and cook, stirring, until soft, about 5 minutes. Stir in the corn and cook for 2 minutes. Add the tomatoes and cook for 1 minute longer. Remove from the heat, stir in the basil, and season to taste with salt and pepper.

Serve the salmon cakes with the salsa.

Shallots

"You won't find shallots that resemble these on the commercial market," says Wally Condon (page 124), as he gestures toward his French gray shallots. "They take too much weeding and too long to grow." But Condon knows that good cooks appreciate these gray, clay-encrusted, tough-skinned bulbs, and once they discover them at his stall, they are quick to buy his other offerings.

Shallots have a sweeter, more distinct, complex, and intense flavor than their other kin in the *Allium* genus. "The shallot of French haute cuisine," explains Condon, "is planted from a bulb that keeps dividing." They are like garlic in this respect. The rounded, coppery red–skinned shallots are more commonly found. But they are also more onionlike and less subtle than the gray or "true" French shallot.

Shallots are thought to have made their way to the Mediterranean from Asia and are sometimes confused with scallions. French-born chef Eric Rippert, of New York's celebrated Le Bernardin restaurant, thinks that shallots add a feminine flavor to foods. They are great in a vinaigrette, mignonette, and other French sauces, and boast a traditional role in the cooking of Southeast Asia.

Season
Dry shallots are available year-round—or as long as the supply lasts at Condon's stall.

Choosing
Look for dry, firm, solid shallots without any wet spots. Discard any that exhibit moldiness, green sprouts, or dustiness.

Storing
Never refrigerate shallots. Instead, keep them in a cool spot in a wire or straw basket that permits good air circulation.

Preparing
Peel away the tough, papery skin with a paring knife.

Ferry Plaza Farmers' Market Shallot Vinaigrette

Serves 4

One of the great Ferry Plaza Farmers' Market's combinations is a vinaigrette made from the products of a trio of vendors, including French gray shallots from Wally Condon, apple balsamic vinegar from The Apple Farm (page 170), and a late-harvest Ascolano olive oil from the Sciabica family (page 290). Make this vinaigrette fresh each time, always allowing the shallots to soften, or macerate, in the vinegar and salt before you add the oil, and toss it with greens. The best way to mix the salad is with your hands, so that you can feel if all the leaves are dressed. Be careful not to overdress the greens. The vinaigrette should lightly cover the leaves and no liquid should be left in the bottom of the bowl.

2 FRENCH GRAY SHALLOTS, MINCED

GENEROUS PINCH OF SALT

2 TABLESPOONS APPLE BALSAMIC VINEGAR OR MILD RED WINE VINEGAR

1/3 CUP EXTRA-VIRGIN OLIVE OIL, PREFERABLY LATE-HARVEST ASCOLANO FROM SCIABICA

In a bowl, combine the shallots and salt and add the vinegar. As you rinse and dry your salad greens, allow the mixture to macerate for about 30 minutes. Just before you are ready to toss the vinaigrette with the greens, pour the olive oil into the shallot mixture and stir well.

Shell Beans

Phaseolus vulgaris

Shell beans are simply the fresh version of various dried beans. Unlike their dried counterparts, they are sold still in their pods. At the market you will see the yellow pods of cannellini, the green pods of flageolets, and the red-streaked pods of cranberry beans. Fava beans (page 39) are shell beans, too, but they appear in spring, and their dried version, while popular in Europe and the Middle East, is not common in the United States. Despite their excellent nutritional properties—good sources of protein, fiber, potassium, and iron—shell beans have virtually disappeared from mainstream markets, leaving farmers' markets the primary source.

Joe Schirmer raises exceptional shell beans on his five-acre organic farm, Dirty Girl Produce, in Santa Cruz. "People in the know wait for the moment that my fresh beans—flageolets, cranberries, Tongue of Fire, and cannellini—appear at the market," Schirmer explains. "They love their creamy texture." Schirmer maintains the integrity of the soil at Dirty Girl by alternating one-half of his vegetable crop with legumes. Once he harvests the beans, he tills the legume plants back into the soil, thereby enriching it with nitrogen.

Season

Late spring to early fall but best in late summer.

Choosing

Seek pods that fit snugly around beans, are tough textured, tightly closed, and plump. The pods should not be wilted, cracked, brown, or bursting. They can be a little leathery, just as long as the beans inside feel firm through the pod.

1 POUND PODS YIELDS ABOUT 1 CUP SHELLED BEANS

Storing

Slip the pods into a perforated plastic bag and store in the vegetable bin of the refrigerator for up to a few days. Look out for mold if you keep them longer.

Preparing

Split the pods open with your thumb and shake out the beans. Keep in mind that tender, subtly flavored shell beans take less time to cook and are more digestible than dried beans.

Freezing

Put the shelled beans into zippered freezer bags, label with weight and date, and freeze for up to 3 months.

Shell beans in the pod

Shell Beans Swirled with Wilted Arugula   Serves 6

Since shell beans take less time to cook than dried beans, they can be cooked along with the rest of a meal as a side dish. They do not absorb as much water as dried beans either, so their volume will not increase dramatically as they cook. Serve with grilled fish or roasts. You can substitute other greens for the arugula, such as spinach, chard, or kale.

3 POUNDS SHELL BEANS IN THE POD, SUCH AS CANNELLI-NI OR CRANBERRY, SHELLED

1 BAY LEAF

2 CLOVES GARLIC

1/2 YELLOW ONION

1/3 CUP EXTRA-VIRGIN OLIVE OIL, PLUS EXTRA FOR DRIZZLING

SALT AND FRESHLY GROUND BLACK PEPPER

2 TO 3 CUPS ARUGULA LEAVES, CHOPPED IF LARGE

In a saucepan, combine the beans with water to cover by about 1 inch. Add the bay leaf, garlic, and onion and bring to a boil. Reduce the heat to a steady simmer and cook, stirring occasionally and skimming off any foam that rises to the top, about 20 minutes. Add the 1/3 cup olive oil, season with salt and pepper, and continue to simmer until tender, 10 to 15 minutes longer. Taste a bean to make sure they are ready.

Remove the bay leaf, garlic, and onion and discard. Add the arugula leaves and swirl them into the beans. They will wilt almost immediately. Drizzle with a little additional olive oil, taste and adjust the seasoning, and serve.

Cranberry beans

Summer Squashes

Cucurbita pepo

Summer squashes are actually gourds harvested at an immature age, when their skins and seeds are edible. They are classified as a fruit, but always eaten as a vegetable; are native to America; and take their name from *askutasquash*, a Narragansett Indian word meaning "eaten uncooked." Common types of summer squashes include cocozelle, pattypan, white scallop, yellow crookneck, straight neck, and, of course, zucchini.

Zucchini is the poster child of the summer squash clan. Even the tiniest of home vegetable gardens boasts one or two of the easy-to-grow, spectacularly prolific plants, with their large, five-pointed leaves and edible yellow-orange flowers. Gardeners who fail to harvest daily will eventually discover baseball bat–sized zucchini hidden under low leaves.

Among the states, California is second only to Florida in summer squash production. Harvested when young, summer squashes have a fresh, bright taste and tender flesh and take well to grilling, sautéing, and roasting, all of which intensify their natural flavor and supple texture.

Season

Summer squashes, as the name implies, are most plentiful from May through September. However, the ubiquitous zucchini is generally available year-round.

Choosing

Summer squashes taste best when small, no more than 5 inches long, or more than 2 inches in diameter in the case of the pattypan. These should be plump, firm, and fairly heavy for their size, with unblemished, smooth, glossy skins. The color should be uniform and bright and the stem ends fresh and green. Select squash blossoms that look full and fresh.

1 POUND SUMMER SQUASHES YIELDS 3 1/2 CUPS SLICED SQUASH

Storing

The skin of summer squash is thin and fragile, so handle carefully. Nicks and punctures can leave the vegetable susceptible to decay. Store in a perforated plastic bag in the vegetable bin of the refrigerator for up to 5 days. Because of their fragility, store the blossoms in the refrigerator, slipping them into a perforated plastic bag and then putting the bag in a closed plastic container to keep them from being "squashed." Use as soon as possible after purchase.

Preparing

Small summer squashes don't need to be peeled or seeded—just trim off the ends. Young squashes can even be thinly sliced and served raw with a drizzle of fruity olive oil, a squeeze of lemon, a sprinkle of salt, and a few grinds of black pepper. Before cooking squash blossoms, reach inside each blossom and pinch off the stamens.

If you do end up with an outsized zucchini, all is not lost: grate it on the large holes of a box grater into a colander, sprinkle it with a couple healthy pinches of salt, allow it to drain for about 30 minutes, squeeze it to release a little more liquid, and then sauté it with whatever seasonings you like.

Chayote, also called mirliton, a pale green, dark green, or white pear-shaped summer squash, is an exception to the rule of no peeling or seeding. Unlike its kin, it has a large, central seed and fairly thick, tough, deeply ridged skin. Peel it with a vegetable peeler, using a sharp paring knife to remove the skin from the deep ridges. (If cooking whole, you can slip off the skin after cooking.) It also requires a longer cooking time. When peeled, chayote exudes a sticky liquid that may burn or even numb the skin, so hold it under cold running water as you work. Halve the chayote and remove the seed; the seed can be cooked with the squash, as it has a pleasant almondlike flavor.

Fried Zucchini Blossoms

Serves 4 to 6

Fry these blossoms plain or stuff them with a little fresh ricotta flavored with a handful of chopped fresh herbs, salt, and pepper and twist the tops closed. Sage leaves prepared the same way are delicious, too.

VEGETABLE OIL FOR DEEP-FRYING

1 1/2 CUPS UNBLEACHED ALL-PURPOSE FLOUR

1 TO 2 CUPS DRY WHITE WINE

12 ZUCCHINI BLOSSOMS, STAMENS REMOVED

SALT

Pour oil to a depth of 3 inches into a heavy, deep skillet, place over high heat, and heat to 375°F on a candy thermometer. (If the oil isn't hot enough, the squash blossoms will absorb too much of it.) While the oil is heating, put the flour in a bowl and whisk in the wine 1/2 cup at a time, always whisking until smooth before adding the next batch. Continue to add wine just until the batter is the consistency of pancake batter.

When the oil is ready, one at a time dip the blossoms into the batter, allowing the excess to drip off, and slide them into the hot oil. Don't crowd the skillet or the temperature of the oil will drop and the blossoms will absorb the oil. Fry, turning frequently, until golden and crisp, 3 to 5 minutes. Remove with tongs or a wire skimmer, drain briefly on paper towels, and sprinkle with salt. Repeat with the remaining blossoms. Serve them piping hot as soon as they are ready. Don't wait for all of the blossoms to be cooked.

Frittata with Zucchini and Onion

Serves 4

A frittata, the Italian answer to the French omelet, can be made with nearly any vegetable. Serve a warm wedge with a green salad for supper, wrap up cold slices for a picnic, or cut tiny squares for hors d'oeuvres.

4 LARGE EGGS

HANDFUL OF CHOPPED FRESH PARSLEY

HANDFUL OF GRATED PARMIGIANO-REGGIANO CHEESE

SALT AND FRESHLY GROUND BLACK PEPPER

4 TABLESPOONS EXTRA-VIRGIN OLIVE OIL

1 YELLOW ONION, FINELY CHOPPED

1 CLOVE GARLIC, MINCED

4 SMALL ZUCCHINI, TRIMMED AND DICED

In a bowl, whisk together the eggs, parsley, cheese, a pinch of salt, and a few grinds of pepper. Set aside.

In a large, well-seasoned omelet pan or nonstick skillet, heat 3 tablespoons of the olive oil over medium heat. Add the onion and garlic and cook, stirring and tossing, until they are browned and a little caramelized, 5 to 10 minutes. Add the zucchini, stir into the onion mixture, and cook for about 2 minutes.

Pour the egg mixture over the vegetables in the pan, stir with a rubber spatula to mix evenly throughout, shake the pan, and then let the eggs and vegetables settle. Cook until lightly browned on the bottom, about 5 minutes. Run the spatula around the edge of the frittata and shake the pan to loosen the frittata from the bottom. Continue to cook until partially set, 2 to 3 minutes.

Remove the pan from the heat, and invert a flat plate larger than the pan over the top. Using a pot holder or folded kitchen towel, hold the plate firmly to the pan and flip them together. Lift off the pan, leaving the frittata on the plate.

Return the pan to medium heat and add the remaining 1 tablespoon oil. When it is hot, slide the frittata, browned side up, into the pan and cook until the bottom has browned, 2 to 3 minutes. Serve warm or at room temperature.

Tomatoes

Lycopersicon esculentum

With names that sound like characters out of a 1950s Western, it is hard to believe that Red Brandywine, Radiator Jack's Mortgage Lifter, Red Oxheart, and Shady Lady actually identify heirloom tomatoes. Nigel Walker of Eatwell Farm (page 39), in Dixon, displays one of the wildest selections of heirloom tomatoes at the market. "Sunshine, complex organic soil with lots of nutrients, and judicious amounts of water make for the best tomatoes," explains the tall Englishman who grows at least fifty varieties yearly of explosively juicy, flavorful tomatoes.

Brandon and Michelle Ross also grow extraordinary tomatoes at their Ella Bella Farm (page 139), in Watsonville, most of them dry farmed. In their case, dry farming, a sustainable alternative to drip irrigation, relies on moisture from previous rainfalls, dew from coastal fog, and an indirect source from adjacent creek beds (by way of tap roots) to keep their plants growing. Heirlooms get minimal drip when needed, but popular Early Girls get this stress treatment, making them fight for survival. The result is concentrated flavor. A smaller yield and thicker skins are not disadvantages when sublime flavor is the reward.

Season
Mid- to late summer through early fall.

Choosing
Tomatoes should be heavy for their size, have a vivid color, and should yield to the touch though not be overly soft. They should also smell like tomatoes—earthy and aromatic. Try to taste before you buy—it's one of the advantages of shopping at a farmers' market.

Storing
Farmers and other experts advise never to refrigerate tomatoes. Refrigeration dismisses their aroma and disables their texture. Store them on a plate away from sunlight on the kitchen counter. Place ripe tomatoes under a mesh screen to avoid tiny fruit flies. If your tomatoes become ripe all at once, eat them quickly or make a sauce or soup.

Preparing
Peeling: For salads and slow roasting, peeling is not necessary. If tomatoes are cooked in a dish where their skins would not taste or look good, remove them by one of two methods, blistering or blanching. To blister tomatoes, place them on the grate of a lit gas-range burner or a charcoal or gas grill and turn as needed to blacken and blister the skins evenly. Let the tomatoes cool and then peel off the blistered skin with your fingers. To blanch tomatoes, drop them into a pot of boiling water for 15 to 20 seconds to loosen their skins. Lift out of

the water with a slotted spoon and, when cool enough to handle, slip off the skins with your fingers or a small knife.

Seeding: Some recipes call for seeding tomatoes, usually for better flavor or appearance. To seed a tomato, cut round tomatoes in half crosswise and plum-shaped tomatoes in half lengthwise. Then, one at a time, hold each half cut side down and squeeze gently, easing the seed sacs out with a fingertip if necessary. Work over a sieve placed over a bowl so you can save the juices but discard the seeds.

Fanny's Tomato Salad with Crispy Shallots   Serves 6

When Fanny Singer, daughter of chef and restaurateur Alice Waters, makes this summery salad (pictured opposite), she adds shallots treated two ways, marinated in vinegar and crisply fried. Use your best extra-virgin olive oil for the dressing, but an everyday extra-virgin olive oil is fine for frying the shallots. A version of this recipe appeared in "Educating Fanny," an article written by Peggy for *Food and Wine* magazine.

5 LARGE SHALLOTS, ABOUT
1/2 POUND TOTAL WEIGHT:
1 MINCED, 4 SLICED CROSSWISE
1/4 INCH THICK AND SEPARATED
INTO RINGS

1 TABLESPOON RED WINE VINE-
GAR

3 TABLESPOONS BEST-QUALITY
EXTRA-VIRGIN OLIVE OIL

SALT AND FRESHLY GROUND
BLACK PEPPER

1/2 CUP EVERYDAY EXTRA-
VIRGIN OLIVE OIL

3 TO 4 POUNDS SMALL TOMA-
TOES OR CHERRY TOMATOES,
SLICED IF SMALL OR HALVED IF
CHERRY

HANDFUL OF SMALL FRESH
BASIL LEAVES, TORN INTO
PIECES

In a small bowl, combine the minced shallot and vinegar and let stand for at least 5 minutes. Whisk in the 3 tablespoons olive oil and season to taste with salt and pepper.

Meanwhile, in a small skillet, heat the 1/2 cup olive oil over medium-high heat until the surface of the oil shimmers and the oil begins to smoke. Add half of the sliced shallots and cook, watching closely so they do not burn, until they are approaching golden brown, only about 2 seconds. Using a slotted spoon, lift the shallots out of the oil and transfer them to paper towels to drain. Sprinkle with salt. Repeat with the remaining sliced shallots. Set aside.

Arrange the tomatoes on a large platter, season with salt and pepper, and drizzle with the vinaigrette right before serving. Scatter the fried shallots and basil leaves over the tomatoes.

Tomatoes

Lycopersicon esculentum

Panzanella

Serves 6

Traditionally, this Italian bread salad is made with day-old or older bread. In the past, it was a way for cooks to stretch out the life of bread that was baked just once a week. Day-old bread will work for this recipe, too, but toasted bread, torn into bits, makes for more crunch. Be sure to use your best extra-virgin olive oil and perfectly ripe tomatoes. This salad makes a terrific summer meal.

2 CLOVES GARLIC, MINCED

1/4 CUP RED WINE VINEGAR

SALT AND FRESHLY GROUND
BLACK PEPPER

2 TO 3 POUNDS TOMATOES,
SEEDED AND CHOPPED, WITH
JUICES RESERVED

1/2 TO 3/4 POUND COUNTRY
BREAD, CUT INTO 1-INCH-THICK
SLICES

6 TO 8 BEST-QUALITY ANCHOVY
FILLETS, RINSED, DRAINED,
AND CHOPPED (OPTIONAL)

1 CUCUMBER, PEELED, SEEDED,
AND CHOPPED (OPTIONAL)

1/3 CUP SALT-PACKED CAPERS,
RINSED (OPTIONAL)

1/2 TO 3/4 CUP EXTRA-VIRGIN
OLIVE OIL

30 FRESH BASIL LEAVES (ABOUT
3/4 CUP) TORN INTO PIECES OR
CUT INTO NARROW STRIPS

In a small bowl, combine the garlic and vinegar. Season with a little salt and pepper and set aside. Place the tomatoes and their juices in a large salad bowl.

Toast or grill the bread slices, let cool slightly, and then tear into bite-sized pieces. Add the bread to the tomatoes. Then add the anchovies, cucumber, and/or capers, if using.

Whisk 1/2 cup of the olive oil into the vinegar mixture to form a vinaigrette. Drizzle the vinaigrette over the tomato mixture and toss to coat all the ingredients evenly. Taste and adjust the seasoning with salt and pepper, if necessary, and scatter the basil over the top. If you make the salad too far in advance, the bread will soak up the dressing, and you may need to add some or all of the remaining 1/4 cup olive oil. The plus, however, is that the flavors will intensify while it sits.

Oven-Roasted Tomatoes

Serves 6 to 8

Make this easy, intensely flavored recipe when tomatoes are plentiful. It is a free-form method that can take an hour or two or up to six hours. The tomatoes should be ripe but not overly juicy. Store them covered with olive oil in a jar for up to a week in the refrigerator. Or, use them immediately in sandwiches, on pasta, or alongside any main dish.

30 SMALL TO MEDIUM TOMATOES

SALT AND FRESHLY GROUND BLACK PEPPER

EXTRA-VIRGIN OLIVE OIL FOR DRIZZLING

Preheat the oven to 250°F if you have plenty of time, or to 350°F if you are in a hurry. Core the tomatoes and cut in half crosswise. Place the halves, cut side up, in a baking dish. Sprinkle with salt and pepper. Drizzle with olive oil.

Bake the tomatoes until they soften and almost collapse, 4 to 6 hours in the 250°F oven or 1 to 2 hours in the 350°F oven. The timing will vary according to the juiciness of the tomatoes.

Serve warm or at room temperature, or store in the refrigerator (see recipe introduction).

Cherry tomatoes at the Market

FALL

HAPPY QUAIL FARMS
of East Palo Alto

Naturally Grown Produce

Eggplant
Pimientos de Padrón
Hot Peppers
Sweet Peppers
804 Green Street, East Palo Alto, CA 94303 – 650 325 0839

(opposite) Peppers and chiles

Almonds

Prunus amygdalus var. *dulcis*

"We're flatlanders," Sally Oliver says emphatically. "My husband George's family bought this farm in 1929—he grew up here. In 1950, when we got married, we joined the family business." Oliver Family Orchards is forty acres of almond and walnut trees in the flat, fertile Sacramento Valley.

Today, a lot of the area's old orchards are gone. George Oliver grew up with many of his trees, he knows and cares for them, and a good number of them are still producing fruit after eighty years. The best time of the farm year for the Olivers is late February. Light breezes send fragrant pink-and-white blossoms drifting down from the graceful, tall almond trees. "It is so beautiful that we can hardly stand it—overwhelmingly beautiful really," says Sally. "We stand in the orchard when the trees are in full bloom and the bees are doing their job, just to hear the buzz."

The almond nut is actually the seed of the leathery almond fruit, and its production is an important part of the state's agricultural bottom line: California is the largest producer of commercially grown almonds in the world. The Olivers grow three varieties on their acreage. Neplus, the darkest and largest, develops a marvelous sweet flavor when cooked. The Mission has the strongest flavor of the three. A particularly old variety, it has a small production and very sweet meat. It outsells the other varieties by fifteen to one. The third type, Nonpareil, has a buttery flavor and light skin.

George manages the orchard and wholesale side of the business, Sally sells almonds and walnuts at the Ferry Plaza Farmers' Market, and the Olivers' daughter, Cathy Mullanix, sells the family's nuts at the Montecito Farmers' Market. The beat goes on.

Season

Almonds are harvested mid-August to mid-September, but they are in the market all year long.

Choosing

Almonds are sold in their shells and out. Whole shelled almonds are sold with their papery brown skin on, called natural almonds, and with the skin removed, known as blanched almonds. Almonds are also sold sliced or slivered (natural or blanched). Look for almonds that are uniform in color and not limp or shriveled. In addition, smell the almonds. They should smell sweet and nutty.

1 POUND SHELLED ALMONDS EQUALS 3 1/2 CUPS NUTS

5 OUNCES ALMONDS EQUALS 1 CUP NUTS

1 CUP WHOLE ALMONDS YIELDS 1 1/4 CUPS FINELY CHOPPED NUTS

Storing

Sally Oliver says without hesitation, "Freeze your almonds." Pack shelled almonds into zippered plastic bags and store in the freezer for up to a year. If you end up with unshelled almonds (they are sold only shelled at the market), keep them in a cool, dark, dry place away from all heat sources. Almonds have a high fat content that makes them susceptible to spoilage. They can easily absorb strong odors and should never be stored in the same room with pungent goods, such as paint and cleaning supplies.

Preparing

Sally Oliver also offers sound advice on blanching shelled almonds, that is removing their thin outer skins: "Place almonds in a bowl and pour enough boiling water into the bowl to cover them. Let the almonds soak for only 1 minute. You don't want them to lose their crispness. Drain, rinse under cold water, and drain again. Pinch each almond between a thumb and forefinger to remove the brown skin. Be careful where you aim, because the almonds tend to shoot across the room."

To grind almonds, use a food processor, or a coffee grinder for an even finer grind, pulsing on and off until finely ground. Work in small batches, and be careful not to overprocess, or the nuts will turn oily and pasty. If the almonds are to be ground for a cake, grind them with a small amount of the flour called for in the recipe.

Sally Oliver at Cache Creek Farms market stall

Sally's Roasted Almonds

Makes 4 cups

George Oliver likes to roast his almonds anointed with olive oil and sprinkled with salt. Sally prefers them prepared this way.

4 CUPS NATURAL ALMONDS

1/2 LARGE EGG WHITE

4 TEASPOONS FINE SEA SALT

Preheat the oven to 275°F. Lightly oil a rimmed baking sheet.

In a large bowl, combine the almonds and egg white and mix until the nuts are evenly coated. Sprinkle with the salt and toss again to coat evenly. Evenly spread the nuts on the prepared baking sheet and roast for 20 minutes. The nuts will be fragrant though their color will change little. Let cool and store in an airtight container.

Macarons

Makes about 5 dozen cookies

The recipe for this airy almond cookie was most likely carried to France by the chefs who accompanied Italian Catherine de Médicis there in the sixteenth century. For the finest grind, use an electric coffee grinder and grind the nuts in small batches, always pulsing to avoid turning them into almond butter.

2 CUPS FINELY GROUND
BLANCHED ALMONDS

2 CUPS CONFECTIONERS'
SUGAR

4 LARGE EGG WHITES

5 TABLESPOONS GRANULATED
SUGAR

1/2 TEASPOON PURE VANILLA
EXTRACT

Preheat the oven to 350°F. Line 2 baking sheets with parchment paper.

Sift the ground almonds and the confectioners' sugar together into a bowl. In a large bowl, using an electric mixer fitted with the whip attachment, beat the egg whites on medium-low speed until frothy, about 2 minutes. Increase the speed to medium-high and beat until the whites form soft peaks, about 2 minutes. Sprinkle in the granulated sugar and vanilla and continue beating until glossy peaks form, 2 minutes more.

Fold the almond mixture, one-third at a time, into the egg whites, being careful not to deflate the whites. Spoon about half of the batter into a pastry bag fitted with a 1/2-inch plain tip. (If you do not have a pastry bag, spoon the batter into a heavy-duty plastic bag, and cut about 1/2 inch off one of the bottom corners.) Pipe cookies about the size of a half-dollar onto a prepared baking sheet, spacing them about 1 inch apart. Repeat with the remaining batter and the second baking sheet.

Bake the cookies until puffed and lightly colored, 10 to 15 minutes. Transfer the pans to wire racks and let the cookies cool completely before peeling them off the parchment. Store in an airtight container.

Apples

Karen Bates won't eat an apple after Christmas. She believes in living and eating in season. Her husband, Tim, their children, and her parents, Don and Sally Schmitt, are three generations who work and live on The Apple Farm near Philo, California.

In 1993, the Schmitt and Bates families bought a dilapidated orchard in the enchanting Anderson Valley and began renovating it. By pruning and coddling the old trees and planting fifty new trees, all heirloom varieties, the thirty-two acre, eighteen-hundred-tree orchard is now thriving. Eighty different apple varieties grow on the farm.

In late summer and through fall, apples are handpicked and packed for market. Bates, who knows her apples, has discovered most early varieties, like Pink Pearl, a crisp and aromatic fruit with deep pink flesh, and thin-skinned, juicy Gravensteins, don't store well. They have low acid and high sugar, which makes delicate and fine-textured eating apples that tend to fall apart when cooked—great for applesauce, not so great for pies.

By the time it's "full on" fall, Bates can't wait for that first magnificent bite of her favorite, the Sierra Beauty, an intensely flavored, crisp, juicy apple with a terrific balance of sweet and tart.

Firm, hard, unblemished late-season apples, like Splendour, Arkansas Black, and Black Twig, are the best keepers. The colder the temperature (above 32°F), the longer they keep. The farm makes the most of their bounty, producing and selling chutneys, jams, jellies, apple cider syrup, and aged apple balsamic vinegar.

No wonder Bates says, "January is my favorite time of the year—the harvest is over, the storeroom is full. We can look back with a little perspective and look forward and imagine the next year. The orchard keeps us where we should be—in the season."

Season

Harvesttime in the Anderson Valley starts in late July and is finished by December, with September and October the peak months. Other vendors at the market may extend beyond December.

Choosing

Look for apples with tight, smooth, unblemished skin (although brown freckles or streaks are characteristic of some varieties) and good color for the particular variety. The fruits should be firm to hard. If they feel slightly soft, the flesh can be mealy and mushy.

Varieties differ in color, texture, taste, and size. Their skin can be green, yellow, or various shades of red, with a texture from tender to tough. Their flesh can range from white, cream, and yellow to pink, and their flavor can be tart or sweet and everything in between. As a general rule, sweet apples are eaten out of hand, while tart apples are used for cooking.

3 MEDIUM-SIZED APPLES WEIGH ABOUT 1 POUND

1 POUND APPLES YIELDS ABOUT 3 CUPS SLICED FRUIT

Storing

Ripe apples can turn mealy if left at room temperature for more than 48 hours, so to preserve their flavor and crispness, store them in plastic bags in the refrigerator for up to 6 weeks. An old-fashioned way to keep apples is to wrap each fruit in tissue or newspaper and store in a cool, dark, dry place. Cold temperatures (above freezing) prevent further ripening (and spoiling) after apples are picked.

Preparing

You don't need to peel apples unless you are using a recipe that directs you to peel. If you will be cooking the apple whole, core it before peeling. To core an apple, use an apple corer, or quarter the fruit and then cut out the semicircular portions that contain the seeds. To peel an apple, use a vegetable peeler or paring knife and remove the thinnest possible layer of skin. (With that skin goes much of the apple's fiber and flavor, so be sure you need to peel the fruit before you begin.) Apple flesh turns brown if exposed to air, so have ready a bowl of cold water to which you have added some lemon juice, and toss the cut fruit into the water as you work.

Gâteau aux Pommes

Serves 6

This very old-fashioned—and very simple—French apple "cake" allows the apple flavor to take center stage.

2 TABLESPOONS UNSALTED
BUTTER

GRATED ZEST AND JUICE OF
2 ORANGES

3 TABLESPOONS SUGAR

4 POUNDS TART APPLES

Preheat the oven to 150°F. Select a 6-cup soufflé dish. Cut out a round of parchment that fits snugly just inside the dish, to use for covering the apples. Butter the bottom and sides of the dish and one side of the parchment with the butter.

In a food processor, combine the orange zest and sugar and pulse until the zest is completely incorporated into the sugar. Put the orange juice in a large bowl.

Working with 1 apple at a time, core the whole apple and, using a mandoline or a very sharp knife, thinly slice it crosswise to create rings. Immediately toss the apple slices in the orange juice to prevent browning. Repeat with the remaining apples, adding them to the bowl.

Arrange the apple slices, overlapping them, in the prepared soufflé dish and lightly sprinkle each layer with the orange zest–sugar mixture. Top with the parchment round, buttered side down. Bake until the apples are meltingly soft, 12 to 14 hours or up to overnight.

Remove from the oven and allow to cool until just warm. Gently press down on the parchment and then pour off any accumulated juices into a small saucepan. Place over medium-high heat and cook until the juices thicken and caramelize slightly, about 10 minutes.

Meanwhile, remove the parchment carefully and invert a flat serving plate larger than the soufflé dish over the top. Holding the plate firmly to the dish, flip them together. Lift off the dish, leaving the cake on the plate. Drizzle the caramelized juices over the cake.

Apples

Malus domestica

The Apple Farm's Applesauce

Applesauce at The Apple Farm is made according to this flexible recipe created by Los Angeles chef Suzanne Goins. You adjust the taste and sweetness according to the type of apples that you use, and you make the amount you need. Serve with pork, game birds, or sausages.

APPLES SUCH AS GRAVENSTEIN, PINK PEARL, JONATHAN, GOLDEN DELICIOUS, SPITZENBERG, SIERRA BEAUTY, OR ASTRACHAN, CORED

APPLE JUICE

SUGAR

SALT

A GENEROUS CHUNK OF BUTTER

CHOPPED FRESH THYME LEAVES

Peel and slice the apples into a heavy pot with a lid. Add apple juice to reach halfway up the sides of the layer of sliced apples. Bring to a simmer, cover, and cook until the apples are soft when pierced with a paring knife. The timing will depend on the type of apple, but plan on 20 to 30 minutes.

Add sugar and salt to taste, the butter, and a generous pinch of thyme and stir vigorously until the sugar has dissolved and butter has melted. Serve warm or cold.

The Apple Farm market stall

Karen's Apple Cake

Makes two 9-inch layers

Karen Bates makes this easy, velvety smooth apple cake using all organic ingredients. Serve it plain, frost it with your favorite cream cheese icing to which you have added a handful of finely chopped fresh basil, or pair with some very fresh goat cheese.

1 TABLESPOON UNSALTED
BUTTER

1 1/2 CUPS COLD-PRESSED
CANOLA OIL

2 CUPS SUGAR

4 LARGE EGGS

2 CUPS UNBLEACHED
ALL-PURPOSE FLOUR

1 TABLESPOON BAKING SODA

2 TEASPOONS GROUND
CINNAMON

1/2 TEASPOON GROUND
NUTMEG

1 TEASPOON SALT

3 CUPS GRATED UNPEELED
TART APPLES

1 TABLESPOON PURE
VANILLA EXTRACT

Preheat the oven to 325°F. Grease two 9-inch round cake pans with the butter.

In a large bowl, combine the canola oil, sugar, and eggs. Using an electric mixer, beat on medium speed until well mixed. In another bowl, sift together the flour, baking soda, cinnamon, nutmeg, and salt. Mix the dry ingredients into the wet ingredients just until well incorporated. Add the apples and the vanilla and again mix well.

Divide the batter evenly between the prepared pans. Bake until a small knife inserted in the center of each cake comes out clean, 35 to 40 minutes. Let cool in the pans on wire racks for 10 minutes, then unmold and let cool completely. If you are icing the cake, use both layers. Otherwise, serve 1 cake and wrap the second cake; it will keep for several days at room temperature or in the freezer for up to 6 months.

Apple Farm apples

Artichokes

Cynara scolymus

Edible thistles of the sunflower family, artichokes are native to the Mediterranean and were carried to California in the 1880s by Italian immigrants. They flourish in coastal climates, where a layer of marine fog, cool summers, and mild winters provide ideal weather conditions. Virtually 100 percent of the U.S. crop is grown in California, thriving in loamy and sandy or clay soil with good drainage.

Mariquita Farm (page 182), near Gilroy, sells large globe artichokes at the market. "We pick them when they are young," says Julia Wiley, who operates Mariquita with her husband, Andy Griffin. "They are best when green and unopened, with a turgid stem that shows no signs of browning." Annabelle Lenderink of Star Route Farms, in Bolinas, harvests Imperial Star globe artichokes, which are lighter colored than traditional globe varieties. "The first artichoke to appear at the top of the plant is the largest," explains Lenderink, "and those picked thereafter are all smaller." The "babies," which grow at the junction of a stem and leaf, are hidden by large, silvery leaves and may not grow bigger than a walnut. Their chokes have barely formed, so they are delicious eaten raw.

An artichoke plant takes up a lot of room in the garden, but when it flowers, it is truly stunning. Some nutritionists claim that these thistly vegetables are good for you, too, lowering blood cholesterol and blood sugar and helping to keep your liver healthy.

Season
March through May with a secondary, smaller crop in the fall.

Choosing
Look for artichokes that feel heavy for their size. The stalk should correspond to the size of the artichoke, and never be spindly. Look for leaves that are dark to acid green without any browning or dryness. Annabelle Lenderink says that fresh artichokes should squeak when firmly rubbed and they should be tightly closed at the tip. The purple, pointed-leaved, thorny-tipped artichokes from Tuscany are becoming more widely available here. Because of their sharp thorns, Warren Weber, also of Star Route Farms, describes them as "a strain that seems to be reverting back to a thistle." They are grown from seed rather than being cloned or picked from the mother plant, so they are random in size and shape. The smaller ones have less of a choke than the bigger ones.

Storing
Artichokes lose moisture quickly after harvesting. Eat them as soon as you can after buying. If you must store them, slip them into a plastic bag and keep in the vegetable bin of the refrigerator for no more than a few days.

Artichokes

Preparing baby artichokes
1. Slicing off top 1 inch of the leaves

2. Trimming the bottom and stem

3. Rubbing with lemon

4. Trimmed, halved artichokes in lemon water

Preparing

If artichokes come into contact with air, iron, or aluminum, they will discolor. To avoid this, always use a stainless-steel or carbon–stainless steel alloy knife and cookware of stainless steel, enameled cast iron, tempered glass, or other nonreactive material. To prevent trimmed artichokes from darkening, drop them into a bowl of water mixed with a splash of white vinegar or a few squeezes of lemon juice. Alternatively, rub the trimmed area with the cut side of a lemon half.

To prepare a large artichoke for boiling or steaming: Pull off and discard the tough outer leaves. With a small, sharp knife, trim off the base of the stem, then peel the stem (a peeled stem tastes as good as an artichoke heart). If you want to remove the thorny tips of the artichoke, slice off the top 1 to 2 inches of the leaves, using a large knife. Rub the cut surfaces with a lemon half. If you will be slipping stuffing into the center of the artichoke (and sometimes between the leaves as well), gently pull apart the leaves at the top. Then, with a sharp, pointed spoon or a small, sharp knife, carefully dig out and discard the choke. Press the leaves gently back into the globe shape.

To slice a large artichoke for grilling, sautéing, or roasting: Trim as directed for boiling or steaming, but pull off the outer leaves until you reach the pale or acid green leaves. Cut the artichoke in half lengthwise. Scoop out the choke with a sharp, pointed spoon or a small, sharp knife. Lay each artichoke half, cut side down, on a work surface and, using a large knife, cut lengthwise into slices, including the stem. You can also leave the artichoke in halves, or cut each half in half again. Drop into lemon water until ready to use.

To prepare baby artichokes for eating raw or for cooking: Cut off the stem flush with the bottom. Pull off and discard a few layers of outer leaves until tender, pale green leaves are visible. Using a large knife, slice off the top 1 inch of the leaves. You can boil, steam, or braise the artichokes whole. To slice the artichokes, cut in half lengthwise. You do not need to remove the choke, as it is not yet prickly. Lay each artichoke half, cut side down, on a work surface and cut lengthwise into slices. You can also leave the artichokes in halves, or cut each half in half again. Drop into lemon water until ready to use.

To prepare an artichoke heart or bottom: Using a large, sharp knife, cut off the leaves where they meet the base. With a sharp, pointed spoon or small, sharp knife, scrape or cut out the fuzzy choke, and neatly trim the exposed area and the bottom. A traditional San Francisco recipe calls for steaming the whole bottom and then filling it with crab or shrimp salad.

Roasted Halibut with Braised Artichokes and Potatoes   Serves 4

Here's a delightful one-dish meal. The earthiness of the artichokes and potatoes riffs off the saltiness of the olives and the mild, sweet flavors of the fish. You don't need to pit the tiny olives, but remind your guests about the pits when you serve the dish. You can use sea bass, salmon, or rock cod in the absence of halibut. Roasting the fish at a high temperature simulates cooking in a wood-burning oven—the fish is done quickly, before it has a chance to dry out. Halibut has almost no fat and cooks very quickly.

1 POUND YELLOW FINN POTA-TOES, PEELED AND CUT INTO 1/2 -INCH-THICK SLICES

SALT

2 POUNDS SKIN-ON HALIBUT FILLET, A SINGLE FILLET OR PIECES

FRESHLY GROUND BLACK PEPPER

12 BABY ARTICHOKES, ABOUT 2 OUNCES EACH, OR 3 GLOBE ARTICHOKES, TRIMMED AND VERY THINLY SLICED

1/4 CUP EXTRA-VIRGIN OLIVE OIL, PLUS EXTRA FOR DRIZZLING

2 CLOVES GARLIC, CRUSHED

1 FRESH ROSEMARY SPRIG

3/4 CUP DRY WHITE WINE

ABOUT 36 NIÇOISE OLIVES

1 LEMON, QUARTERED

Preheat the oven to 500°F.

In a saucepan, combine the potatoes with water to cover, add some salt, and bring to a boil. Cook until nearly tender, 8 to 10 minutes. Drain well.

Season the fish generously on both sides with salt and pepper. In a bowl, combine the potatoes, artichokes, 1/4 cup olive oil, garlic, rosemary, and wine and toss to mix evenly. Turn into an oval gratin dish or other baking dish just large enough to hold the mixture and the fish.

Measure the fish fillet at its thickest point. Nestle the fish, skin side up, in the vegetable mixture, and drizzle with a little olive oil. Roast until the fish is opaque when tested with a fork and the skin is browned, about 7 to 9 minutes per inch of thickness.

Remove from the oven and lift off and discard the skin from the fish. Pick out and discard the rosemary. Scatter the olives around the fish and serve directly from the dish, or transfer the fish and vegetables to a warmed platter and scatter the olives around the fish. Serve with lemon wedges on the side and olive oil for drizzling.

Slivered Raw Artichokes with Olive Oil and Shaved Pecorino   Serves 4 to 6

Rose Pistola, a Ligurian restaurant in the heart of San Francisco's North Beach, serves these slivered artichokes with mild extra-virgin olive oil and shards of pecorino as an antipasto. Use only tight-tipped, tender, perfectly fresh baby artichokes for this recipe.

2 LEMONS

24 BABY ARTICHOKES, ABOUT
2 OUNCES EACH

EXTRA-VIRGIN OLIVE OIL AS
NEEDED

SALT AND FRESHLY GROUND
BLACK PEPPER

1/4 -POUND WEDGE PECORINO
CHEESE

Fill a bowl with water. Halve 1 lemon, squeeze the juice from both halves into the water, and then throw in the spent halves. Trim the baby artichokes, then using a mandoline fitted with the slicing blade, and with the hand guard in place, or using a sharp knife, slice as thinly as possible. As the artichokes are cut, slip the slices into the lemon water.

When all the artichokes are sliced, drain, pat dry, and place in a shallow bowl. Halve the remaining lemon and squeeze the juice over the artichokes. Pour in olive oil just to cover and toss to coat evenly. Season with salt and pepper and toss again.

Using a vegetable peeler, shave curls of the pecorino cheese over the top, then serve.

Baby Artichokes Braised in White Wine and Thyme   Serves 4

Another way to keep trimmed artichokes from turning black is to coat them with olive oil, instead of imposing the flavor of lemon. Here's a delicious side dish to go with fish, fowl, or meat.

1/2 CUP EXTRA-VIRGIN
OLIVE OIL

12 BABY ARTICHOKES, ABOUT
2 OUNCES EACH

1 LARGE WHITE ONION

1 CLOVE GARLIC, CRUSHED

SALT AND FRESHLY GROUND
BLACK PEPPER

1 FRESH THYME SPRIG

1/2 CUP DRY WHITE WINE

Pour the olive oil into a bowl. Trim and quarter the artichokes lengthwise. As you cut the artichokes, place them, cut side down, in the oil and leave them there while you chop the onion.

Drain off the olive oil into a skillet and warm it over medium heat. Add the onion and garlic and cook, stirring constantly, until the onion has softened, about 2 minutes. Add the artichokes to the onion mixture and cook uncovered, stirring occasionally, until golden brown, about 10 minutes.

Sprinkle the artichokes with salt and pepper and throw in the thyme sprig. Pour in the wine, and then add water just until the artichokes are barely covered. Cover and continue to cook until the artichoke bottoms offer little or no resistance to a fork tip, 10 to 15 minutes, depending on the toughness of the artichokes. If the liquid does not evaporate, remove the lid and continue to cook until it does.

Remove from the heat and serve warm or at room temperature.

Broccoli and Broccoli Rabe

Brassica oleracea and *Brassica rapa*

Ask Andy Griffin of Mariquita Farm a question and be prepared to get an informed, definitive answer. Griffin is a passionate farmer-philosopher-activist—and a writer extraordinaire. He and his wife, Julia Wiley, publish a weekly e-newsletter on what's cooking in their kitchen, what's growing on their farm, what's coming to market, and what's going on in Andy's head. He should run for political office. But if he did, it would be our loss, because he grows and sells some of the best and most interesting vegetables around. Though Griffin has been farming organically for over twenty years, and is an expert on everything he grows, his specialty is broccoli.

Before the 1920s, broccoli was not widely known in the United States. Italian immigrants introduced it, and it was first grown commercially in their California market gardens. In the mid-1920s, Castroville's D'Arrigo family packed the mild-flavored Calabrese variety in ice on railcars and sent it across the country to East Coast markets. America was soon sold on broccoli, and today, the large-headed Calabrese is the primary commercial crop.

Griffin grows the self-sprouting Broccoli di Cicco, an antique variety of Calabrese. With consecutive planting and twice-weekly harvest, he can bring broccoli to the market all year. (Each successive picking yields smaller but still flavorful florets.) This careful farm management has also enabled him to keep his same crew working full-time for nine years. And this matters to Griffin, who can see the social consequences where others only see broccoli.

Mariquita Farm cultivates broccoli rabe (also known as rapini, *cima di rapa*, *broccoletti di rape*, and many colloquial names), too. Despite the name, it is more closely related to turnips than broccoli. It is a pleasantly bitter vegetable, with cooks putting more emphasis on its spicy, slender flower stalks and leafy greens than on its small flowering heads. Leafier wild varieties grow in Italy, where they are prized for their strong, bitter flavor.

Season

Broccoli and broccoli rabe are available just about year-round, with peak season from October through April.

Choosing

Look for broccoli with tight, compact bud clusters that are deep green or green tinged with purple and fresh-looking leaves. Yellow flower buds are a sign of age. The leaves of broccoli rabe should look crisp and fresh.

A 1 1/2 -POUND BUNCH OF BROCCOLI YIELDS 4 CUPS TRIMMED BROCCOLI

Storing

Put all types of broccoli in perforated plastic bags and store in the vegetable bin of the refrigerator for up to 4 days.

Preparing

For broccoli, peel the tough outer skin from the stalks. This not only makes the stalks more tender, but also ensures that the stems and florets will cook in the same amount of time. Cut off 1 to 2 inches from the bottom of the stalk or any split portions and discard. Divide the stalks into lengthwise spears or trim even further if your recipe calls for florets. For broccoli rabe, simply trim off the tough stem bottoms and any wilted leaves and then cut as directed in individual recipes.

Broccoli rabe

Broccoli and Broccoli Rabe

Brassica oleracea and *Brassica rapa*

Julia's Essential Rapini Recipe

Serves 4

Andy Griffin prefers rapini to the other many names for this vegetable because "it alludes to the vegetable's roots as a turnip (*rapa*), but it ends in a cute "ini" diminutive. This classic preparation is how Julia Wiley most often cooks the intensely flavored rapini grown on the farm. She likes to use penne or *spaghettini* for the pasta.

SALT

1 POUND RAPINI, TRIMMED

1/2 POUND PASTA

2 TABLESPOONS EXTRA-VIRGIN OLIVE OIL

1 OR 2 CLOVES GARLIC, CHOPPED

RED PEPPER FLAKES

FRESHLY GROUND BLACK PEPPER

GRATED PARMIGIANO-REGGIANO CHEESE (OPTIONAL)

Bring a large pot of salted water to a boil over high heat. Add the rapini and cook for about 3 minutes. Using a long-handled sieve, carefully scoop the rapini out of the water and set aside to cool for a minute.

Meanwhile, add the pasta to the boiling water. While the pasta cooks, heat the olive oil in a skillet over medium heat, add the garlic, and cook just until soft, about 2 minutes. Do not let it get brown. Add the rapini and season to taste with the red pepper flakes, salt, and black pepper.

When the pasta is ready, drain it, return it to the pot, and then add the rapini along with the garlic-pepper oil in the skillet. Toss, taste for seasoning, and add some grated Parmigiano if you like.

Broccoli and Broccoli Rabe

Brassica oleracea and *Brassica rapa*

Simple Green Soup

Serves 4

Make this soup for lunch or supper when you have some good homemade stock on hand.

SALT

2 POUNDS BROCCOLI RABE, TRIMMED AND COARSELY CHOPPED

1/2 CUP ORZO OR OTHER SMALL PASTA SHAPE

2 CLOVES GARLIC, SPEARED TOGETHER ON A TOOTHPICK

4 CUPS RICH HOMEMADE CHICKEN STOCK

FRESHLY GROUND BLACK PEPPER

GRATED PARMIGIANO-REGGIANO CHEESE FOR SERVING

Bring a large pot of salted water to a boil over high heat. Add the broccoli rabe and cook for about 3 minutes. Using a long-handled sieve, carefully scoop the broccoli rabe out of the water and set aside.

Add the pasta to the boiling water and cook until al dente. While the pasta cooks, combine the garlic and stock in a saucepan and bring to a simmer over high heat. Season the stock to taste with salt and pepper. Remove and discard the garlic.

Drain the pasta and add the broccoli rabe and pasta to the simmering stock. Simmer for 1 minute, then ladle into bowls. Sprinkle with lots of cheese and serve.

Jon's Sautéed Broccoli

Serves 4

After a long day in the garden, landscape designer and renowned gardener Jon Carloftis finds that cooking relaxes him, but he is still always looking for ways to simplify recipes. Most often broccoli is blanched before sautéing, but Carloftis skips that step and allows the broccoli to "stew in its own juice," which intensifies its flavor.

3 TABLESPOONS EXTRA-VIRGIN OLIVE OIL

1 YELLOW ONION, THINLY SLICED

1 CLOVE GARLIC, THINLY SLICED

2 OLIVE OIL–PACKED ANCHOVY FILLETS, CHOPPED AND MASHED

2 POUNDS BROCCOLI, TRIMMED AND FLORETS AND STALKS CUT CROSSWISE INTO 1/2 -INCH-THICK SLICES

SALT AND FRESHLY GROUND BLACK PEPPER

In a large skillet, heat the olive oil over medium-high heat. Add the onion, garlic, and anchovies and cook, stirring often, until the onion is soft and lightly browned, about 5 minutes.

Add the broccoli and toss well to mix with the onion and oil. Reduce the heat to medium, cover, and cook until the broccoli is tender but still green and still has a little texture, about 10 minutes.

Season to taste with salt and pepper and serve.

Cardoons

Cynara cardunculus

Cardoons, like their close cousins artichokes, are members of the thistle family and native to the Mediterranean. Some food scholars believe that the relationship is more than simply close, however. They insist that the artichoke was born in fifteenth-century Europe as a result of cultivating a cardoon. Still relatively unknown in the United States, cardoons look like gigantic, overgrown celery stalks with artichoke tendencies, and they taste almost like a tangy cross between artichokes and celery. While the artichoke plant is prized for its edible flowers, the cardoon plant holds the promise of pale, cloudy gray-green stalks.

A damp, mild climate is ideal for cultivating cardoons, and they are grown as a food crop in Italy, France, Spain, Australia, and Northern California, among other places, and primarily as ornamentals in England. Very cold weather is said to make the stalks tender. At the market, you can find cardoons at Tairwa Knoll Farm (page 106).

High in potassium, iron, and vitamins A and C, cardoons are too bitter and tough to eat raw, but once cleaned and cooked, they are an unusual, tender delight. The stalks are dipped into the wonderful Piedmontese *bagna cauda*, a hot dip of olive oil and anchovies, and take well to frying, roasting, and making into soup.

Season
Typically November through February but sometimes into April.

Choosing
Select bunches with firm, fresh, turgid stalks, fresh-looking leaves, and lots of available inner stalks. Keep in mind that the very tough outer stalks must be removed and discarded. So a good batch of inner stalks is important.

Storing
Place cardoons in a plastic bag or wrap in damp kitchen towels and keep in the refrigerator for a day or two. They are best when very fresh, and since they take up a lot of space in the refrigerator, it is wise to prepare them soon after purchase.

Preparing
Strip away and discard the tough outer stalks. Using a stainless-steel or carbon–stainless steel alloy knife, strip the inner stalks of any thorny spurs and fibrous strings, much like you clean celery. Cut the stalks as directed in individual recipes and, if not put into liquid to cook immediately, immerse in water to which lemon juice has been added to stave off browning. You will usually need to simmer the cardoon pieces in liquid for 40 to 60 minutes, or until they are tender, before frying them or using them in a gratin or soup.

Cardoon Gratin

Serves 4 to 6

Here's an easy, delicious way to cook cardoons in the French style with luscious cream and rich cheese. You do not need to soak the cardoons in lemon water to prevent browning, as they go directly into the cream mixture. You can assemble the dish fully up to a couple hours in advance and then put it in the oven about a half hour before dinner.

3 CUPS HEAVY CREAM

1 CUP CHICKEN STOCK, PREFERABLY HOMEMADE

1 BAY LEAF

SALT AND FRESHLY GROUND BLACK PEPPER

3 POUNDS CARDOONS

BUTTER FOR PREPARING GRATIN DISH

1 CUP SHREDDED GRUYÈRE CHEESE

In a large saucepan, combine the cream, stock, and bay leaf, and season with salt and pepper.

Trim the cardoons and cut into 2-inch pieces, placing the pieces immediately into the cream mixture as you go to prevent them from discoloring.

When all of the cardoons are in the pan, place the pan over medium heat and bring to a simmer. Cook, stirring occasionally, until the cardoons are tender, about 1 hour. Meanwhile, butter a 4-cup gratin dish.

When the cardoons are tender, using a slotted spoon remove them from the cream mixture and transfer them to the prepared dish, mounding them up slightly if necessary to make them fit. Reduce the cream mixture to about 3/4 cup over medium heat, about 30 minutes. Discard the bay leaf and pour the reduced sauce over the cardoons. Sprinkle the Gruyère on top.

About 15 minutes before you are ready to bake the gratin, preheat the oven to 350°F. Bake until the top is golden and the gratin is bubbling, about 30 minutes. Remove from the oven, let cool for about 5 minutes, and serve directly from the dish.

Cardoons at the Market

Chiles and Sweet Peppers

Capsicum spp.

In 1492, Columbus, looking for a shortcut to the East Indies and its lucrative spice trade, wound up way off track in the Caribbean. There, the locals were spicing up their food with hot chiles. So instead of bringing home a boatload of *pimienta* (Spanish for black pepper), he returned with his version of pepper, *pimientos*. He also got credit for discovering the Americas.

The words *chile* and *pepper* can be confusing: which is what? As a general rule, sweet peppers have no heat and chiles have varying degrees of it. Originally all wild peppers had heat, but it has been bred out of certain varieties for more diversity in the marketplace. Scoville heat units are used to measure "the burn": sweet bell peppers register 0 units on the scale, while habaneros can hit a searing 300,000 units.

All chiles and sweet peppers start out pale yellow or green and then ripen to bright yellow, orange, red, or chocolate brown. The more mature the chile, the hotter it will be. Its heat is found in tiny blisters of clear, odorless, and flavorless but fiery capsaicin on the white pithy veins and membranes inside the fruit. (Yes, these vegetables are fruits, and members of the nightshade family.)

For the last twenty-five years, Wayne James and his sister, Lee, have been growing sweet peppers and chiles on their farm, Tierra Vegetables, outside of Santa Rosa. From August to November, they bring to market eighteen varieties of fresh sweet peppers and forty different fresh chiles of varying heat. In the winter, they sell jams and jellies and dried chiles. When pressed to choose a couple of favorites, Lee chooses fat, round, sunny yellow Cheese Pimentos, with a sweet, intense flavor and nice thick flesh, and long, green Anaheims, with their mildly hot, good green flavor.

Season

Fresh chiles and sweet peppers are available August through November. Dried chiles are sold year-round.

Choosing

"Look for beautiful peppers," advises Lee James. "You can almost tell from a distance if they're good." A fresh pepper should be well shaped, shiny, hard, and have a full, weighty feel to it. Its stem should be fresh and green. Avoid peppers with dark or soft spots and cracks, except for jalapeños, which can display shallow cracks at their stem ends. Dried chiles should be glossy and intact, and never broken or dusty.

Chiles and Sweet Peppers

Capsicum spp.

Store unwashed peppers in a cool place loosely covered with a kitchen or paper towel. Don't store them in the refrigerator; it's too cold, and while they will continue to look good, the low temperatures will destroy their flavor, leaving them watery and bland. Never store peppers in plastic, which can cause moisture that will spoil them. Even if peppers lose their crunch and get soft overall, their flavor is not affected. On the contrary it becomes more concentrated.

Thin-walled chiles can be successfully dried by stringing them and then hanging the string in a warm, dry place.

Preparing

Be careful when handling chiles. The capsaicin contained in pithy veins and membranes can cause a painful burning sensation. Wear thin rubber gloves or, in a pinch, thin plastic bags to keep this fiery alkaloid off your hands. After removing the gloves, wash your hands thoroughly with soapy water.

Wash chiles just before using them. Remove and discard the seeds. If you want to temper the heat of the chile, remove some or all of the membrane. After handling a chile, Lee James licks one of her fingers. This simple test lets her know how hot it is.

"I'll just tell you how I roast the peppers and chiles," says Evie Truxaw, who has worked for Tierra Vegetables for fifteen years. "I put a bunch of them in the broiler and cook them until they're nice and black. Next, I put them on a plate and cover with a cloth until cool. Then I peel away."

To make chile flakes and powder, wipe off dried chiles with a damp cloth and grind in a mortar and pestle, a spice grinder, or a coffee grinder dedicated to spices. To soften the texture of whole dried chiles, soak them in hot water for about 20 minutes.

To prepare chiles for stuffing: Roast and peel Anaheims or other large, mild chiles according to Evie Truxaw's directions (above). Cut a 2-inch slit near the stem. Holding on to the stem, reach into the chile and detach the core with the seeds attached. Scrape out and discard any remaining seeds.

Lee's Sweet Pepper Sandwich

Makes 1 sandwich

Lee James likes this simple, satisfying open-faced sandwich that lets the sweet roasted flavor come through. It is more of a suggestion than a recipe, with flexibility for the amounts.

EXTRA-VIRGIN OLIVE OIL

LONG ITALIAN SWEET PEP-
PERS, STEMMED, SEEDED,
AND SLICED LENGTHWISE
INTO STRIPS

SLICED GARLIC

SALT AND FRESHLY GROUND
BLACK PEPPER

1 SLICE GOOD SOURDOUGH
BREAD, TOASTED

In a skillet, heat a generous amount of olive oil over medium-high heat. Add the peppers and garlic and season with salt and pepper. Cover and cook, stirring occasionally, until soft, about 10 minutes.

Spoon the pepper mixture onto the toasted bread and serve.

Chiles at Tierra
Vegetables market stall

Chiles Rellenos, Tierra Vegetables Style

Serves 4

Prepare these rustic, delicious stuffed chiles in their traditional manner, fried in oil, as described here, or in a casserole (see variation).

8 LONG, GREEN FRESH CHILES SUCH AS ANAHEIM, ROASTED, PEELED, SLIT, AND SEEDS REMOVED

8 SLICES MONTEREY JACK CHEESE, THE LENGTH AND WIDTH OF THE CHILES

4 LARGE EGGS, SEPARATED

1/4 CUP UNBLEACHED ALL-PURPOSE FLOUR

1/4 CUP WATER

SALT

CANOLA OIL FOR FRYING

SOUR CREAM AND FRESH TOMATO SALSA FOR SERVING (OPTIONAL)

Stuff each chile with a cheese slice and set aside.

In a bowl, whisk together the egg yolks, flour, water, and a little salt. In a large bowl, using a balloon whisk, whisk the whites until they are stiff but not dry. Fold the yolk mixture into the whites in three batches just until combined. Take care not to deflate the whites.

Pour a little canola oil (1/4 inch or so) into a large skillet and place over medium-high heat. When the oil is hot, drop 4 dollops of the egg batter, each large enough to fit a chile on, into the pan. Place a chile on top of each dollop of batter, then spoon more batter on top of each chile. Cook until the batter is browned on the bottom, about 2 minutes. Using a spatula or 2 forks, carefully turn the chiles over and cook until the second side is browned, about 2 minutes longer. Transfer to paper towels to drain briefly.

Serve the chiles hot with sour cream and salsa, if you like.

Variation: To bake the stuffed chiles, preheat the oven to 350°F. Lightly oil a 9-inch square baking pan. Stuff the chiles with cheese and make the batter as described above. Spoon half of the batter onto the bottom of the dish. Put the stuffed chiles on top of the batter (they can overlap), and cover evenly with the remaining batter. Bake until browned, about 25 minutes. Serve with sour cream and salsa.

Evie Truxaw adds that she "often uses a *lot* of roasted peppers, both sweet and chile. I usually lay them flat, cover them with cheese, and then make another layer of the peppers and cheese. I top them off with the fluffy egg batter and bake them."

Mae's Stuffed Peppers   Serves 4

Christopher's grandmother, Mae Lundy, who was born in San Francisco at the end of the nineteenth century, used to make these stuffed peppers with a sweet tomatoey ketchup sauce on cold, foggy nights for her granddaughter.

4 LARGE BELL PEPPERS

SALT

1/4 CUP EXTRA-VIRGIN
OLIVE OIL

1 YELLOW ONION, CHOPPED

3 CLOVES GARLIC, CHOPPED

1 POUND GROUND BEEF CHUCK

11/2 CUPS COOKED
WHITE RICE

1 CUP CANNED CHOPPED
TOMATOES

1 TEASPOON CHOPPED FRESH
OREGANO

FRESHLY GROUND BLACK
PEPPER

1/2 CUP KETCHUP

6 TABLESPOONS PLUS
1/4 CUP WATER

Preheat the oven to 350°F.

Slice the top off of each pepper and remove the seeds. Bring a large pot of water to a boil over high heat and salt the water. Add the bell peppers and parboil for 3 minutes. Remove the peppers with tongs or a slotted spoon and stand them upside to drain well and cool.

In a large skillet, heat the olive oil over medium heat. Add the onion and garlic and cook, stirring, until soft and golden, 10 to 15 minutes. Add the beef, breaking up the lumps with the back of a spoon, and cook, stirring occasionally, until the meat just turns from red to pink, about 3 minutes. Remove the skillet from the heat and add the rice, tomatoes, and oregano. Generously season with salt and pepper and then mix well.

Arrange the peppers, cut side up, in a baking dish in which they fit snugly. Spoon the filling into the peppers, dividing it evenly. In a small bowl, stir together the ketchup and the 6 tablespoons water and drizzle the mixture evenly over the filling in each pepper. Pour the 1/4 cup water into the baking dish.

Bake the peppers, basting with the juices in the dish once or twice, until the peppers have softened and turned a dull green, about 1 hour. Serve with the juices from the dish spooned over the top.

Grapes

Vitis vinifera and *V. labrusca*

Lots of different table-grape varieties show up at the Ferry Plaza market, but John Lagier's Bronx Seedless is legendary. (There is some irony that arguably the best table grape grown in California is named the Bronx Seedless.)

"My Dad was a grape grower," says Lagier. "He grew wine grapes commercially. When I left home I wanted to be a farmer, too, so I started out managing a ten-acre farm for a guy who worked in the Silicon Valley. That farm was a botanical Garden of Eden. The owner was from the East Coast, and so we grew a table-grape variety developed at Cornell in New York State—the Bronx Seedless. I loved those grapes, so I took cuttings and propagated vines for my own farm."

Today, Lagier has five acres of grapes growing on double-wire trellises. A vigorous grower with large leaves, the Bronx Seedless is a cross between *Vitis vinifera* (thin-skinned wine grapes) and *V. labrusca* (grapy-flavored native American grapes). It is thin skinned, very fruity, and has a deep floral essence and refreshing mouthfeel. These long clusters of sweet red grapes aren't suited for shipping. "They are just too finicky," Lagier says. "But gosh they're great—just killer." When they show up at the end of summer at Lagier's booth, people stand in line to buy them.

Season

Many grape varieties come to market in late summer through fall. Lagier's Bronx Seedless are harvested and available mid-August through September.

Choosing

Look for plump, full grapes with no softening or deterioration near the stem end. Avoid wrinkled or mushy fruit. A white bloom is an indication that the grapes have been handled carefully.

Storing

Store grapes unwashed, on a paper towel, in a perforated or open plastic bag in the refrigerator for up to 1 week. Grapes do not continue to ripen after picking.

Preparing

"Wash grapes in cold water," John Lagier says. "A cool 60°F is the perfect temperature to bring out their full, sweet flavor. I love to eat them out of hand, but many of my customers freeze them for a cooled, refreshing treat." You can also serve them at the end of a meal, in a large bowl filled with ice and water.

Freezing

Rinse the grapes, remove and discard the stems, and pat dry with paper towels. Arrange them in a single layer on a tray or pan that will fit in your freezer, then slip them in to freeze until solid, about 2 hours. Transfer the frozen grapes to a zippered plastic bag, squeeze out all the air, and seal closed or put in an airtight container. They will keep for up to 2 weeks.

Green Grapes in Sour Cream and Brown Sugar

Serves 4

This seemingly odd combination is an easy and delicious way to finish a meal. The creamy tartness of the sour cream makes the grapes taste that much sweeter.

1 POUND SEEDLESS GREEN
GRAPES, STEMMED

2 GENEROUS PACKED TABLE-
SPOONS BROWN SUGAR

1/2 TEASPOON GROUND
CARDAMOM

1 CUP SOUR CREAM

4 FRESH MINT SPRIGS
(OPTIONAL)

Put the grapes in a bowl. Sprinkle the brown sugar and cardamom over them, and use your hands to mix gently together until the grapes are evenly coated. Set aside until the sugar dissolves and is no longer grainy, 10 to 15 minutes.

Using a rubber spatula, fold the sour cream into the grapes, coating evenly. Cover and chill for several hours.

To serve, spoon the well-chilled grapes into individual dishes and garnish with the mint sprigs, if you like.

Grapes at the Market

Grapes

Vitis vinifera and *V. labrusca*

Grape Jelly

Makes 3 half pints

This soft-set luscious grape jelly is perfect to serve on buttered toast in the morning or with a pork roast for supper. Use any grape variety, as long as the grapes are plump and delicious. You can use this same recipe to make a clear, beautiful jelly with any type of berry. The apples add the pectin that the jelly needs to set.

3 QUARTS GRAPES WITH STEMS
INTACT (ABOUT 6 POUNDS)

SKINS FROM 2 GREEN APPLES

ABOUT 3 CUPS SUGAR

In a large, heavy enameled cast-iron or other nonreactive pot, combine the grapes and apple skins. Gently crush the grapes with the back of a wooden spoon. Place over medium-low heat, bring just to a simmer, and cook until the grapes collapse slightly and lose their vibrant color, about 1 hour.

Transfer the fruit and juice to a large jelly bag suspended over a bowl. (You may have to do this in batches). Don't press on the grapes, or the jelly could end up cloudy. When the juice stops running, discard the contents of the jelly bag. Measure the juice. Each quart of fruit should yield about 1 cup juice.

Have ready 3 sterilized half-pint jars. Pour the juice back into the pot, and add 1 cup sugar for every cup of juice. Place over medium heat, bring to a boil, and boil, skimming off any foam, until the liquid reaches 220°F on a candy thermometer, about 10 minutes. Stir occasionally to prevent sticking. If you don't have a thermometer, slip a couple of small saucers into the freezer to chill well before you begin boiling the juice. Then, when you think the juice is ready, spoon a few drops onto a chilled saucer and leave for about 2 minutes; if it sets up and wrinkles slightly when you push it with your finger, it is ready.

Ladle the hot jelly into the steriziled jars, screw on the lids, and let cool undisturbed on the kitchen counter for 24 hours. Store in the refrigerator for up to several months (you are only making 3 half pints, so you are sure to eat it faster).

Persimmons

Diospyros kaki

Persimmons are available mainly in two varieties on the West Coast. Fuyus, short, squat, and shaped like a small apple, are eaten when crisp, usually out of hand, while the acorn-shaped Hachiya must ripen to a nearly gelatinous state to be edible, and is then usually turned into a pudding, cookies, or a cake. Native to Asia, and the season's most underappreciated fruits, persimmons are beguiling on the tree: amber globes dangling from spare, leafless, woody limbs.

"Most farmers can't give them away," says Stan DeVoto, who is also known at the market for his splashy array of cut flowers and Sebastopol apples. "Every year I pull up more trees so that I can make room for flowers and apples. Customers seem to prefer the Fuyus because they can be eaten out of hand. But the Hachiyas are best for baking."

Bill Crepps of Everything Under the Sun, in Winters, has been farming persimmons organically for fifteen years. Market shoppers know him best for selling unusual sun-dried or dehydrated fruits, including persimmons, which keep their vibrant color and taste.

The only persimmons native to North America (*Diospyros virginiana*), found primarily in the eastern Midwest and in some Atlantic and Southern states, are unlike the varieties of California, the Mediterranean, or Asia. They are small and dark and considered ripe once they fall to the ground. They are far too puckery before that point. You won't find them at the market, but if you should come across them elsewhere, they are good eaten out of hand or used in cakes and puddings.

Season
Fall and Winter.

Choosing
Both the Hachiya and Fuyu should be a rich orange. You can purchase Hachiyas when they are still firm and ripen them at home, or purchase them soft and ripe. Fuyus should be firm and the small leaves surrounding the stem should be fresh looking.

Storing
Arrange firm Hachiyas, point side up, on a windowsill or as a centerpiece on a platter and wait for them to ripen. Once ripe, they can be stored in the refrigerator for a few days. If you are in a hurry, place firm Hachiyas in the freezer as is for 24 hours. Then thaw them in the refrigerator and use them for baking: scoop the flesh from the peel, remove any seeds, and purée the flesh in a food processor. If you have too many Hachiyas ripening at the same time, scoop out the flesh, measure it, place in zippered plastic bags, label and date, and freeze for up to 2 months. Store Fuyus at room temperature for a day or two, or in the refrigerator for longer.

Persimmons

Diospyros kaki

Preparing

Fuyus, which are essentially seedless, can be eaten peel and all, or you can peel and slice them for salads. You need to peel Hachiyas and remove any small, dark seeds from the pulp.

Fuyu Persimmon and Radicchio Salad with
Feta and Pomegranate Seeds

Serves 4 to 6

The colors of this salad (pictured opposite)—red, orange, and white—are dazzling. The sprinkle of pomegranate seeds provides a good crunch, and the feta adds a nice saltiness, riffing against the sweet persimmon. Serve as a first course, or as a main course for lunch.

FOR THE VINAIGRETTE

2 TABLESPOONS APPLE
BALSAMIC VINEGAR (PAGE 170)
OR 2 TABLESPOONS RED WINE
VINEGAR AND A FEW DROPS
AGED BALSAMIC VINEGAR

1 SHALLOT, MINCED

SALT AND FRESHLY GROUND
BLACK PEPPER

1/3 CUP EXTRA-VIRGIN
OLIVE OIL

3 FUYU PERSIMMONS, PEELED
AND THINLY SLICED CROSSWISE

1 HEAD RADICCHIO, CORED AND
THINLY SLICED

2 CUPS SMALL ARUGULA
LEAVES

1/4 CUP CRUMBLED FETA OR
BLUE CHEESE

HANDFUL OF POMEGRANATE
SEEDS

To make the vinaigrette, in a small bowl, combine the vinegar, shallot, and a little salt and pepper. Let stand while you get the salad ready. Just before using, whisk in the olive oil to make a vinaigrette.

In a salad bowl, combine the persimmons, radicchio, arugula, and about two-thirds of the cheese. Drizzle the vinaigrette over the top and toss to coat evenly. Scatter the remaining cheese and the pomegranate seeds over the top and serve.

Fuju persimmons

Persimmons

Persimmon Pudding

Makes one 8- or 9-inch pudding; serves 8 to 10

Make sure the persimmons are completely soft. The flesh should be translucent—almost like jelly. This satisfying pudding is inspired by a recipe in *Chez Panisse Fruit* by Alice Waters.

ABOUT 1 1/2 POUNDS HACHIYA
PERSIMMONS

3/4 CUP SUGAR

3 LARGE EGGS

1 1/2 CUPS WHOLE MILK

1/4 CUP HEAVY CREAM

1 TABLESPOON HONEY

1 1/4 CUPS UNBLEACHED
ALL-PURPOSE FLOUR

3/4 TEASPOON BAKING SODA

3/4 TEASPOON BAKING
POWDER

1/8 TEASPOON SALT

1 TEASPOON GROUND
CINNAMON

6 TABLESPOONS UNSALTED
BUTTER, MELTED

WHIPPED CREAM OR CRÈME
FRAÎCHE FOR SERVING

Preheat the oven to 325°F. Butter an 8- or 9-inch springform pan. Line the bottom with parchment paper and then butter the parchment.

Slit the skin of the persimmons and scrape the flesh into a food processor, discarding any seeds. Purée until smooth. Pour into a large bowl, add the sugar, eggs, milk, cream, and honey, and stir until smooth.

In another bowl, stir together the flour, baking soda, baking powder, salt, and cinnamon. Stir the dry ingredients into the wet ingredients. The mixture will be thin at first, but set it aside and allow it to thicken for about 20 minutes. Then add the melted butter and stir well.

Pour the batter into the prepared pan. Bake the pudding until it is set when pressed gently with a fingertip and the edges begin to pull away from the sides of the pan, 1 to 1 1/2 hours. Transfer to a wire rack and let cool for about 30 minutes.

Remove the pan sides and slice the pudding onto a serving plate. Serve warm or at room temperature. The top will be a glossy brown and needs no more embellishment than a little whipped cream or crème fraîche.

Poultry

The Hoffman family has lived on their thirty-five-acre San Joaquin Valley ranch in Manteca for more than a half century. Until 1980, they grew walnuts and alfalfa hay, but then they found their calling. "My husband, Bud, really started all this when he began raising game birds for the California Department of Fish and Game," explains Ruth Hoffman. The male birds were released for hunting, and the Hoffmans sold the females to restaurants. Alice Waters of Chez Panisse was their first customer. Bud Hoffman passed away in 1999 and now Ruth, her son Joe, and her grandson Jeremy carry on the business of raising chickens, quail, wild turkeys, and pheasants for restaurants and the farmers' market.

Hoffman birds are raised in flight pens measuring fifty by three hundred feet, where they are free to roam and forage on native grasses that grow up to three feet tall. All the birds are from the Hoffmans' own breeding stock and are fed only whole grains. They grow more slowly and longer than industrially raised birds, and their muscular meat is moist, lean, and flavorful.

Large-scale poultry farming has had its share of bad press in recent years. Overcrowded conditions and feed made of recycled animal by-products (which encourage the growth of salmonella) have made shoppers lose confidence in "supermarket" poultry. Small growers, like the Hoffmans, know their birds, raising them and processing them according to a higher set of standards.

When asked why her poultry tastes so good, Ruth Hoffman answers without hesitation, "Because we raise our birds right and they come to the market so fresh." The Hoffmans process on Wednesday and Thursday and then pack up their birds in ice-filled coolers and bring them to the Ferry Plaza market early Saturday morning. They usually sell out by noon.

Season

Chicken, guinea hens, ducks, and quail are available year-round. Pheasants are seasonal and can be found at the market mid-September through Christmas.

Choosing

Buy birds with pink, fresh-looking skin and no off odor. If you know you're going to buy poultry, throw a cooler in your car with a few frozen ice packs to keep the birds cold on the ride home.

Storing

Keep poultry in the coldest part of the refrigerator (the ideal temperature is as close to 32°F as possible), and cook within 3 days of purchase.

Poultry

Preparing

Remove any excess fat from inside the bird, then rinse inside and outside under cold running water. Dry well with paper towels.

Brining chickens makes them juicier and more tender. Make a solution of salted water (2 tablespoons kosher salt for every 1 quart water), submerge the bird completely in the brine, and then cover and refrigerate for 24 hours. Alternatively, sprinkle a rinsed bird generously with kosher salt, about 1 tablespoon for a 3-pound bird.

Poultry should be cooked to an internal temperature of 160°F to kill bacteria. Always be sure to use hot, soapy water to wash your hands, cutting boards, and knives after handling raw poultry.

Freezing

Cut the birds into pieces and then arrange in a single layer, not touching, on a tray. (Pieces freeze much faster than a whole bird, preserving the quality of the meat.) Freeze until frozen solid. Remove from the freezer, wrap pieces individually in heavy plastic, put in zippered plastic bags, and squeeze out all the air before sealing. Freeze for up to 3 months. Thaw in the refrigerator; it may take longer than putting it on the kitchen counter, but the chance of bacterial growth is minimized and the quality of the meat remains high.

Varieties

Ducks weigh 3 to 5 pounds, are sold whole, breasts only, or legs only. The flesh is dark and has a rich meaty flavor. Guinea hens, which weigh about 3 pounds, are similar in size and flavor to a chicken, but have leaner, darker flesh and a richer flavor. Pheasants weigh 2 to 3 pounds and have light, moist, tender mild-flavored meat. Quail are small birds, about 6 ounces each, with white, delicately flavored meat.

Herb-Roasted Guinea Hen with Mushrooms   Serves 4

Guinea hens aren't quite as meaty as chickens, but their flesh is far more flavorful.

1 GUINEA HEN, ABOUT
3 POUNDS

SALT

HANDFUL OF FRESH ROSE-
MARY SPRIGS, CHOPPED

HANDFUL OF FRESH THYME
SPRIGS, CHOPPED

2 BAY LEAVES, BROKEN INTO
SMALL PIECES

EXTRA-VIRGIN OLIVE OIL
FOR BRUSHING

1 CUP WATER

2 TABLESPOONS BUTTER

3 LEEKS, WHITE AND PALE
GREEN PARTS, FINELY
CHOPPED

FRESHLY GROUND BLACK
PEPPER

1/2 POUND FRESH CREMINI
MUSHROOMS, STEM ENDS
TRIMMED AND CAPS SLICED

1/4 POUND FRESH SHIITAKE
MUSHROOMS, STEMS
REMOVED AND CAPS SLICED

1/2 CUP PORT

At least 4 hours (and as much as 24 hours) before cooking, cut down along both sides of the backbone of the guinea hen and remove it. Rinse the hen in cold running water and pat dry with paper towels. Sprinkle both sides of the hen with 1 tablespoon salt and all the herbs, rubbing them all over the bird. Lay the hen flat on a plate, cover loosely with waxed paper, and refrigerate.

When you are ready to cook the guinea hen, preheat the oven to 450°F.

Brush most of the salt and herbs off the guinea hen and pat dry with paper towels. Lay the hen, skin side up, on a rack in a roasting pan and brush the skin with a little olive oil. Pour the water into the pan. Roast until skin is crispy and well browned, about 1 hour. Remove from the oven, transfer the hen to a plate, and let rest for 10 minutes.

About 15 minutes before the hen is ready to remove from the oven, melt the butter in a skillet over medium heat. Add the leeks, sprinkle with salt and pepper, and cook, stirring often, until soft, about 10 minutes. Add the mushrooms and cook, stirring occasionally, until they are soft and most of the juices they release have been reabsorbed, about 10 minutes.

Remove the rack from the roasting pan and put the pan on the stove top over medium heat. Add the port and deglaze the pan, stirring with a wooden spoon to loosen any browned bits stuck to the bottom. Pour the deglazed pan juices into the skillet holding the mushroom mixture and stir to mix well.

Spoon the mushroom mixture onto a serving platter. Cut the hen into serving pieces, arrange the pieces on top of the mushrooms, and serve.

Poultry

Ruth's Grilled Quail

Allow 1 or 2 quail per person

Ruth Hoffman says that her quail are the perfect "fast food" because they cook in 7 to 8 minutes. Here is her favorite recipe for the succulent birds.

"Marinate quail in soy sauce, peeled and grated fresh ginger, and a little extra-virgin olive oil in a covered pan in the refrigerator for a few hours. Remove the quail from the marinade and dry with paper towels. Grill over hot glowing coals for 2 to 3 minutes per side, or sear in a skillet over high heat for 2 to 3 minutes per side. Serve with lots of napkins for these finger licking tidbits."

Pimentón Chicken with Preserved Lemons

Serves 4 to 6

Pimentón, the smoky Spanish paprika sold in three varieties, sweet, medium-hot, and hot, adds a deep, rich flavor to this recipe (pictured opposite). Serve with roasted potatoes, or on top of wide noodles to soak up the cooking juices.

8 CHICKEN THIGHS

1 TABLESPOON SALT

1 TABLESPOON SPANISH PIMENTÓN

1 TABLESPOON BUTTER

1 TABLESPOON OLIVE OIL

3 RED ONIONS, PEELED AND CUT IN HALF CROSSWISE

1 PRESERVED LEMON (PAGE 244), CUT INTO 8 WEDGES

FRESHLY GROUND BLACK PEPPER

A FEW FRESH THYME SPRIGS

Rinse the chicken thighs under cold running water and pat them dry. In a small bowl, stir together the salt and *pimentón*. Rub the chicken thighs evenly with the mixture.

In a large, heavy skillet, melt the butter with the olive oil over medium-high heat. Add the onion halves cut side down and cook until browned, about 5 minutes. Turn the onion halves and cook on the second side until browned, about 5 minutes longer. Add the chicken thighs, skin side up, and cook until browned, about 10 minutes. Turn the chicken thighs over, nestle the lemon wedges in among the chicken and the onions, reduce the heat to medium, cover, and cook until the chicken is tender, about 30 minutes.

Season the chicken and onions with pepper and transfer to a serving platter. Garnish with the thyme and serve.

Swiss Chard

Beta vulgaris subsp. *cicla*

Swiss chard goes by many names, including leaf beet, silver beet, sea kale beet, and simply chard. The use of the term *Swiss* came about in Europe because of the need to distinguish chard from a similar French green. Chard can be traced back to the Hanging Gardens of Babylon, and Aristotle spoke of it in 350 B.C. The broad, fanlike, slightly crinkled leaves remind some chard partisans of beet greens and others of spinach, though chard is usually more bitter and pungent, and the stalks can taste slightly salty. Beets and chard are varieties of the same species, and reveal the same betaine pigment in the veins of their leaves and in their colored stems.

You can now buy Swiss chard with rainbow stalks in psychedelic yellow, orange, and pink, but most of the chard at the market has the more conventional white or red stalks. Regardless of the color, chard is good for you, with high concentrations of potassium and other minerals, and lots of vitamins A and C. It is thought to reduce risks of certain cancers and cataracts, too, and provides an excellent source of dietary fiber.

Stuart Dickson of Heirloom Organics, near Watsonville, is committed to genetic preservation. "Most heirlooms," Dickson explains, "come from seeds that have been passed down from generation to generation and village to village for over a hundred years." His chard is exceptional, he says, because he has "carefully chosen to plant the right variety, for the right soil, at the right time. I have figured out the best habitat for my heirlooms to flourish. Chard likes a rich, dark, loamy soil with good drainage. It's a hearty plant that can be turned under with a tractor and revives itself in no time."

Dickson learned his trade working on farms in England, Israel, and France, picking up sound sustainable farming practices along the way. They include, among other things, creating habitats for beneficial insects, careful water management, and the use of flames to singe weed seedlings.

For cooking, Dickson suggests separating the stalk from the chard leaves, as they cook at different rates. He cuts chard leaves into a chiffonade (see note, page 41) and swirls them into wintry soups and scatters them on top of baked pizzas. "Young, tender leaves have an affinity for eggs," he says, so he folds them into omelets. He also tosses them with a vinaigrette as a salad green, much like spinach.

Season
Available all year, but is best from early October to early April.

Choosing
Check for moist, crisp, brilliant green leaves with crisp stems and no evidence of browning.

Storing

To revive slightly limp chard, stand the bunch upright, stalks down, in a jar of cold water for an hour. Then, dampen the leaves, wrap in a damp towel, and store in the vegetable bin for up to 4 days.

Preparing

Swirl the leaves in a bowl of cold water to shake off any sand or dirt. Trim off any brown spots from the stems or leaves. Because they cook at different rates, separate the leaves from the stalks: fold each leaf in half lengthwise; then, holding the leaf, pull the stalk off or cut it away with scissors or a knife. If the ribs or stalks are tough, peel them as you would celery, then cut them into small pieces.

To blanch chard before using in a baked dish, drop the stems, cut into 1-inch pieces, into boiling salted water and boil for 3 minutes. Add the cut leaves and continue to cook for another minute, or until tender, then drain promptly.

Red Swiss Chard

Braised Swiss Chard Armistead

Serves 4 to 6

Here's an easy, delicious side dish for just about any meat, fowl, or fish main course, or you can swirl it into a pot of cooked beans. Keep in mind that the chard cooks way down, so using two or even three bunches is not an unreasonable amount.

2 BUNCHES YOUNG, TENDER CHARD, STEMS AND LEAVES SEPARATED

3 TABLESPOONS EXTRA-VIRGIN OLIVE OIL

1 MEDIUM ONION, SLICED

1 CLOVE GARLIC, CRUSHED

2 OLIVE OIL–PACKED ANCHOVY FILLETS

SALT AND FRESHLY GROUND BLACK PEPPER

GRATED PARMIGIANO-REGGIANO CHEESE FOR TOPPING (OPTIONAL)

Cut the chard stems into bite-sized pieces, and cut the leaves into 2-inch-wide strips. Bring a large pot of water to a boil over high heat and then salt the water. Add the chard stems and boil for 3 minutes. Add the leaves and cook for about 1 minute longer. Drain well and press out any excess moisture.

In the same pot, heat the olive oil over medium heat. Add the onion and cook until it becomes translucent, about 4 minutes. Then, add the garlic and anchovies and stir until the anchovies melt into the oil and the garlic is translucent, 1 to 2 minutes. Add the chard and continue to cook, stirring occasionally, until tender, about 10 minutes. Season to taste with salt and pepper.

Transfer to a serving dish, sprinkle a little cheese over the top, if desired, and allow it to melt in. Serve warm.

Swiss Chard

Swiss Chard Flan

Serves 6 to 8

This delicate chard flan is a cousin to both the quiche and the frittata: it lacks the crust of a quiche, and it is a little wobblier than a frittata. It's a great choice for a light vegetarian supper with a green salad and warm, crusty bread. Prepare it ahead of time as a side dish to go with meat or fowl.

2 BUNCHES YOUNG, TENDER CHARD, STEMS AND LEAVES SEPARATED

4 TABLESPOONS EXTRA-VIRGIN OLIVE OIL

1 LARGE YELLOW ONION, CHOPPED

1 CLOVE GARLIC, MINCED

5 LARGE EGGS

1 CUP HALF-AND-HALF

1/2 CUP HEAVY CREAM

SALT AND FRESHLY GROUND BLACK PEPPER

1 CUP GRATED PARMIGIANO-REGGIANO OR GRUYÈRE CHEESE

Cut the chard stems into 1/2 -inch pieces and cut the leaves crosswise into 2- to 3-inch-wide strips. Set aside.

In a large skillet, heat 2 tablespoons of the olive oil over medium heat. Add the onion and garlic and cook, stirring occasionally, until tender and translucent, about 3 minutes. Add the chard stems, cover, and cook for about 7 minutes. If the mixture becomes dry, add a few splashes of water. Add the chard leaves, cover, and continue cooking until the leaves have wilted, about 5 minutes longer.

While the chard cooks, crack the eggs into a bowl and whisk in the half-and-half and cream.

When the chard is ready, remove from the heat and season to taste with salt and pepper. Select a 10- to 12-inch nonstick skillet that can also be used in the broiler and place over medium heat. Add the remaining 2 tablespoons olive oil and swirl the oil in the skillet to coat evenly. Transfer the chard mixture to the skillet, spreading it out evenly. Pour the egg mixture over the chard and season with salt and pepper. Reduce the heat to medium-low, cover, and cook until the custard has just set, about 10 minutes. As the flan cooks, occasionally pull the edges gently toward the center with a rubber spatula to ensure even cooking. It may be a little loose in the center. Meanwhile, preheat the broiler.

Remove the flan from the heat and sprinkle the cheese evenly over the top. Slip the flan under the broiler to brown, a minute or so. Remove from the broiler and loosen the edges with a knife or a spatula. If the flan still seems too loose, return it to the broiler for another minute. It should not be perfectly dry, however, as it will continue to cook in the pan once you remove it from the broiler.

Serve the flan directly from the pan, cutting it into wedges, or slide it onto a serving plate and then cut into wedges. Serve warm or at room temperature.

Winter Squashes

Cucurbita spp.

Buy a handsome winter squash when its beauty strikes you and allow it to sit on the table until the whim to cook it hits. Winter squash is the name for the many varieties of hard-skinned squash of South and Central America, such as the sturdy fall-colored delicata, Gold Nugget, Hubbard, Red Kuri, acorn, buttercup, kabocha, and all sorts of pumpkins. They all have a hard, indigestible skin in common and, like gourds, cucumbers, and melons, belong to the all-embracing Cucurbitaceae family. Whereas every bit of a summer squash is edible, winter squashes have a fleshy, usually golden to flaming orange interior with lots of big, hard seeds that are inedible unless hulled and roasted. In fact, today most pumpkins in the United States are ornamentals, primarily jack-o'-lanterns of the pepo species. These are direct relatives of Mexican pumpkins that were first cultivated for their seeds rather than their flesh.

Luckily for shoppers at the market, All Star Organics, a three-and-a-half-acre farm in Marin County, brings exceptional heirloom winter squashes to market every fall and winter. Farmers Marty Jacobson and Janet Brown are dedicated to growing heirloom and open-pollinated varieties of squash (and other crops) with a primary focus on diversity. "We are interested in providing our customers with the experience of diversity that exists within any category of food crop," explains Brown, who also has a day job at the Center for Ecoliteracy in Berkeley. They nourish their soil in part with sea kelp, which promotes strong growth; compost for nitrogen; ground up oyster shells for calcium; and granite rock powder for micronutrients. Wildflowers attract beneficial insects.

"The amount of nutrition stored in a winter squash is formidable," says Brown, "and they will keep for months without refrigeration. No wonder so many cultures all over the world depend in part on squash for their diet." All Star gives market shoppers a chance to try a variety of these nutritional powerhouses, among them Long Island Cheese squash, which is squat shaped, fawn colored, and has a soft suede finish. Its dark reddish orange interior is densely flavored. The extraordinary French Rouge vif d'Etamps, which dates back to the 1840s and is also known as the Cinderella pumpkin (because it is shaped like Cinderella's carriage), is fantastic for making soup baked in the squash shell.

All Star Organics also raises delicious examples of more mainstream squashes, such as the butternut and buttercup. The butternut is the most common all-purpose squash, with firm, abundant, bright orange, creamy flesh and a thick neck that gives way to a bulbous, smooth bottom. Brown describes the buttercup as "squat and dark green, with an occasional scattering of warts. Blazing orange inside, the flesh is dry and flaky after baking, like a baked potato." The handsome delicata, with its yellow, green, and orange stripes and distinctive, nutty flavor (somewhere between a sweet potato and a butternut squash) is also popular and sold by other vendors at the market.

Winter Squashes

Season
Late summer through March.

Choosing
Squashes should be heavy for their size and free of soft spots.

Storing
Store whole at cool room temperature for up to a few months. Janet Brown advises arranging squashes "in a single layer in a cool, dry place with at least modest air circulation." If the squash is cut, store it in the refrigerator wrapped in plastic wrap. It molds quickly if not chilled.

Preparing
Typically, winter squashes are halved or cut into wedges, the seeds and strings are removed, and then the pieces are peeled. A large metal spoon is ideal for scooping the seed cavities clean. A microwave can make seeding and peeling go more quickly: Prick the squash in several places with a knife so it won't explode. Place the squash in the microwave and microwave on high for 4 minutes for small squashes and about 10 minutes for larger squashes, then halve, seed, and peel.

Don't throw away your pumpkin seeds. Wash them in a colander under cold running water, rinsing away any strings, and then pat dry and toss with a little olive oil or melted butter and salt or other seasoning. Spread the seeds on a rimmed baking sheet and toast in a 325°F oven until golden brown and crisp, 30 to 45 minutes. Let cool and store in an airtight container.

Oven-Roasted Delicata Squash

Serves 4

Here is a quick, easy, and delicious recipe for a fall or winter side dish that will please kids and grown-ups alike.

2 DELICATA SQUASHES, EACH
5 TO 7 INCHES LONG

3 TABLESPOONS BUTTER

SALT AND FRESHLY GROUND
BLACK PEPPER

2 TABLESPOONS HONEY

Preheat the oven to 350°F.

Cut the squashes in half lengthwise, but leave the seeds intact. In a large, heavy ovenproof skillet, melt the butter over medium heat. Place the squash halves, cut side down, in the butter and cook for a few minutes until browned. Turn the squash halves cut side up and transfer the skillet to the oven. Cook until tender when pierced with a fork, about 25 minutes.

Remove from the oven and carefully scoop out the seeds with a spoon. Season with salt and pepper and drizzle the honey evenly among the 4 halves and serve.

(right) Cinderella pumpkins
(far right) Delicata squash

French Pumpkin Soup Baked and Served in the Shell

Serves 6 to 8

For a festive meal, serve this soup as a main course for a light supper or lunch on a chilly autumn day. The heavy, dense flesh of the pumpkin helps it to hold its shape during baking. As it cooks, its juices are slowly released into the stock, where their flavor intensifies.

1 ROUGE VIF D'ETAMPS (CINDERELLA) PUMPKIN, 8 TO 10 POUNDS

1/2 CUP (1/4 POUND) UNSALTED BUTTER, INCLUDING 1 TABLESPOON AT ROOM TEMPERATURE

SALT

3 LEEKS, WHITE PART AND 2 INCHES OF GREEN, CUT INTO 1-INCH-THICK ROUNDS

6 SLICES COUNTRY BREAD, EACH 1 INCH THICK, TORN INTO BITE-SIZED PIECES AND TOASTED

1/2 TEASPOON GROUND DRIED SAGE

1/2 TEASPOON FRESHLY GRATED NUTMEG

FRESHLY GROUND BLACK PEPPER

2 CUPS SHREDDED GRUYÈRE CHEESE

ABOUT 5 CUPS CHICKEN STOCK, PREFERABLY HOMEMADE

2 BAY LEAVES

Preheat the oven to 350°F.

Using a large, sharp knife, cut off the top of the pumpkin, creating a lid about 4 inches in diameter. Set the lid aside. Using a large metal spoon, scoop out any seeds and strings. Rub the cut side of the lid and the inside of the pumpkin with the 1 tablespoon room-temperature butter. Season the lid and the inside of the pumpkin with salt and place the pumpkin, cut side up, in a good-looking deep baking dish or pan that you can bring to the table. Set the lid aside.

In a skillet, melt the remaining 7 tablespoons butter over medium heat. Add the leeks and cook, stirring, until soft, about 8 minutes. Add the toasted croutons and sprinkle them with the sage, nutmeg, and a little salt and pepper. Stir well and remove from the heat.

Spoon a layer of the seasoned croutons into the pumpkin. Sprinkle a layer of the cheese on top of them. Repeat the layers until you have used up all the croutons and cheese. Pour in stock to within 1 inch of the rim. Lay the bay leaves on top, and then fit the lid onto the pumpkin.

Bake until the pumpkin begins to soften and brown on the outside and the stock bubbles on the inside, 1 1/2 to 2 hours. Carefully remove the baking dish from the oven.

With a long-handled spoon, gently scrape the flesh from the bottom and sides of the pumpkin into the soup, being careful not to puncture the walls. Ladle the soup, including tender chunks of pumpkin flesh, into warmed bowls and serve.

WINTER

(opposite) Carrots and parsnips

Arugula

Arugula, variously called rocket, *roquette*, *ruchetta*, and *rucola*, is a member of the big Cruciferae family and a relative of the radish, turnip, and watercress. It has been used as a spice, food, medicine, aphrodisiac, digestive, and deodorant, and its seeds are, at times, treated as mustard.

While this versatile green has long enjoyed widespread appeal throughout the Mediterranean, it has gained acceptance only recently in the United States, where cooks now like to mix it with other salad greens, add it to a beet salad, or pair it with goat or blue cheese, figs, tomatoes, or citrus. Its American name, arugula, may be a mangled version of the Italian *rucola* or perhaps is taken directly from a southern Italian dialect. Nobody knows for sure. Wild rocket used to refer to the type foraged in the Mediterranean, but today the term refers to a garden species (*Diplotaxis erucoides*). It tends to have more stem to leaf, and its leaf tends to be sharper and slimmer and often more peppery.

Lovers of arugula wait for the moment every winter when Nancy Gammon's lovely, diminutive bouquets of mild, slow-growing arugula hit her Four Sisters Farm stall (page 36). Warren Weber of Star Route Farms (page 176) also sells arugula, offering various types throughout the year. "The green flourishes in frost-free zones and in most soils," according to Weber, who sells loose-cut, prewashed, nutty-flavored arugula in big wicker baskets at his stall. During the warmer months, the fingerlike, jagged leaves grow quickly, producing a hotter, more peppery flavor.

Arugula's pale ivory blossoms are a springtime reward that not only make delicate additions to salads and to pizzas fresh from the oven, but also beautiful bouquets. Food writer Deborah Madison explains that the cream-colored blooms have tiny blood-red veins with four single petals in the shape of a cross—the perfect symbol for this crucifer.

Season
Available year-round from growers in coastal areas.

Choosing
Reach for deep, dark green leaves and avoid faded yellow or wilted ones.

Storing
Weber suggests rinsing arugula in several changes of water, then draining, drying, and placing in zippered plastic bags, forcing out all the air before sealing. (If the leaves are very tender, do not spin them dry; instead wrap in clean kitchen towels.) Store in the vegetable bin of the refrigerator for 4 to 5 days.

Preparing

If you have already rinsed the arugula for storing, you only need to check for any wilted or discolored leaves, and break off any tough stems. While arugula is most often consumed raw, either in salads or as a finishing touch on beans, pizzas, and pastas, it can also be sautéed (especially if it is a little tough).

Arugula

Arugula

Eruca sativa

Penne with Wilted Arugula, Olive Oil, and Goat Cheese

Serves 4

For a quick, fresh, simple meal, toss arugula with pasta, a good extra-virgin olive oil, and a sprinkle of grated cheese.

1/2 POUND ARUGULA

SALT

1 POUND PENNE

1 CLOVE GARLIC, MINCED

RED PEPPER FLAKES

1/3 CUP EXTRA-VIRGIN OLIVE OIL, PLUS EXTRA FOR SERVING

3/4 CUP GRATED AGED GOAT CHEESE OR PARMIGIANO-REGGIANO CHEESE

If the arugula leaves are large, tear them into bite-sized pieces, removing any tough stems. Bring a large pot of water to a boil over high heat and then salt the water. Add the pasta and cook until al dente. Scoop out and reserve about 1/2 cup of the pasta water and then drain the pasta.

Place the pasta in a warmed serving bowl and add the garlic. Season well with salt and add a sprinkle of pepper flakes. Splash in the 1/3 cup olive oil and about two-thirds of the reserved pasta water and toss well. Add more pasta water as needed to create a nice sauce consistency. Sprinkle in the arugula leaves and one-half of the grated cheese and gently toss again.

Serve the pasta and pass a bottle of olive oil and the rest of the grated cheese at the table.

Arugula Salad with Shaved Aged Gouda and Satsumas

Serves 4

The combination of peppery arugula, sweet mandarins, and aged Gouda tossed with a simple vinaigrette makes a sophisticated salad that takes seconds to make. You can substitute a good dry Jack or even Parmigiano-Reggiano for the Gouda.

1 SHALLOT, MINCED

2 TABLESPOONS RED WINE VINEGAR

FEW DROPS BALSAMIC VINEGAR

1/3 CUP EXTRA-VIRGIN OLIVE OIL

SALT AND FRESHLY GROUND BLACK PEPPER

4 CUPS TORN ARUGULA

3 SATSUMA OR OTHER MANDARIN ORANGES, PEELED, PITH AND SEEDS CAREFULLY REMOVED, AND SECTIONED

1/4 -POUND WEDGE AGED GOUDA CHEESE

In a small bowl, combine the shallot and the red wine and balsamic vinegars and let stand for at least 5 minutes while you prepare the other ingredients for the salad. Whisk in the olive oil and season to taste with salt and pepper to finish the vinaigrette.

In a salad bowl, combine the arugula and mandarin sections. Drizzle the vinaigrette over the salad and toss to coat evenly. Using a vegetable peeler, shave the cheese over the top, then serve.

[– cheese]
+ red onion also good.

Brussels Sprouts

Brassica oleracea var. *gemmifera*

If Dr. Seuss conjured up a vegetable, it couldn't look more eccentric than a field full of Brussels sprouts. The plants send up elongated three-foot stalks along which twenty to forty sprouts grow in tight spiral patterns. The heavily loaded stalks are capped with plumes of large leaves—a picture straight out of Whoville. Each Brussels sprout looks like a tiny head of cabbage (they're both members of the *Brassica* genus). At harvest, sprouts are cut, twisted, or snapped off the stalk. The stalk continues to grow more sprouts and several harvests can be made in succession from one plant.

Lore has it that Brussels sprouts were first cultivated in northern Europe in the fifteenth century (and thus named for Brussels, Belgium). Today, almost all of the Brussels sprouts grown commercially in the United States are cultivated in California. The plants do best where the growing season is long and cool. Louis Iacopi grew them for twenty years on his Half Moon Bay farm—it has the perfect climate. But it is a tricky crop, susceptible to every bug and disease that wants to settle inside its tightly furled leaves. So now he takes the sprouts grown by neighboring Cabrillo Farm to the market to sell on Saturday mornings.

Brussels sprouts have a denser texture than their cabbage cousins and a wonderful bitter-sweet, bright, nutty flavor. "Very tasty," says Iacopi, who likes to sauté the sprouts with garlic in olive oil, throw a handful of them around a pork roast (they absorb all those delicious juices as they cook), or braise them in butter with fresh bread crumbs.

Season

August through March.

Choosing

Look for 1-inch sprouts: the smaller they are, the more tender they are. They should all be about the same size so that they will cook evenly. Yellow leaves and tiny holes can be signs of bugs or worms, so choose bright green, compact heads with clean, white stem ends.

Storing

Keep unwashed and untrimmed Brussels sprouts stored in a perforated or open plastic bag in the vegetable bin of the refrigerator for up to 1 week.

Preparing

Remove stems and any yellow or discolored leaves, then rinse well under cold running water. If you are concerned that bugs may have taken up residence in the inner leaves, soak the sprouts in a bowl of cold water for about 20 minutes to force them out.

Brussels Sprouts

Brassica oleracea var. *gemmifera*

Some folks suggest cutting a shallow X in the bottom of Brussels sprouts so they will cook evenly, but they will cook just fine without it. Cut them in half lengthwise if you want them to cook more quickly. If you are not a fan of the bittersweet taste of Brussels sprouts, tone down the flavor by halving the sprouts and cooking them in a large pot of boiling water to leach out some of the strong flavor.

Pan-Roasted Brussels Sprouts with Bacon

Servers 4

Use bacon, pancetta, or ham in this dish (pictured opposite) to add salt and/or smoke to the sprouts. Or, simply brown the sprouts and add a splash of balsamic vinegar right at the end.

SALT

1 POUND BRUSSELS SPROUTS, TRIMMED AND HALVED LENGTHWISE

1 TABLESPOON EXTRA-VIRGIN OLIVE OIL

3 OUNCES BACON, DICED

FRESHLY GROUND BLACK PEPPER

Bring a large pot of water to a boil over high heat and then salt the water. Add the Brussels sprouts and parboil for about 3 minutes. Drain, rinse under cold running water until cool to preserve their green color, and drain again.

In a large, heavy skillet, heat the oil and fry the bacon, stirring with a wooden spoon, until browned, 3 to 5 minutes. Add the Brussels sprouts and sauté, stirring occasionally, until they begin to brown, about 15 minutes. Do not stir too much or the flat sides will not brown, but always keep a close eye on them so they don't burn.

Season with salt and pepper and serve.

Brussels Sprouts Salad

Serves 4

Chef Mark Ladner makes this delicious salad at well-known chef Mario Batali's Lupa restaurant in New York City. Brussels sprouts are not the only choice here. Ladner suggests using nearly any vegetable in season that can be eaten raw.

1/2 CUP WARM WATER

1/2 CUP EXTRA-VIRGIN OLIVE OIL

1/4 CUP GRATED PARMIGIANO-REGGIANO CHEESE

1/4 CUP GRATED PECORINO ROMANO CHEESE

FRESHLY GROUND BLACK PEPPER

1 POUND SMALL BRUSSELS SPROUTS, TRIMMED, HALVED, AND SLICED INTO FAT SLIVERS

In a bowl, stir together the warm water, olive oil, cheeses, and a few good grinds of pepper. If the mixture is too dry, add a little more water and oil in equal parts. It should be, in Chef Ladner's words, an "emulsified slurry." The oil and water, which usually don't mix, are held together by the grated cheese. Add the Brussels sprouts and toss until they are well coated. Taste and add more pepper, if you like, and serve.

Carrots

Daucus carota

The flavor of a well-grown carrot is rich, sweet, and *all* concentrated carrot! That full taste is no surprise. The carrot is a swollen edible taproot—the very essence of a plant. With the exception of the beet, the carrot has a higher sugar content than any other vegetable. The most familiar of all root vegetables, it is related to parsley, dill, fennel, celery, parsnip, and the wildflower Queen Anne's Lace.

Slender, orange carrots are the most common, but their colors can range from purple to palest yellow and their shapes from fat nubbins to long, slim beauties. Those ubiquitous bags of "baby carrots" you see in supermarkets aren't babies at all. They are milled and stamped from large carrots into identical two-inch pieces. Baby carrots look just like miniature carrots, but they aren't really worth the trouble, because their flavor has not had the chance to develop. Although raw carrots are popular, cooking them softens their cell walls and opens up their sweet taste.

Beta-carotene gives a carrot its color, and vitamin A is derived from beta-carotene. Carrots are the leading source of this necessary nutrient in the American diet. Low levels of vitamin A have been linked to the formation of cataracts, proving the old wives' tale that carrots are good for your eyes.

Season

You'll find carrots at the market year-round, while more unusual varieties are for sale late summer through fall.

Choosing

If buying carrots with their green tops intact, make sure the leaves are moist and bright colored. The carrot itself should be firm and smooth. Avoid those with cracks, signs of withering, and a soft feel. Young carrots are likely to be mild flavored and tender, but mature carrots are typically sweeter. The core of the root has the least flavor because the natural sugars are stored in the outer layers.

Storing

If you buy carrots with their tops, twist or cut off the bulky leaves before storing. While the carrots will last a long time, the greens wilt and decay and drain the roots of their flavor and moisture. Refrigerate carrots in perforated or open plastic bags in the vegetable bin of the refrigerator. Avoid storing them near apples or pears. They emit ethylene gas as they ripen, which will turn the carrots' natural sweetness bitter.

Preparing

Trim off leafy green tops and stem ends, rinse well, and then peel with a swivel-bladed vegetable peeler. Leave whole or cut into sticks, strips, or coins. Trim away any green on the "shoulders," as it will be bitter.

A ubiquitous part of every relish tray, along with celery sticks and radishes, raw carrots have a good crunch. But cooking them, even just until crisp-tender, helps break down their cellular structure, which allows their nutrients to be more easily absorbed into the body.

Beef Stew with Carrots

Serves 4 to 6

One of the specialties at Aux Amis du Beaujolais, a lively Parisian bistro, is *boeuf aux carottes*. Although homey in taste and style, the preparation is involved and sometimes the meat can still be dry. We changed this French classic from a pot roast into a hearty stew loaded with sweet carrots. Serve it over pasta or with potatoes to absorb all the juices.

3 POUNDS BONELESS BEEF CHUCK, TRIMMED OF FAT AND CUT INTO LARGE PIECES OF ABOUT 2 INCHES EACH

SALT AND FRESHLY GROUND BLACK PEPPER

EXTRA-VIRGIN OLIVE OIL AS NEEDED

2 CUPS DRY RED WINE

1 CLOVE GARLIC, SLICED

1 LONG STRIP ORANGE PEEL

BOUQUET GARNI OF 4 FRESH THYME SPRIGS, 2 BAY LEAVES, AND A FEW PARSLEY STEMS, TIED TOGETHER WITH KITCHEN STRING

2 BUNCHES CARROTS, TRIMMED, PEELED, AND CUT INTO 2-INCH PIECES

6 TO 12 SMALL YELLOW ONIONS, PEELED AND LEFT WHOLE

2 CUPS CHICKEN STOCK, PREFERABLY HOMEMADE

Preheat the oven to 325°F.

Season the beef generously with salt and pepper. In a large nonstick skillet, heat about 2 tablespoons olive oil over medium-high heat. Add the beef and cook, turning as needed, until well browned on all sides, about 10 minutes. Do not crowd the beef, or it will steam instead of brown; work in batches if necessary and add more oil as needed. As the beef is ready, remove it from the pan and set aside.

Add 1 cup of the wine to the pan over medium-high heat and cook, stirring with a wooden spoon to loosen any brown bits stuck to the bottom, until the wine is reduced to about 1/2 cup, about 10 minutes.

Meanwhile, select a large enameled cast-iron or flameproof earthenware pot with a lid and heat 2 tablespoons olive oil over medium heat. Add the garlic and orange peel and cook, stirring often, until the garlic is soft but not browned, 1 to 2 minutes. Add the browned beef to the pot along with the bouquet garni, carrots, onions, stock, and the remaining 1 cup wine. When the wine in the skillet has reduced, add it to the pot as well.

Cover the pot, put in the oven, and cook until the beef is tender, about 11/2 hours. Remove from the oven and use a large spoon to remove as much of the fat floating on the surface as possible. Remove and discard the orange peel and bouquet garni.

Season to taste with salt and pepper and serve.

Carrots

Roasted Carrots

Serves 4 to 6

You can substitute nearly any root vegetable—parsnips, turnips, rutabagas—for the carrots in this recipe. You can also coat the carrots with the flavorings and cook them in the same pan with a chicken, beef, or lamb roast.

2 BUNCHES CARROTS, TRIMMED
AND PEELED

2 TABLESPOONS BUTTER, MELTED

1 TABLESPOON BROWN SUGAR,
MOLASSES, OR HONEY

SALT AND FRESHLY GROUND
BLACK PEPPER

1/2 CUP RICH BEEF STOCK

CHOPPED FRESH PARSLEY FOR
GARNISH

Preheat the oven to 375°F.

Put the carrots in a baking dish, drizzle with the butter, sprinkle with the brown sugar or other sweetener, and season with salt and pepper. Roll the carrots around to be sure that they are evenly coated. Pour in the stock.

Put the dish in the oven and roast the carrots, basting every 15 minutes or so with the dish juices, until they are very soft when pierced with a knife tip, about 45 minutes. Serve garnished with the parsley.

Gingery Carrot Soup

Serves 4 to 6

Adding a potato to a puréed soup makes it smoother and creamier, without the addition of heavy cream. This soup (pictured opposite) makes a satisfying winter lunch or light supper main course, and is equally delicious served cold on a warm summer day.

3 TABLESPOONS BUTTER OR
OLIVE OIL

3 LEEKS, WHITE PART AND
2 INCHES OF GREEN, CHOPPED

1 YELLOW ONION, CHOPPED

1 HAND OF GINGER, ABOUT
5 OUNCES, CUT INTO 8 PIECES

2 POUNDS CARROTS, TRIMMED,
PEELED, AND CHOPPED

1 RUSSET POTATO, PEELED
AND QUARTERED

SALT AND FRESHLY GROUND
BLACK PEPPER

4 CUPS CHICKEN STOCK,
PREFERABLY HOMEMADE

In a large, heavy pot, melt the butter over medium heat. Add the leeks and onion and cook, stirring often, until soft, about 10 minutes. Add the ginger, carrots, and potato, season with salt and pepper, and stir with a wooden spoon to mix together. Pour in the stock, raise the heat to medium-high, and bring to a boil. Reduce the heat to low, cover partially, and simmer until the carrots are very soft, about 1 hour.

Remove from the heat and remove and discard the ginger. Let the soup cool slightly. Working in batches, process until very smooth in a food processor or blender. Return to the same pot, reheat until hot, and add water or a little more stock if the soup is too thick. Season to taste with salt and pepper, ladle into warmed bowls, garnish with a swirl of sour cream and a sprinkle of chives, and serve.

SOUR CREAM FOR GARNISH

MINCED FRESH CHIVES FOR
GARNISH

Or, let the puréed soup cool completely, thin if needed, cover, and refrigerate until well chilled. Just before serving, season to taste with salt and pepper, ladle into chilled bowls, and garnish with a swirl of sour cream and a sprinkle of chives.

Cauliflower

Brassica oleracea var. *botrytis*

Louis Iacopi's fields lie next to Half Moon Bay Airport. All day long when coastal fog has not "socked in" the runway, planes take off and touch down as Iacopi tends his crops. Cauliflower is among the many vegetables he cultivates for farmers' markets. He plants seedlings that take sixty to ninety days to mature in the cool, moist marine climate that is perfect for this vegetable. Big, deeply ribbed leaves grow up around the thick, white clusters of undeveloped flower buds that form its compact head. The leaves shield the head from the sun, preventing chlorophyll from developing so that it remains white. Sometimes Iacopi gives Mother Nature a hand, tying up the leaves around the head or placing a leaf on top to shade it. Too much sunlight changes the color and texture of cauliflower and gives it an unpleasantly strong flavor.

Cauliflower, like such other cruciferous vegetables as broccoli, cabbage, and kale, is known for its antioxidant properties. Some evidence suggests that these kin may also help in the fight against rheumatoid arthritis. All of them seem to contain compounds that aid the body in its efforts to neutralize potentially toxic and carcinogenic substances, which makes Louis Iacopi's crop a boon to market shoppers in search of a healthful diet.

Standing in the field, taking a moment from his work, Iacopi shares his favorite cauliflower recipe. "You make it just like fried zucchini," he says. "Blanch it, dip it in an egg batter, then fry it in a skillet in olive oil with some garlic." His voice trails off and you can tell that he can just taste that cauliflower. "It's worth all the trouble it takes to grow it right," he adds, and then he hurries off. There is talk of rain for the coming weekend and he needs to finish planting.

Season

Although traditionally thought of as a cool-weather crop, cauliflower can be found in the market most of the year now.

Choosing

Select clean, firm, compact heads that are white or creamy white. The size of the head doesn't affect its quality. Leaves should be fresh and green.

A 2-POUND CAULIFLOWER ABOUT 6 INCHES IN DIAMETER WILL SERVE 4 TO 6

Storing

Place a cauliflower stem side up on a paper towel (to keep the crown moisture-free) and slip inside a perforated or open plastic bag. Store in the vegetable bin of the refrigerator for up to 5 days.

Preparing

Remove any outer leaves and cut off the protruding stem flush with the base of the head. You can leave the head whole or divide it into florets. Use nonreactive pots and skillets, such as stainless steel or enameled cast iron. If cooking in unlined cast iron or aluminum, add a squeeze of lemon, a splash of vinegar, or a cup of milk to the water to keep the cauliflower from turning brown. If cooking whole, submerge the head, stem side down, in boiling salted water. A whole head (depending on size) will cook in about 15 minutes; florets will cook in about half the time.

Cauliflower heads

Cauliflower

Penne with Crispy Cauliflower

Serves 4 to 6

This easy dish cooks in no time. While you are boiling the water for the pasta, you can begin browning the cauliflower. Then all you need to do is cook the pasta, combine it with the cauliflower, drizzle on a little of your best olive oil, sprinkle with grated cheese, and dinner is ready.

1/3 CUP EXTRA-VIRGIN OLIVE OIL, PLUS EXTRA FOR DRIZZLING

4 OLIVE OIL–PACKED ANCHOVY FILLETS

1 HEAD CAULIFLOWER, TRIMMED AND BROKEN OR CUT INTO BITE-SIZED FLORETS

SALT AND FRESHLY GROUND BLACK PEPPER

1 POUND PENNE

GRATED DRY JACK OR OTHER GRATING CHEESE FOR SERVING

Bring a large pot of water to a boil for cooking the pasta.

Meanwhile, in a large skillet, heat the 1/3 cup olive oil over medium-high heat. Add the anchovy fillets and use a wooden spoon to smash the anchovies once they begin to melt into the oil. Add the cauliflower and cook until soft and browned, about 10 minutes. Season to taste with salt and pepper.

While the cauliflower is cooking, add salt to the boiling water and then add the pasta and cook until al dente. Scoop out and reserve about 1 cup of the pasta water and then drain the pasta.

Pour the drained pasta into the pan with the cauliflower over medium-high heat, add a little of the pasta water, and stir together for a couple of minutes. Add more of the pasta water if the mixture seems dry.

Pour the pasta onto a platter or into a big bowl, drizzle with olive oil, and serve. Pass the cheese at the table.

CITRUS
Blood Oranges

Citrus sinensis

Blood oranges belong to the clan of sweet oranges, the same as Washington navels or Valencias, as opposed to the sour or bitter oranges often used in marmalades. They were first brought to California by Sicilian immigrants and farmed on a small scale. The red blush of the skin seems to be light related and develops independently of the startling scarlet of the interior. The inside hue is caused by anthocyanin pigments, which seem to contribute the deepest coloration in years of cold winters and hot, dry summers.

Yuk Hamada has found a niche at farmers' markets selling fruits that are slightly out of the ordinary, including the blood orange. He had previously sold underripe fruits to whole-sale packinghouses, as his father had since 1908, but when he saw the renewed interest in unusual citrus—Meyer lemons, satsuma mandarins, pomelos—Hamada changed his approach, moving from wholesale to retail.

During the winter, from a total of forty trees, Hamada sells six to seven crates of blood oranges weekly at the market. He carries three varieties: the Moro, the most reliably blood colored, darkening as the season progresses; the Sanguinelli, which sports a bright cherry red rind; and the Tarocco, prized for its full flavor with berry overtones.

Season
December through March or April.

Choosing
Even if small, a blood orange should feel hefty for its size. The flesh can range from deep crimson to pale pink, depending on the variety, and the rind can be flushed with red or can be deceptively orange, like a navel.

Storing
Store blood oranges loose in the vegetable bin of the refrigerator for up to a month. Or, you can store them in a cool, dark spot in the kitchen for a week or so, but watch to make sure no mold starts to form on the citrus. If mold does appear, discard any affected fruits and store the remaining oranges in the refrigerator. The juice does not keep well, becoming muddy and developing an off flavor after only a few hours.

Preparing
Treat blood oranges as you would any orange—grating the zest, squeezing the juice, section-ing the flesh—but use them where their color is most impressive: for juice, in a granita or sorbet, in a salad with beets and blue cheese. Or, for a festive aperitif, pour a splash of blood orange juice into a Champagne flute and fill with sparkling wine.

Blood oranges at the Market

Blood Orange Granita

Serves 6

This classic Sicilian dessert brings a tart, cleansing sweetness to the end of a meal. It takes a couple of hours to freeze, but only a few minutes to prepare. You will need to be present as the granita freezes, as it needs to be agitated every half hour or so.

3 CUPS SPRING WATER

1/2 CUP SUGAR

ZEST OF 1 BLOOD ORANGE, CUT INTO LONG STRIPS

2 1/4 CUPS FRESH BLOOD ORANGE JUICE (FROM 8 TO 10 ORANGES)

In a small, heavy saucepan, combine the water, sugar, and orange zest over medium heat. Bring to a gentle simmer, stirring until the sugar dissolves, 1 to 2 minutes.

Remove from the heat, let cool, and then cover and refrigerate until chilled. Strain the syrup through a fine-mesh sieve into a bowl. Stir in the orange juice.

Pour the mixture into a large, shallow pan or dish, such as a 9-by-13-inch pyrex baking dish or similar vessel. The liquid should be about 1 inch deep. Place uncovered in the freezer.

After about 30 minutes, stir the mixture with a fork, scraping down the crystals from the sides of the dish, and return to the freezer. Repeat the stirring every 30 minutes. When the granita is slightly slushy but definitely frozen hard with small firm granules of ice, it is ready. This will take about 2 hours from the time you first put it in the freezer.

Serve at once in dessert bowls or glasses. Or, transfer the granita to an airtight container and place in the freezer for up to 2 hours. Take the granita out of the freezer about 10 minutes before serving so it is easy to spoon.

Grapefruit

Citrus paradisi

While it is assumed that the grapefruit is a hybrid between a sweet orange and a pomelo, (the largest member of the citrus family), it turns out that information about its origin is murky. It's a good breeder that crosses easily with other citrus. For example, the tangelo, appreciated for its good flavor and few seeds, is a hybrid of the grapefruit and the tangerine.

Grapefruit, which are thought to take their name from their tendency to grow in clusters, require more heat than other citrus to reach peak quality. The climate of Southern California is ideal, and eight varieties of specialty grapefruit flourish in the deep sandy, loamy soil at Bernard Ranches in Riverside. "The cool ocean breezes from some twenty miles away bring up the pigment of our Star Ruby and Rio Red varieties to a deep red," explains Vince Bernard, who's been raising citrus for over a quarter century.

Vince Bernard is at an advantage by being able to leave the fruit on the trees until hours before going to market, unlike large commercial growers, who harvest their crops and keep them in cold storage before they are sold, with sharp deterioration in flavor the result. "The flavor of our fruits," Bernard believes, "is further enhanced by spraying the plants with a nutritional seaweed solution that gets absorbed by their leaves."

Bernard Ranches harvests all year long. And how does Vince Bernard know when a grapefruit is ready to be picked? "We do a taste test, and make sure that the skin is as smooth as a baby's bottom."

Grapefruit are available in two basic types, pigmented and white fleshed. The color of pink varieties comes from the presence of lycopene pigment, which requires steady exposure to high growing temperatures to do its work. The types can be used interchangeably, and the only cautionary note applies to both: grapefruit can interfere with the body's ability to metabolize certain drugs, so check your prescription labels.

Season
All year.

Choosing
Look for grapefruit that are heavy for their size and have thin skins.

Storing
Store grapefruit loose—never in plastic—in the refrigerator for up to 2 weeks. Or, arrange them on a large platter placed where air circulates freely for up to 1 week. If they show signs of molding, discard the moldy fruits and refrigerate the rest.

Grapefruit

Citrus paradisi

Preparing

Here is an easy way to section a grapefruit—or nearly any other citrus fruit—so that flesh is free of any bitter white pith: Cut a slice off both the stem and blossom end and stand the grapefruit upright on a cutting board. Following the contour of the fruit, slice off the peel in wide strips, taking as much of the white pith with the peel as possible. Then, holding the grapefruit in one hand and working over a bowl, cut along both sides of each segment to release it from the membrane and then coax it free, letting it drop into the bowl. Use the tip of the knife to pry out any seeds from the sections.

If you are juicing grapefruits, use the juice right away, as it turns bitter if it stands for too long.

Grapefruit Varieties

Vince Bernard usually brings four different varieties, depending on what is ripe and juicy at the moment, to the market each week. Deep red Star Ruby is crisp and clean tasting, seedless, and has easy-to-peel skin. It is smaller and less acidic than most other rosy varieties. Rio Red is lighter and slightly larger, has a smooth rind blushed with red, and a sweet-tart taste. It's excellent for juicing. Marsh is the most popular white grapefruit, with a juicy, aromatic, rich flavor. It's seedless and great for juicing. Finally, Oroblanco, a cross between a pomelo and a grapefruit, is paler and thicker skinned than the Marsh. It has a nonbitter, juicy quality and a faintly astringent finish.

(right) Slicing off grapefruit peel
(far right) Cutting segments

Pink Grapefruit Marmalade   Makes 1 pint

This small-batch marmalade is an ideal way to make a preserve. Cooking large amounts of fruit yields too much juice for good jam or marmalade; it must be boiled for so long to reduce the liquid that the fruit breaks down too much and the consistency is never quite right. So the small-batch solution is easier and produces excellent results.

Make sure you start out with organic grapefruit, since you will be eating the peels. Use a wide, heavy pot so the juices will reduce quickly and the fruit pieces will stay plump and not turn to mush. Just put the jars in the refrigerator when the marmalade is cool.

1 PINK GRAPEFRUIT

3 1/3 CUPS WATER

2 1/2 CUPS SUGAR

JUICE OF 1 LEMON

Halve the grapefruit crosswise and squeeze the juice through a fine-mesh sieve into a bowl. Gather the seeds from the sieve and tie them up in a small square of cheesecloth. Cover and refrigerate the juice until ready to use. Using a small metal spoon, scoop out and discard the pulp and membrane from the spent halves, leaving the thick white pith attached to the peel.

Halve the grapefruit halves and slice them into strips about 1/4 inch wide. Put the strips, the bundle of seeds, and the water into a wide, heavy enameled cast-iron or other nonreactive pot. Place a plate that just fits inside the pot on top of the peels to hold them under water. Set aside to soak at room temperature for at least 4 hours or up to overnight. (The seeds contain pectin and will help the marmalade to gel.) Remove and discard the seed bundle.

Put the pot with the peels and water over medium-low heat, bring to a simmer, and simmer, uncovered, until the peels are soft, about 25 minutes. Add the sugar, lemon juice, and reserved grapefruit juice to the pot and stir well. Raise the heat to high and bring to a boil, stirring often.

Reduce the heat to medium or medium-low to retain a gentle simmer and cook, stirring frequently, until the peels are translucent, the mixture thickens and turns amber, and the temperature registers 212°F to 214°F on a candy thermometer, about 40 minutes.

Have ready 2 sterilized half-pint jars. When the marmalade is done, remove the pot from the heat. Spoon the hot marmalade into the jars, let cool, cover, and store in the refrigerator for up to 4 weeks.

Avocado and Grapefruit Salad with Frisée

Serves 4 to 6

Try this wonderful old-fashioned winter salad before a fish course. The contrast of textures and colors is sublime.

2 RIPE HASS AVOCADOS, HALVED, PITTED, PEELED, AND SLICED 1/2 INCH THICK

2 GRAPEFRUIT, PREFERABLY PINK, SECTIONED

2 SCALLIONS, WHITE PART AND ABOUT 2 INCHES OF THE GREEN, MINCED

FEW DROPS AGED BALSAMIC VINEGAR

SPLASH OF EXTRA-VIRGIN OLIVE OIL

SALT AND FRESHLY GROUND BLACK PEPPER

3 HANDFULS OF FRISÉE

In a bowl, combine the avocados and grapefruit and scatter the scallions over the top. In a small bowl, whisk together the vinegar, olive oil, and salt and pepper to taste to make a vinaigrette.

In another bowl, drizzle one-third of the vinaigrette over the frisée and toss to coat the leaves. Arrange the frisée in a bed on a platter. Pour the remaining vinaigrette over the avocado-grapefruit mixture and toss gently with your hands to coat evenly. Arrange the mixture on the bed of frisée and serve.

CITRUS
Mandarin Oranges

Citrus reticulata

Dave Fredericks's family has been farming north of Winters since 1852, when his great-grandfather traveled there from Hamburg, Germany. He came by ship to Panama, which he crossed on foot, and eventually made his way up to the Sacramento Valley. GEM, the name of the Fredericks farm, conveniently stands for Genuine Exotic Melons (page 120) in the summer and Genuine Exotic Mandarins in the winter. He sells four hundred pounds of clementines and five hundred pounds of satsumas a week, brightening an otherwise sparse winter market. Besides their remarkable flavor, Fredericks's satsumas (called zipper fruit by his daughter because they are easy to peel) are sought after for their absence or near absence of seeds.

Like so many of the farmers at the Ferry Plaza market, Fredericks (sadly, now deceased) came to farming by way of other creative pursuits. Like his father, John, he studied at the San Francisco Art Institute. While John studied painting under Diego Rivera in the 1930s, Dave studied photography while Annie Leibowitz was there in the 1970s.

In 1973, Dave Fredericks went back to the land to farm organically. Over the years, his farming practices have included mixing together compost from a nearby chicken farm and kelp. He controls bugs with the use of sticky traps and bats (bat houses), and he simply mows his weeds.

His methods have proved successful, with shoppers eager for his mandarins in the late fall and early winter. Mandarins are as sweet as oranges but slightly less acidic. They have loose, easy-to-peel skin, and, since they are small, are an ideal, nonmessy fruit for eating out of hand. The Latin name *reticulata* means "netted," and refers to the stringy web of pith that encircles the fruit under the skin. Most mandarins have fewer seeds than oranges, or no seeds.

Clementines, sometimes called Algerian tangerines, are a cross between a sour orange and a Mediterranean orange. They can be seedy, but have a delicate flavor. Popular in Europe, they were introduced to California as early as 1914. Tangerines, which are a type of mandarin orange, came to Europe first via Tangiers. They are slightly tart and, like clementines, generally have loose-fitting skins. Satsumas arrived in Japan from China in the mid-sixteenth century and today are the most common mandarin in the United States.

Satsumas are the first mandarins to appear at the market, in late fall. They are seedless because their weak pollen is unable to fertilize the ovum of other, similar trees. Since pollen produces seeds, the satsuma trees are purposely segregated from the stronger pollen of grapefruit or lemon trees, which might produce unwanted seeds in the mandarins.

Season
November through spring.

Choosing

Mandarins should be heavy for their size and have deep orange, glossy skin. Pass up fruits with soft or wet spots. The skin of the Owari, the most widely available satsuma, should be slightly puffy but not loose (an indication of being overripe). They should feel puffy and soft compared to oranges.

Storing

Mandarins lose flavor when refrigerated and can get moldy when stored in plastic bags. Use a net or mesh bag and, if you can, hang the bag in a cool, dry spot. A wire basket is a good alternative, as air can freely circulate between the fruits. Check them often and discard any that start to mold, as the mold will spread and spoil all adjacent fruits.

Clementines in Syrup

Makes about 4 pints

Here's a favorite Fredericks family recipe. Use small, firm, unblemished clementines. Spoon the small fruits, cut crosswise into rings and then half-moons, on top of your favorite vanilla or other ice cream or yogurt. Use only organic fruits for this recipe, as you will be eating the peels.

2 CUPS SUGAR

1 CUP WATER

2 1/2 TO 3 POUNDS SMALL CLEMENTINES

COGNAC (OPTIONAL)

Select a heavy enameled cast-iron or other nonreactive pot large enough to accommodate the clementines in a single layer. Combine the sugar and water in the pot, place over medium-low heat, and heat, stirring occasionally, until the sugar dissolves. Then continue to heat, stirring, until a thickened syrup forms, 8 to 10 minutes. Meanwhile, prick each clementine with a wooden skewer or a fork in several spots.

Carefully drop the clementines into the sugar syrup, reduce the heat to low, and simmer gently, swirling the pot every so often, until the syrup becomes quite thick and the clementines are very tender when pierced with a skewer, about 11/2 hours.

Have ready 4 sterilized pint jars. When the clementines and syrup are ready, spoon them into the jars, leaving a little space at the top of each jar for a splash of Cognac, if you like. Let cool, cover, and store in the refrigerator for up to 2 months.

Meyer Lemons

Citrus meyeri

Meyer lemons originated in China, where they were discovered by American agricultural researcher Frank Meyer, who introduced them to the United States in 1908. Likely a cross between a mandarin orange or an orange and a lemon, they tend to be rounder than Eureka or Lisbon lemons and have smoother, darker, more tender skin, usually tinged with orange. Their flavor is less acidic and more flowery—not as puckery as a lemon nor as sweet as an orange—and their flesh is juicier.

"San Franciscans love Meyer lemons," exclaims Art Lange of Honeycrisp Farm. "For every one box I sell at the Beverly Hills market, I sell twenty at the Ferry Plaza market." He has about fifty Meyer lemon trees on his ranch in Reedley, twenty-two miles southeast of Fresno, where he has been farming some two hundred varieties of fruit trees and vines since 1970.

The trees are easy to grow (usually to about six feet) and are not overly sensitive to cold. "Meyer lemons get sweeter while their tasty skin changes from golden yellow to an orange tinge as they move through the season. There's a sporadic burst of growth sometimes in the summer," explains Lange, "so consumers get a bonus crop just when they are not expecting it."

Season
October through April.

Choosing
Look for Meyer lemons free of spots and with good heft for their size. They should be shiny and bright yellow-orange. Do not buy Meyers with a greenish tinge.

Storing
Store in a paper bag in the refrigerator for no more than a week.

Candied Lemon Peel

Makes about 50 strips

This delightful dessert is perfect to serve with coffee or a tisane after dinner. The candied peels also make a superb present in a small box or a little ceramic container. You can use oranges or grapefruit, instead of lemons. Buy only organic citrus, as you will be eating the peels. This recipe is adapted from one for candied orange peels in the *Chez Panisse Fruit Book*.

6 MEYER LEMONS

5 CUPS WATER

3 1/2 CUPS SUGAR

Trim 1/2 inch off both ends of each lemon. Using a small, sharp knife, remove the peel from each lemon in strips about 2 inches wide. Try to cut away only the colored portion, or zest, avoiding as much of the white pith as possible. Place the strips in cold water to cover for 30 minutes. Drain.

In a saucepan, bring 1 cup of the water to a boil over high heat. Add the citrus strips, reduce the heat to medium-low, and simmer gently for 10 minutes. Drain. Repeat the process twice with 1 cup water each time. The final time, when the peels are almost translucent and can easily be pierced with the tip of a knife, remove them from the water with a slotted spoon and drain them in a colander until they are cool enough to handle. Discard the liquid.

Using a teaspoon with sharp edges, scoop out any remaining white pith. Cut the peels into uniform strips 1 inch wide. Now the peels are ready to candy.

In the same saucepan, bring the remaining 2 cups water to a boil over high heat. Add 3 cups of the sugar and stir until it dissolves. Drop the peels into the sugar water and cook them in the rapidly bubbling syrup until they become translucent, or until the syrup reaches 225°F on a candy thermometer. Remove from the heat and let the peels steep in the syrup for 20 to 30 minutes.

Line a rimmed baking sheet with parchment paper or waxed paper. Using the slotted spoon, lift the peels from the syrup, allowing the excess syrup to drip back into the pan, and place the peels on the prepared baking sheet. Spread them out in a single layer, or they will clump together. Allow them to cool, uncovered, in the kitchen, for several hours or up to overnight. If it is humid outside, it will take longer for the strips to lose their moisture.

When the peels are no longer wet, toss them with the remaining 1/2 cup sugar and store in an airtight container for up to 4 months—though chances are they will be gone in no time.

Meyer Lemons

Citrus meyeri

Preserved Lemons

Preserved lemons (pictured opposite) are an indispensable ingredient in Moroccan cooking, in *tagines*, cooked with fish, added to salads, and as a relish. They keep well in the refrigerator, covered with a splash of olive oil to prevent the growth of mold. A big jar of preserved lemons looks beautiful in your refrigerator—always there for inspiration. The whole preserved lemon is used—peel and interior—adding a delicious, slightly astringent, salty taste.

16 LARGE MEYER LEMONS

1 CUP COARSE SEA SALT OR KOSHER SALT

EXTRA-VIRGIN OLIVE OIL

Have ready a sterilized 2- or 2 1/2 -quart jar with a lid with a wire bale closure. Cut 8 of the lemons lengthwise into eighths. Place in a large bowl, add the salt, and toss together. Transfer the lemons to the jar. Juice the remaining 8 lemons and pour the juice into the jar to cover the lemon wedges. If it doesn't cover, you will need to juice more lemons, or you will need to turn the jar more frequently during the first week. Cap the jar and allow the lemons to remain in a cool, dark spot for 1 week, agitating the jar every couple of days to distribute the salt throughout.

Float a little olive oil on top of the lemons, and then store the jar in the refrigerator for up to 6 months.

Italian Light Lemon Custard

Serves 4

Here's a fluffy, light, utterly appealing dessert from artist Beverly Mills, former president of the board of directors of the Ferry Plaza Farmers' Market. She adapted the recipe from a book called *Roma*, by Julia Della Croce.

3 EXTRA-LARGE EGGS, SEPARATED

1 1/4 CUPS GRANULATED SUGAR

GRATED ZEST OF 1 1/2 MEYER LEMONS

1/3 CUP FRESH MEYER LEMON JUICE

PINCH OF SALT

In the top pan of a double boiler, whisk together the egg yolks, sugar, lemon zest, lemon juice, and salt. Place over simmering water in the bottom pan and whisk until the mixture is a somewhat airy and thickened cream, about 5 minutes. Remove from the heat and transfer to a bowl, cover with plastic wrap, and refrigerate until cool, about 30 minutes.

In a large bowl, using an electric mixer or a balloon whisk, beat the egg whites until stiff peaks form. Fold the whites into the yolk mixture in 3 batches, folding just until no white streaks remain.

Spoon into dessert bowls or glasses. Cover and chill before serving.

Cress

"The cress we grow and bring to market is called upland cress," explains Nancy Gammon of Four Sisters Farm (page 36). "It has the same pungent, peppery flavor and shape as watercress, but the growing conditions are different. Upland cress is grown in fields and watered daily with a drip misting system. Better-known watercress grows wild in sandy creek bottoms or alongside streams, but given the state of many of our waterways these days, cultivated cress is a safer bet."

Cresses belong to the mustard family and have a strong flavor when eaten raw. Cooked cress loses its heat, but still has a good green fresh taste.

Season
Cultivated cress is available year-round.

Choosing
Look for crisp, deep green leaves with no yellowing.

1 BUNCH CRESS USUALLY WEIGHS ABOUT 6 OUNCES

Storing
Refrigerate in an open plastic bag (or stems down in a glass of water covered with a plastic bag) for up to 3 days. Or, rinse, spin dry in small batches, and refrigerate in a closed plastic bag for up to 5 days.

Preparing
Rinse and shake dry just before using. Trim off the tough bottom half of the stem ends. If the leaves look tired, soak them in cold water to revive them.

Cress and Blue Cheese Toasts

Makes about 12 toasts

You can also smear this delicious blend of fresh cress and blue cheese on thinly sliced white bread, with the crusts cut off, in the style of a traditional watercress sandwich.

1 BUNCH UPLAND CRESS, WATERCRESS, OR OTHER CRESS, ABOUT 6 OUNCES, TRIMMED AND COARSELY CHOPPED

HANDFUL OF FRESH CHIVE BLADES, FINELY CHOPPED

1/4 POUND BLUE CHEESE, AT ROOM TEMPERATURE

2 TABLESPOONS BUTTER, AT ROOM TEMPERATURE

FRESHLY GROUND BLACK PEPPER

6 SLICES RUSTIC WALNUT BREAD OR ANY DENSE COUNTRY BREAD, TOASTED

In a bowl, combine the cress, chives, cheese, butter, and a few grinds of pepper and mix with a wooden spoon until smooth. Spread on toasted bread slices and serve.

Cress

Leeks

Leeks, the sweetest, mildest members of the *Allium* genus that also includes garlic, shallots, and onions, are one of the world's oldest vegetables. They look like overgrown scallions but are much milder, and people who have difficulty digesting onions find leeks a good alternative. Long considered poor man's fare, the versatile leek has been used in European cooking for centuries, usually in stocks, soups, stews, and poached or steamed and dressed with a vinaigrette.

Star Route Farms (page 176) cultivates a leek variety called the American Flag that grows quickly. It is not allowed to get huge, however, as customers nowadays prefer a younger, more tender stalk. With fields in both the California desert and in coastal Bolinas, Star Route could harvest leeks year-round, though for now they are a winter and spring crop.

Season

October through May.

Choosing

For large leeks, look for firm, upright green tops. Keep in mind that the white section and about 2 inches of the pale green are the desirable parts for cooking. Bend the lower part of the pale section to test its give. If it doesn't bend slightly, the leek has a woody heart that won't soften during cooking. Ideally, choose leeks with the largest percentage of white to green. In late spring, look for smaller, pale spring leeks. They will be particularly tender.

Storing

Wrap in a damp towel, place in an open plastic bag, and store in the vegetable bin of the refrigerator for 3 to 5 days. Unlike longer-lasting garlic and onions, leeks are eaten fresh. Wash when ready to use.

Preparing

Grit hides within the tight folds of a leek's leaves, making thorough cleaning essential. For large leeks, cut off the spindly roots, keeping the base intact, and pull off the tough green outer leaves, then rinse vigorously under cold running water. Split lengthwise, cutting almost all of the way through and keeping the root base intact for easier rinsing. Holding the leek under running water, open the leaves, as if fanning the pages of a book, and let the grit flood out. Cut off and discard the dark green tops, or both the dark green and light green tops if only the white base is called for in a recipe. Alternatively, trim off the roots and the green tops, cut the leek into rounds, place the rounds in a colander, and rinse thoroughly under cold running water. Small, tender leeks can be trimmed of their roots, split lengthwise, and rinsed in the same way. They are not as tiresome to clean as larger leeks, nor is their flavor as intense.

Be careful not to overcook leeks, as they can become unappetizingly slippery and slimy. Also, leeks do not caramelize as readily as onions, so you will need to be patient.

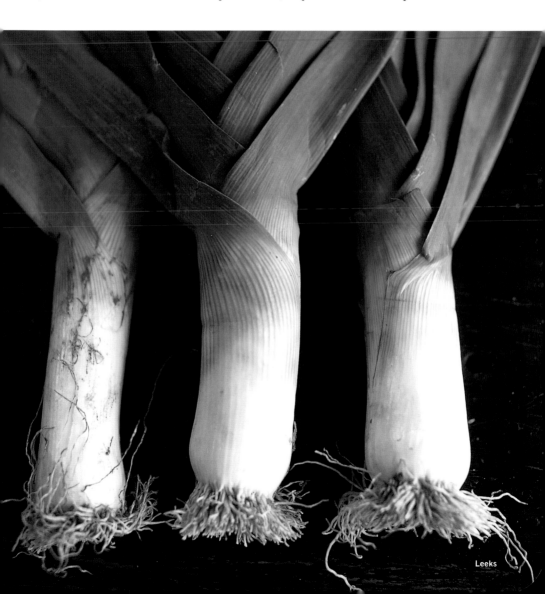

Leeks

Vichyssoise

Serves 6 to 8

Vichyssoise sounds as French as the Eiffel Tower, but it was actually created in America by French chef Louis Diat at New York's Ritz-Carlton hotel in 1917. Here is a slightly revised version of the one in *Mastering the Art of French Cooking: Volume One*, by Simone Beck, Louisette Bertholle, and Julia Child.

3 RUSSET POTATOES, PEELED AND SLICED

4 LEEKS, WHITE PART AND ABOUT 2 INCHES OF THE GREEN, TRIMMED, CLEANED, AND CUT CROSSWISE ABOUT 1 INCH THICK

6 CUPS CHICKEN STOCK, PREFERABLY HOMEMADE

SALT

1/2 CUP HEAVY CREAM

6 FRESH CHIVE BLADES, MINCED

In a large, heavy pot, combine the potatoes, leeks, stock, and a little salt and bring to a simmer over medium heat. Cover partially and simmer until the vegetables are tender, about 45 minutes.

Remove from the heat and, using an immersion blender, purée the soup. Alternatively, mash the vegetables with a fork, or pass the soup through a food mill. If you want the soup to have a very refined consistency, pass it through a fine-mesh sieve. Cover and refrigerate until nice and cool, at least 1 hour.

Remove from the refrigerator and stir in the cream. Taste and adjust the seasoning with salt. Serve in individual bowls or from a soup tureen. Either way, sprinkle the chives on top.

Grilled Leeks

Serves 4

Serve these delicious charred leeks alongside grilled fish, chicken, or steak.

8 YOUNG, TENDER LEEKS

ABOUT 4 CUPS WATER

EXTRA-VIRGIN OLIVE OIL FOR BRUSHING

SALT AND FRESHLY GROUND BLACK PEPPER

Prepare a medium-hot fire in a charcoal grill, or preheat a gas grill to medium-high.

Trim the leeks and clean well. If they are very small, leave them whole. If they are large, halve them lengthwise.

In a large, heavy skillet, bring the water to a boil over medium-high heat. Add the leeks and parboil for 6 or 7 minutes for large leeks and 3 minutes for smaller leeks. Remove the leeks from the water and drain briefly on clean kitchen towels.

Brush the leeks with olive oil and season with salt and pepper. Arrange them on the grill rack directly over the fire and grill, turning with tongs as needed, until tender and nicely charred on all sides, 5 to 7 minutes.

Transfer to a platter and serve warm or at room temperature.

Pears

It seems like no fruit is sweeter than a ripe pear. Its soft, succulent flesh is all sugar, with no acidic tang. Pears can range in texture from meltingly soft to crisp and slightly granular, but they are always sweet.

In this country, pears play second fiddle to their cousin the apple (they are both members of the rose family). Perhaps the round, shiny, crisp character of the apple makes it seem more virtuous than the sensually shaped, succulent pear. Pears in the United States today date to the introduction of French stock during colonial times. In France, growers had developed the art of espalier to improve the growing conditions in orchards, and though American fruit farmers did not duplicate these practices fully, some contemporary pruning techniques recall the early French influence.

Pears are picked and arrive at the market when fully mature but still unripe. That's fortunate, because ripe pears are so fragile and prone to bruising that they don't transport well.

Season
Fall through spring, with specific months varying according to variety. Anjou and Bosc are available fall through spring, Bartlett and Comice fall through winter, and Asian pears are in season from midsummer until late fall.

Choosing
Pears are picked before they ripen, so they will still feel hard at the market. Choose fruits with no bruising or blemishes and according to how they will be used, for cooking or eating raw.

3 MEDIUM-SIZED PEARS WEIGH ABOUT 1 POUND

1 POUND PEARS YIELDS ABOUT 3 CUPS SLICED FRUIT

Storing
Stand unripe fruits on their blossom ends on a tray or platter in a cool place in your kitchen (about 75°F) and allow them to ripen. Store ripe pears in the refrigerator in a perforated plastic bag for up to 1 week. They bruise easily, so handle with care. Traditionally pears were individually wrapped in tissue paper and stored in a cool cellar where the cold slowed, but didn't stop, the ripening process. You can refrigerate unripe pears and then remove them from the refrigerator several days before you plan to eat them.

Bosc and Anjou pears

Preparing

Fresh pears can be eaten peeled or unpeeled. If cooking pears, use a swivel-bladed vegetable peeler to remove the skin, which gets tough and leathery when cooked. Pears turn brown once they are peeled, so rub with lemon juice or place in a bowl of water to which lemon juice has been added to keep the flesh from darkening.

Pears, like apples, have a seeded core. If keeping the pears whole, use an apple corer, melon baler, or a small, sharp knife to scoop out the core from the blossom end of the fruit. If cutting the pear into halves or quarters, cut away the core from each portion.

Varieties

Anjou pears are oval, sweet, and juicy, with a mild flavor and smooth green or red skin. They are good for both cooking and eating. Asian pears look like large greenish beige apples with a matte finish. They are prized for their crispness and have a delicate, refreshing flavor. Bartletts, the most popular pears, have juicy flesh and smooth golden skin with a rosy blush. Boscs have an elongated neck, heavy, pear-shaped bottoms, russeted golden brown skin, and crisp, dense cream-colored flesh that tastes sweet and has a great perfume. They hold their shape well in cooking. Comice pears are large, squat, and have yellowish green skin with a red blush and a matte finish. Considered the best eating-out-of-hand pear, they are sweet, with a fine texture and full aroma.

Roasted Pears with Vanilla

Serves 6

This recipe is easy to prepare, delivers an unusual and intense flavor, and looks beautiful on a dessert plate.

6 BOSC PEARS

3 LEMONS, PREFERABLY
MEYER

1 CUP SUGAR

1/2 CUP (1/4 POUND) CHILLED
UNSALTED BUTTER, CUT INTO
SMALL CUBES

1 OR 2 VANILLA BEANS, SPLIT
LENGTHWISE

3 CUPS DRY WHITE WINE

Preheat the oven to 375°F.

Peel the pears, and then cut a thin slice off the blossom end so they will stand upright. Juice 1 lemon and rub the peeled pears with the juice. Stand the pears upright in a nonaluminum or other nonreactive baking pan in which they fit fairly snugly. Sprinkle the pears evenly with the sugar, allowing it to scatter onto the bottom of the pan. Scatter the butter around. Thinly slice the remaining 2 lemons crosswise and scatter the slices around the pears. Add the vanilla bean(s) and the wine to the pan.

Place the pan in the oven and roast the pears, basting every 15 to 20 minutes with the liquid in the pan, until they are tender, 1 to 1 1/2 hours. Add more wine (or water) to the pan if it begins to dry out.

Remove the pan from the oven and remove and discard the vanilla bean(s). Transfer the pears to individual plates. Drizzle the pan sauce over the pears and scatter a few of the lemon slices on each plate. Serve warm.

Radicchio

Radicchio, cousin to endive and escarole, is a colorful and singularly flavorful member of the chicory clan. It has everything: its color is vibrant, its texture is smooth, and its taste is refined and sophisticated. When it is not festooning salad bowls, this indelibly Italian vegetable is sensational grilled or sautéed, mixed into pasta sauces and risottos, or simply dipped in *bagna cauda*, the celebrated hot anchovy–olive oil dip of Italy's Piedmont.

Radicchio was developed from various local chicory varieties in the Veneto region of northern Italy in the late 1860s by visiting Belgian gardener Francesco Van Den Borre. Today, Italy is home to about a dozen different types. The two most common—both in Italy and in America and both named after towns in the Veneto—are Chioggia, with its tight, red-and-white cabbage-shaped head, and Treviso, with a head reminiscent of Belgian endive. Two other varieties gaining ground in America, and again both named for towns, are Castelfranco, a mottled-green radicchio flecked with red that unfurls like a rose, and the egg-shaped Verona, which is small and loose leaved.

A late-maturing offspring of Treviso radicchio, known as *radicchio rosso di Treviso tardivo,* has thin, curled leaves and a hook at the tip. It is typically sweeter than its parent because the heads are blanched with tarps or boxes as they grow, shielding them from the light that would darken the leaves, rendering them bitter. You can also find Pan di Zucchero at the market, pale green, furled leaves on an oval head.

Annabelle Lenderink brings back fine Italian seeds from Italy's Veneto to cultivate a vivid variety of radicchio on her Star Route Farms in Bolinas (page 176). The coastal climates of both regions are ideal for growing the full range of dapple-leaved radicchios, and a stop at Lenderink's wintertime market stall offers shoppers a chance to shop as if they are in Italy.

Season

Late November throughout the winter and sometimes into spring.

Choosing

Look for full, heavy heads, an indication of lots of vibrant interior leaves. If the heads are floppy, they may be over the hill. Avoid wilted or browned leaves. Generally, the darker the color, the more bitter the taste.

Storing

Discard any deep colored, tough, or browned leaves. Keep whole heads in a perforated plastic bag in the vegetable bin of the refrigerator for up to 1 week.

Radicchio

Cichorium intybus

Preparing

For salad, cut heads in half lengthwise and cut out the central core. Separate and trim the leaves. Wash, spin dry, and use immediately, or store, wrapped in clean kitchen towels and then slipped into a plastic bag, in the refrigerator for no more than 1 day.

For grilling, cut Treviso or Chioggia heads in half lengthwise, keeping the core intact.

Radicchio rosso di treviso (left) and radicchio rosso di chioggia (right)

Grilled Radicchio and Apple Salad with Balsamic Vinaigrette   Serves 6 to 8

Radicchio leaves are great in a salad with a good vinaigrette or an anchovy dressing (see Crunchy Puntarella Salad with Anchovy Dressing and Chopped Egg, page 269). Here is a tasty way to incorporate the pleasure of tawny grilled radicchio in a seasonal salad from San Francisco chef Stephen Whalen. Choose a blue cheese that crumbles well.

4 HEADS TREVISO OR CHIOGGIA RADICCHIO, HALVED LENGTHWISE

OLIVE OIL FOR BRUSHING

SALT AND FRESHLY GROUND BLACK PEPPER

2 FUJI OR OTHER CRISP APPLES, HALVED AND CORED

2 SHALLOTS, MINCED

SPLASH OF BALSAMIC VINEGAR

1/3 CUP EXTRA-VIRGIN OLIVE OIL

1/3 POUND BLUE CHEESE

1/3 CUP WALNUT PIECES, TOASTED

Prepare a medium-hot fire in a charcoal grill, or preheat a gas grill to medium.

Brush the radicchio halves with olive oil and season with salt and pepper. Place on the grill rack directly over the fire and grill, turning once, until the leaves have softened and grill marks are visible, 3 to 5 minutes total. At the same time, place the apple halves, cut side down, on the grill rack, and grill, turning as needed, until slightly softened and grill marks are visible, about 4 minutes. Remove the radicchio and apple halves from the grill and let them cool until they can be handled.

Meanwhile, in a small bowl, combine the shallots, vinegar, and a little salt and pepper and let stand for at least 5 minutes, then whisk in the extra-virgin olive oil to make a vinaigrette.

Cut the radicchio into 2- to 3-inch-wide strips, discarding the tough core, and transfer to a salad bowl. Core the apple halves and then cut lengthwise into thin slices. Add to the salad bowl.

Drizzle the vinaigrette over the radicchio and apples and toss to coat evenly. Crumble the cheese and scatter the cheese and the walnuts over the top and serve.

Variation: Substitute 2 grilled Fuyu persimmons, peeled and thinly sliced, for the apples.

Fettuccine with Radicchio

Serves 4

Here is a sophisticated, yet simple recipe from a story that appeared in *Saveur* magazine a decade ago. Steven Wagner, an Italian-born radicchio enthusiast, has agreed to let us use it here.

3 TABLESPOONS EXTRA-VIRGIN OLIVE OIL, PLUS EXTRA FOR DRIZZLING

1/4 POUND SLICED PANCETTA OR BACON, CUT INTO 1-INCH-CUBES

1 YELLOW ONION, CHOPPED

SALT AND FRESHLY GROUND BLACK PEPPER

3 HEADS CHIOGGIA OR TREVISO RADICCHIO, CORED AND JULIENNED

1 POUND DRIED FETTUCCINE OR *PAPPARDELLE*

GRATED PARMIGIANO-REGGIANO CHEESE FOR SERVING

In a large skillet, heat the 3 tablespoons olive oil over medium-high heat. Add the pancetta or bacon and cook, stirring occasionally, until browned, about 5 minutes. Reduce the heat to medium-low, add the onion, and season with salt and pepper. Cook, stirring often, until the onion is soft, 8 to 10 minutes. Add the radicchio and cook, tossing constantly, until wilted, about 3 minutes.

Meanwhile, bring a large pot of salted water to a boil over high heat. Add the pasta and cook until al dente. Scoop out and reserve about 1 cup of the pasta water and then drain the pasta.

Pour the pasta into the radicchio mixture, add a little of the pasta water, and stir and toss to incorporate, adding more pasta water as needed to create a nice saucelike consistency. Season to taste with salt and pepper.

Transfer the pasta onto a warmed serving platter, drizzle with olive oil, and serve. Pass the cheese at the table.

WINTER GREENS
Cavolo Nero

Brassica oleracea

Also known as lacinato kale, dinosaur kale, black cabbage, and Tuscan kale, *cavolo nero* just might be the ideal winter green. Andy Griffin, who sells beautiful bunches of it that he grows at his Mariquita Farm (page 182), begs his customers not to call it by its American epithet, dino kale. It's easy to digest and it's said to be great for hangovers, it barely needs any washing, and it keeps a long time. It tastes and looks stunning in soups, pastas, with beans, and on polenta, and can be braised and made into a pesto with garlic and olive oil for serving on top of toast.

Cavolo nero has long been known as Tuscany's peasant winter green. The slightly spicy, dark green, long-leaf borecole is closely related to curly kale. The plants look like miniature palms. In the United States, *cavolo nero* is picked by the leaf and bundled. In Italy, the tip of the young plant is cut off, the tough stem is trimmed, and the leaves are sliced and used as an essential ingredient in an authentic *ribollita* (Tuscan bean-and-vegetable soup) and other dishes.

The leaf rosettes of *cavolo nero* can withstand temperatures below freezing, making this hardy kale an ideal winter vegetable. In fact, its flavor is best after the first freeze, which converts the starches to sugars and makes the greens more digestible.

Season
Fall through winter.

Choosing
Look for plump, crisp leaves and avoid any that are yellow or have a strong odor. The stems should be vibrant and nonfibrous. Since kale contains a high percentage of water, it will shrink considerably when cooked, so buy more than you think you will need.

Storing
Keep in a plastic bag in the vegetable bin of the refrigerator for up to 5 days. Wash just before using.

Preparing
Rinse *cavolo nero* by grasping the stems and shaking the leaves under cold running water. Separate the leaves of the bundle. Holding a leaf at the stem, cut along either side of the spine and discard it.

Removing ribs from cavolo nero leaves

Cavolo Nero Swirled into Gigandes Beans

Serves 6 to 8

Gigandes beans, popular in Greece and Spain, are large, white, and substantial. In this simple, tasty wintertime dish (pictured opposite), deep green *cavolo nero* is swirled through a platter of the steaming white beans for a stunning presentation. Serve as a main course with a salad for a light supper, or offer as a side dish to roast pork or lamb or grilled steak. Rancho Gordo sells a wide variety of dried beans at the market.

1 POUND GIGANDES OR OTHER DRIED WHITE BEANS

2 OR 3 FRESH THYME SPRIGS OR 1 FRESH ROSEMARY SPRIG

SALT

2 TO 3 BUNCHES *CAVOLO NERO*, LEAVES SEPARATED, SPINES REMOVED, AND LEAVES CUT INTO 2- TO 3-INCH-WIDE STRIPS IF LARGE

A FEW TABLESPOONS EXTRA-VIRGIN OLIVE OIL FOR SAUTÉING, PLUS EXTRA FOR DRIZZLING

2 CLOVES GARLIC, CRUSHED

FRESHLY GROUND BLACK PEPPER

GRATED PARMIGIANO-REGGIANO CHEESE FOR SERVING

Pick over the beans, rinse well, place in a bowl, cover with cold water, and let soak for at least 4 hours or up to overnight. Drain the beans and place in a saucepan. Add water to cover by a few inches, add thyme or a rosemary sprig, and bring to a gentle boil over medium-high heat. Reduce the heat to medium-low, cover, and simmer gently until the beans are tender, 1 to 2 hours. The timing will depend on how long the beans were soaked and how long they sat on the shelf.

Just before the beans are ready, bring a large pot of salted water to a boil over high heat. Add the *cavolo nero* and parboil for about 5 minutes. Drain well.

In a large, heavy pot, heat the olive oil over medium-high heat. Add the garlic and the *cavolo nero* and cook until tender, 10 to 15 minutes. Season with salt and pepper, remove the herb sprigs, and discard the garlic. Keep warm.

When the beans are ready, scoop out and reserve about 1 cup of the cooking water and then drain the beans. Season the beans with salt and pepper. Place the beans in a warmed deep platter with a lip and swirl in the *cavolo nero* and enough of the reserved cooking water to make the dish juicy. Drizzle generously with olive oil and pass the cheese at the table.

WINTER GREENS
Escarole

Cichorium endivia

Organic farmer Andy Griffin of Mariquita Farm (page 182) explains, "There are two distinct classifications of chicory, *Cichorium intybus*, which includes a galaxy of radicchio types and Belgian endive, and *C. endivia*, which includes escarole, curly endive, and frisée." Griffin has an array of international chicories to choose from and will happily discuss their particular merits with customers.

Over at Star Route Farms (page 176) in Bolinas, where Andy first learned to farm, you can see fields, close to the road, dotted with plastic blanching caps that look as if they were designed by Jean-Paul Gaultier. The Madonna-type brassierelike caps cover the escarole heads during the winter months, keeping the light off of them, thereby reducing bitterness.

Escarole is a nutty, slightly bitter, lettucelike winter green, ideal for salads, soups, and braises. Its outwardly flaring leaves are smooth and broad and range from near white to a creamy pale yellow to pale green. They are purposely blanched almost white at the center of the head to yield a mild flavor and gentler texture. As the color darkens, the leaves become sharper and sturdier.

Season
December through April.

Choosing
Look for full, nonspindly heads. If the outer leaves seem tough and raggedy, they can be torn off to reveal the white tender center leaves that curl randomly. (The outer leaves actually protect the inner leaves, acting as a blanching agent themselves.) If you buy a very large head, cut off just what you need, leaving the rest well wrapped for later use.

Storing
Place in a plastic bag in the vegetable bin of the refrigerator for up to 5 days.

Preparing
Slugs love escarole, so soak the leaves in several changes of cold water to rinse them clean. Spin dry, wrap in kitchen towels, and refrigerate until using. If the outer leaves are brown and tough, discard them. If they are in good shape, cut or tear them into manageable-sized pieces.

Braised Escarole Stew with Potatoes and Leeks   Serves 6

"Escarole is one of my favorite humble greens. I like to simmer it in long-cooked soups and stews," says Boston chef Steve Johnson, an occasional visitor to Ferry Plaza market stalls. He often adds salt cod to this dish, which you can, too. Just soak about 1 pound salt cod in water to cover for a few hours, then add it to the stockpot whole and flake it as it cooks. Hold back on the addition of salt until the last minute. Or, instead of salt cod, at the last minute, he adds Niman Ranch brand long, slender frankfurters, cutting them into bite-sized pieces. "The hot dogs deliver a bonus," explains Johnson. "They flavor the broth in a back-ended way, adding another whole layer of pleasant flavor to the dish."

1 LARGE YELLOW ONION, SLICED

2 LEEKS TRIMMED AND CLEANED, WHITE PART AND 2 INCHES OF THE GREEN, SLICED ON THE DIAGONAL

4 RUSSET POTATOES, PEELED, HALVED LENGTHWISE, AND CUT CROSSWISE INTO HALF-MOONS

1 HEAD ESCAROLE, CORED, TOUGH LEAVES REMOVED, AND ROUGHLY CHOPPED

4 CLOVES GARLIC, CHOPPED

1 TEASPOON FRESH THYME LEAVES, CHOPPED

1 CUP EXTRA-VIRGIN OLIVE OIL, PLUS EXTRA FOR DRIZZLING

2 CUPS DRY WHITE WINE

2 QUARTS WATER

SALT AND FRESHLY GROUND BLACK PEPPER

6 WEDGES PLAIN FOCACCIA, TOASTED, OR 6 SLICES COUNTRY BREAD, TOASTED

In a stockpot, combine the onion, leeks, potatoes, escarole, garlic, thyme, 1 cup olive oil, wine, and water. Place over medium-high heat and bring to a boil. Reduce the heat to medium-low and simmer gently, uncovered, for about 1 1/2 hours. All the vegetables will be tender, melting into one another. The starch from the potatoes should just be starting to thicken the soupy stew.

Season to taste with salt and pepper. Place a piece of focaccia or toasted bread in the bottom of each warmed soup plate and ladle the stew over the top. Drizzle each serving with olive oil and serve.

Quick Skillet-Braised Escarole

Serves 4 to 6

Here is one of chef Steve Johnson's very fast treatments for escarole. It is wonderful served alongside grilled meat or fish.

3 TABLESPOONS EXTRA-VIRGIN
OLIVE OIL, PLUS EXTRA FOR
DRIZZLING

1 LARGE ONION, THINLY SLICED

1 SMALL CLOVE GARLIC,
THINLY SLICED

2 HEADS ESCAROLE, CORED,
QUARTERED THROUGH THE
STEM END, AND TOUGH OUTER
LEAVES DISCARDED

SALT AND FRESHLY GROUND
BLACK PEPPER

In a large, heavy skillet with a lid, heat the 3 tablespoons olive oil over medium-high heat. Add the onion and cook, stirring, until translucent, about 4 minutes. Add the garlic and cook, stirring, for 1 minute until fragrant. Add the escarole, season lightly with salt and pepper, cover, and reduce the heat to medium-low. Allow the escarole to cook gently until it is wilted and easily pierced with a fork, 4 to 5 minutes.

Remove from the heat, transfer to a serving dish, and drizzle lightly with olive oil. Serve hot.

WINTER GREENS
Puntarella

Cichorium intybus 'Puntarelle di Galatina'

When this spiky Roman chicory first shows up at the market, buy it. The heads become hollow and tough later in the season. Crunchy *puntarella* is sold from January through early spring at the Ferry Plaza market and in the fall in Italy. The name comes from the Italian *punta*, meaning "point" or "tip." The long, slender leaves grow outward from the pale head, becoming darker and more bitter toward the tips.

Siblings Lee and Wayne James of Tierra Vegetables, in Healdsburg, were introduced to *puntarella* by a customer who gave them some seeds from Italy. When they saw that chefs and people who had enjoyed *puntarella* in Italy loved the opportunity to buy it here, they started getting seeds from Italy. "Chicories flourish in our deep, rich Yolo silt loam soil," explains Lee James, and they like the frost that comes with a rough winter."

In Rome's age-old outdoor market, Campo dei Fiore, purveyors sell *puntarella* trimmed and ready for cooking, the lovely white and green curls floating in ice water. No such luck in San Francisco. At the Ferry Plaza market, Tierra Vegetables and Rick and Kristie Knoll of Tairwa Knoll Farm (page 106), the only vendors who carry it, sell the white-based, green-tipped chicory whole. "*Puntarella* differs from other chicories in that you eat the flower stalk rather than the leaf," says Lee James. The leaves actually look like dandelion leaves."

Season

Winter through early spring.

Choosing

Look for bright green, perky tips and solid stems. The smaller the heads are, the better. Larger heads have tough leaves and stems.

Storing

Store the whole head, with green part well covered to avoid wilting, in a plastic bag in the vegetable bin of the refrigerator for no more than 3 or 4 days.

Preparing

Pull off any tough or brown outer leaves. Cut the head in half lengthwise and cut off the feathery green tips. If they are very short and tender, save them for salad. If the green parts are longer and not too tough, store them in a damp kitchen towel in the refrigerator and sauté them later, as you would other greens, in a little olive oil with garlic.

To prepare the tips for salad, fill a bowl with cold water and ice cubes. Working with one segment at a time, trim the tough stem bases off and discard. Pull off and discard any tough or discolored outer leaves. Pull off the tender leaves and, using a small, sharp knife, cut them lengthwise through the white part. Cut the pieces into 3-inch julienne. Cut the white central core, the part that was above the tough stem base, into similar lengths. Taste as you go for tenderness, and include anything that is tender and good. Place the sliced white parts and the white part of the central core into the ice water. They will curl slightly while you continue trimming the remaining leaves and stalks.

After the stalks and tender green leaves have been revitalized in the ice water, drain them well and use immediately or wrap them in clean kitchen towels, refrigerate, and use within 3 days.

Puntarella

Crunchy Puntarella Salad with Anchovy Dressing and Chopped Egg

Serves 2 to 4

Here is one of the great wintertime salads. It takes a bit of work to trim the *puntarella*, but it is well worth the trouble for its wonderful crunch and slightly bitter flavor. This same dressing goes beautifully with escarole.

1 POUND *PUNTARELLA*

FOR THE ANCHOVY DRESSING

2 CLOVES GARLIC, MINCED

PINCH OF SALT

4 OLIVE OIL–PACKED ANCHOVY FILLETS, CHOPPED

3 TABLESPOONS FRESH LEMON JUICE

1/2 CUP EXTRA-VIRGIN OLIVE OIL

2 LARGE HARD-BOILED EGGS, PEELED AND YOLKS AND WHITES GRATED

FRESHLY GROUND BLACK PEPPER

Trim and cut the *puntarella* for salad as described on facing page.

To make the anchovy dressing, combine the garlic and salt in a mortar and pound with the pestle into a paste. Add the anchovies and pound again to mix well. Add the lemon juice and mix to incorporate thoroughly. Whisk in the olive oil. Alternatively, using a food processor, add the garlic, salt, and anchovies to the bowl and pulse to mash. Add the lemon juice and pulse again. With the motor running, slowly drizzle in the olive oil. Scrape down the sides of the container and pulse again. Transfer the dressing to a bowl.

Place the *puntarella* in a salad bowl. Blot any excess moisture from it with paper towels. Drizzle the dressing over the greens and toss to coat evenly. Scatter the egg over the top. Season with pepper and serve.

ALL YEAR LONG

Saturday morning market

Beef

Before World War II, most American beef was grass fed. Then, with readily available grain surpluses after the war, ranchers found that they could expeditiously and inexpensively fatten their herds at feedlots before slaughter. Grain finishing produced marbled meat that Americans grew to love, and a new dietary chapter in animal husbandry was opened.

Soon cattle ranchers were not just finishing their cattle at feedlots, however. They were practically raising them there from the moment they left their mothers. Cows digest grass easily and turn it into fuel effectively throughout their lives. But the digestive tracts of young cows are not evolved to deal with grain (mostly cheap corn), according to journalist Michael Pollan, who has written extensively on the subject. Corn is too rich and fatty and can lead to serious medical complications in the digestive tract. So cows are given antibiotics to ward off these ills, and the antibiotics get passed on through the food chain to us.

And now, as if going backward, another chapter is slowly opening, some fifty years later. Third-generation farmer David Evans founded Marin Sun Farms, his Point Reyes grass-fed beef operation, in 1998 on a two-thousand-acre family parcel dating back to 1939. There, he raises a Hereford-Angus cross best suited for his particular grass-fed model.

His cattle roam and graze on West Marin native grasses, without benefit of growth hormones or antibiotics, until they are two years old. "At that age, the meat attains a level of intermuscular fat that appeals to the American palate," Evans explains. Grass-fed beef contains substantially less fat than grain-fed meat, and it contains fewer omega-6 fatty acids (linked with heart disease) and more healthful omega-3 fatty acids.

"It's not too lean, but it must be cooked with attention," Chez Panisse chef Jean-Pierre Moullé explains. "We needed to relearn how to cook grass-fed beef with its sweeter flavor and its tendency to be less tender and tighter textured. Cooking must be precise. It is best if cut into thinner pieces, so there's not too much resistance to the teeth, and it must be cooked rare."

"Experts consider grass-fed beef to be a seasonal artisanal product," says Chez Panisse meat forager Sue Moore, who visits farms to taste meats and then makes recommendations to the restaurant based on her findings.

West Marin grass is green and vibrant from March or April through June, and David Evans's cattle graze on it during those months, making grass-fed beef a kind of seasonal product. During the winter months, these fields are too wet, and the animals are sent to the hills so that they do not compact the soil, which would hurt the grass that comes in the spring. Then, in the summer, the fields turn golden, until the rains begin. During the months when grazing on the natural grasses is not possible, the cattle are fed silage or hay or are moved to irrigated pastures. It is the integrity and taste of the grass that influences the ultimate taste of the meat. "In a way, the ranchers are also grass farmers," explains Moore.

Beef

Season

March through June, or longer if irrigation or alternative green pastures are available.

Choosing

The best cuts, according to Jean-Pierre Moullé and Thom Fox at the Acme Chophouse, are short ribs, rib eyes, New Yorks, and ground meat. Most of the meat available at the Ferry Plaza market is frozen shortly after slaughter.

Storing

Frozen meat is sold at the market in zippered plastic bags that can be put directly in the freezer and kept for up to 4 months (but I'd say 2 months is best). To thaw, place on a plate (to capture any juices) in the refrigerator a day before you plan to use it. Or, immerse the meat in its plastic bag in a bowl of room-temperature water and leave on the countertop until thawed.

Preparing

When cooking, use a hot pan, watch carefully, and shorten the normal cooking time. Make sure to have enough olive oil or fat in the pan so that the meat does not dry out. Always cook rare to barely medium-rare.

Marin Sun Farms market stall

Beef

Individual Classic Meat Loaves

Serves 6

In the 1980s, cooks began putting all sorts of spices and seasonings in meat loaves, taking the familiar and making it new. This old-fashioned recipe steps back into the past, to create a flavorful meat loaf good any time. The cream adds a certain lightness and juiciness to the grass-fed beef.

FOR THE MEAT LOAVES

1 1/2 POUNDS GROUND
GRASS-FED BEEF

3/4 POUND GROUND ORGANIC
PORK

1/2 CUP HEAVY CREAM

3 TABLESPOONS TOMATO
PASTE

1 LARGE EGG, LIGHTLY BEATEN

1 YELLOW ONION, MINCED

1 TABLESPOON BEAU MONDE
SEASONING OR CELERY SALT

PINCH OF SALT

PINCH OF FRESHLY GROUND
BLACK PEPPER

FOR THE SAUCE

1/3 CUP KETCHUP

SPLASH OF PICKAPEPPER OR
WORCESTERSHIRE SAUCE

Preheat the oven to 350°F. Put six 6-by-3-by-2-inch nonstick loaf pans on a baking sheet.

To make the meat loaves, in a large bowl combine the beef, pork, cream, tomato paste, egg, onion, Beau Monde seasoning or celery salt, salt, and pepper. Mix together with your hands until all the ingredients are evenly distributed. Divide the meat mixture evenly among the loaf pans, mounding it in the center.

To make the sauce, in a small bowl stir together the ketchup and Pickapepper or Worcestershire sauce. Brush the top of each loaf with the sauce.

Bake the loaves until a small incision in the center of a loaf reveals the palest pink inside, 30 to 45 minutes. Remove from the oven and let the loaves rest for a few minutes. Then turn out the loaves onto individual plates or onto a platter and serve.

Joe's Special

Serves 2 to 4

This dish has appeared on San Francisco restaurant menus for decades, and is still regularly ordered at Original Joe's on Taylor Street, which dates to 1937. Some believe it was introduced as a late-night supper for carousing drinkers in the Barbary Coast days of the nineteenth century, while others claim it was invented in the late 1920s by dance-band musicians. Regardless of its origin, it has long been considered a good hangover cure. This satisfying mélange of ground grass-fed beef, spinach, onions, and eggs makes a hearty meal for lunch or supper for two. To serve four, accompany with a substantial salad or a potato side dish.

3 OR 4 LARGE EGGS

SALT AND FRESHLY GROUND BLACK PEPPER

4 TABLESPOONS EXTRA-VIRGIN OLIVE OIL

1 POUND GROUND GRASS-FED BEEF

1 CLOVE GARLIC, MINCED

1 LARGE ONION, ANY KIND, FINELY CHOPPED

1 POUND SPINACH, TOUGH STEMS REMOVED AND LEAVES CHOPPED

1/2 TEASPOON DRIED OREGANO

In a bowl, lightly beat the eggs until blended and season with salt and pepper. Set aside.

In a large, heavy skillet, heat 2 tablespoons of the olive oil over medium-high heat. Crumble the beef into the pan and cook, stirring, until some of the red is gone but not a minute longer. This will take only a few minutes (keep it pink). Pour off the excess fat and transfer the meat to a bowl. Set aside and keep warm.

Meanwhile, add the remaining 2 tablespoons olive oil to the skillet and place over medium heat. Add the garlic and onion and cook, stirring occasionally, until the onion is translucent, 3 to 4 minutes. Add the spinach and cook, stirring occasionally, until it wilts and is tender, 3 to 5 minutes. Season with salt and pepper. Return the meat to the pan, add the oregano, and taste and adjust the seasoning.

Add the eggs, reduce the heat to low, and cook, stirring constantly, just until the eggs are set, another minute or two, then serve.

Acme Chophouse Short Ribs

Serves 6

Acme Chophouse chef Thom Fox, who is a frequent shopper at the Saturday Ferry Plaza market, has a way with grass-fed beef. His short ribs are meltingly tender and packed with flavor, with the meat falling off the bone. At Acme Chophouse, the short ribs are accompanied by roasted cipollini onions and baby heirloom carrots. Serve the meat and its luscious juices over a slice of crisp garlic-rubbed toast to soak up all the flavors.

You can use your everyday extra-virgin olive oil for browning the ribs. Since the meat is a fatty cut, the dish benefits from being placed in the refrigerator after cooking, so the fat hardens on the surface and can be removed. You will need to start the recipe at least a day in advance of serving, as the meat must marinate overnight, but the short ribs can be cooked up to 2 days ahead and gently reheated, making them a great party dish.

5 POUNDS BEEF SHORT RIBS, CUT INTO PIECES 2 1/2 TO 3 INCHES LONG

FOR MARINATING

1 1/2 YELLOW ONIONS, DICED

2 CARROTS, PEELED AND DICED

2 CELERY STALKS, DICED

6 CLOVES GARLIC, SLICED

6 BAY LEAVES

1 BUNCH FRESH THYME

1 BOTTLE (750 ML/3 CUPS) FULL-BODIED RED WINE, OR AS NEEDED

FOR BRAISING

3 TABLESPOONS UNBLEACHED ALL-PURPOSE FLOUR

SALT AND FRESHLY GROUND BLACK PEPPER

4 TABLESPOONS EXTRA-VIRGIN OLIVE OIL

6 CUPS CHICKEN OR BEEF STOCK

To marinate the meat, put it in a large glass or ceramic bowl. Lay the onions, carrots, celery, garlic, bay leaves, and thyme over the top and pour in the bottle of wine. If the meat is not covered completely by liquid, add more wine as needed. Cover and refrigerate overnight.

The next day, remove the meat from the refrigerator and preheat the oven to 325°F. Lift the meat out of the marinade, reserving the marinade, pat the ribs dry with paper towels, and place on a large platter.

To braise the meat, in a small bowl mix the flour with a little salt and pepper. Sprinkle the flour mixture over the ribs, covering all sides. Heat 2 large, heavy skillets over medium-high heat. Add 2 tablespoons olive oil to each skillet. Shaking any excess flour off the short ribs, add them, one by one, to the pans, being careful not to crowd the pieces. Sprinkle the ribs with salt and pepper and cook, turning them with tongs and seasoning them with salt and pepper as you do, until browned to a deep mahogany on all sides, about 10 minutes in all. Transfer to a deep, heavy baking dish or roasting pan with a lid.

Return 1 of the skillets to the stove top over medium heat. Pour in the marinade, including the vegetables and aromatics and, using a wooden spoon, dislodge the crispy bits stuck to the bottom of the pan. Then cook until the wine reduces and the vegetables become tender at the edges, about 15 minutes. Pour the vegetables, aromatics, and wine on top of the browned ribs, and pour in the stock. Cut a piece of parchment paper

FOR SERVING

6 SLICES COUNTRY BREAD

1 OR 2 CLOVES GARLIC

5 FRESH CHIVE BLADES, FINELY
CHOPPED, OR HANDFUL OF
CHOPPED FRESH FLAT-LEAF
PARSLEY

to fit just inside the rim of the baking dish, place the parchment over the ribs, and then cover the dish with the lid.

Place in the oven and cook until the meat is falling off the bones, 3 to 3$1/2$ hours. Remove from the oven and let the meat cool in the liquid. Transfer the ribs to another fairly deep baking dish. Pour the liquid and vegetables through a fine-mesh sieve placed over a bowl and discard the contents of the sieve.

Place the bowl of liquid in the refrigerator until the fat settles on the surface, at least 1 hour. Scoop off and discard the fat. Return the cooking liquid to a pot and reduce again for about 15 minutes. Pour it over the ribs. The dish can be cooled and refrigerated at this point for a day or two.

To serve, bring the meat to room temperature and warm it in a pot over medium-low heat. Meanwhile, toast the bread slices and rub 1 side of each slice with the garlic clove. Place the bread slices in shallow soup plates and spoon the ribs and their cooking liquid over the top. Scatter with chives or parsley and serve.

Bread

Sourdough starter was a treasured commodity to miners during the California gold rush of the 1850s. They carried it from San Francisco to the goldfields, where they made the good bread that they remembered from their homelands and that they had grown accustomed to in San Francisco. Its distinctive flavor began San Francisco's long and legendary history of sourdough bread, which can be attributed to wild yeasts and certain bacteria that were captured in the area's naturally fermented starter.

More than a century later, in the 1960s, change began fermenting in the communes and kitchens of a counterculture that was unwilling to settle for the mass-produced, plastic-wrapped white breads that had first crept into America's diet in the 1920s, and were now on dinner tables from coast to coast. A whole-grain bread-baking revival soon took hold in the Bay Area and eventually spread to the rest of the nation.

Then, in the 1970s and 1980s, as Americans began to travel widely and see what the rest of the world was eating, a new wave of bread baking was born on the West Coast. It combined American ingenuity and Old World techniques, and a new standard for bread baking was born. Steve Sullivan, of Acme Bread Company, was among the pioneers.

ACME BREAD COMPANY

"We have maintained the same starter that was inoculated with yeast from wine grapes some twenty years ago," explains Steve Sullivan, the handsome, innovative West Coast bread-baking forerunner. Sullivan, founder and owner of the now-celebrated Berkeley bakery Acme Bread Company, started baking bread as a sideline, having been inspired on his honeymoon in France. While working as a busboy at Chez Panisse, his breads caught the attention of owner Alice Waters, who hired him to bake breads for the restaurant. Five years later, in 1983, Steve and his wife, Susie, opened the bakery.

The Sullivans' avocation turned into a vocation. Acme set the standard for long-fermented, large-crumbed sour and sweet breads with dark, crackly crusts. Sullivan filled a niche in the dynamic food world created by Waters, Baywolf founding chef Michael Wild, and others in the East Bay and in San Francisco in the early 1970s.

Acme Bread Company was one of the first vendors at the original Ferry Plaza Farmers' Market, and today, on Saturdays, there is always a line at both the permanent, marble-topped stall inside the Ferry Building and the stand outside on the east side of the market. The same hearth-made breads—*pain au levain*, *épi*, baguette, walnut bread, New York rye, Italian— that helped establish the Bay Area as a food lovers' axis are selling at the rate of some fifteen thousand loaves a day.

Acme, which uses only organic flours, works closely with farmers to select the best grain varieties for its artisanal breads. The breads are baked around the clock in the original

PAIN HERBE

Bread at Della Fattoria market stall

Bread

Berkeley site, at a second Berkeley site, at an outpost in Mountain View, and at the Ferry Building Marketplace. The Ferry Building has provided needed room for Acme to bake traditional flaky croissants.

Just as Chez Panisse has generated a flourishing progeny, Acme has been the starting point for many bakers, including Michael Gassen of San Francisco's Noe Valley Bakery, Jeff Dodge of La Farine in Berkeley, and the original bakers at the Bread Workshop, also in Berkeley.

DELLA FATTORIA

"We have the best customers at the Ferry Plaza market," says Kathleen Weber of Della Fattoria, whose bread sells out most Saturdays before the market closes. "They come in the dead of winter and in the rain to get our bread." And they brave the elements with good reason. Kathleen and Ed Weber are making some of the region's best handmade loaves. They emerge from wood-fired stone ovens, designed by well-known oven builder Alan Scott, on the fourteen-acre family farm in Petaluma. Della Fattoria means "from the farm," named for the former chicken farm on which Ed Weber was born and where the family now lives and works.

As with Steve Sullivan, Kathleen Weber's avocation quickly turned into a vocation. Weber, a former oncology nurse and a retail salesperson, felt as if she had bread baking in her genes and soon followed her instincts. She mixes, kneads, shapes, and bakes bread made from a naturally fermented starter inoculated with yeast from grapes grown on the farm. All of the breads are made with organic flours, Brittany sea salt, and spring water.

Kathleen began by working on recipes for Meyer lemon–rosemary bread, country-style French bread, *ciabatta*, and baguette, among others. Before long, son Aaron, who was chef at a local restaurant, took her breads to work. Shortly after, the Webers had the bread account at the restaurant, and others quickly followed, including the legendary French Laundry.

For the first five years, it was strictly a family affair. Ed would stoke the fire in the early evening with eucalyptus wood in an oven that stayed hot for twenty-four hours a day. Once the oven was ready, Kathleen would rise just after midnight to mix the dough that she and Aaron would shape into loaves and bake. The bakery grew and Della Fattoria acquired a loyal, sophisticated following. Aaron's wife, Linda, was soon baking light, flaky pastries in the ambient heat of the bread ovens (in a small oven snuggled between them).

In 2001, Della Fattoria appeared at the Ferry Plaza Farmers' Market one Saturday morning, taking about six hundred loaves of their high-quality bread to a built-in clientele. "As a result of selling there," Kathleen explains, "we are more in the public eye and have gained credibility in a place where the best of everything is sold. The market draws a cross section of people who care about what they eat. Somehow this translates into caring about how they live. We realize every Saturday how much we have in common with our customers."

Storing

Keep in a paper bag wrapped in a kitchen towel. Putting bread in plastic ruins the crust and makes the interior and the crust all taste and feel the same. But if you plan to store sliced bread in the freezer, a zippered plastic bag is the way to go. Freeze whole loaves in their paper bags.

You can revive a loaf of hard day-old bread by slipping it into a hot oven for a few minutes. Failing that, slice and toast it. Della Fattoria's bread keeps fresh and tasty in its brown bag for a couple of days.

Kathleen and Ed Weber at Della Fattoria market stall

Cheese

Various artisanal culinary enterprises in California today can be traced back to the Franciscan monk Father Junipero Serra. He planted the first olive trees in the gardens of the California missions, brought the first cows here, and introduced cheese making at the missions in 1769. Some historians believe he had a hand in the burgeoning wine industry as well.

During the gold rush, newcomers arrived with dairy cows attached to their covered wagons, which meant there was a lot of milk waiting to be made into cheese. In 1857, one of the first cheese-making operations in the country was started in Point Reyes, just north of San Francisco. For many years, the dairy business flourished in that region, expanding over time, until it slowly started moving south through the state's vast valleys and along the coast where land was cheaper. Before long, Monterey Jack was developed (1915), named after cattle owner and land baron David Jacks. Dry Jack was created when a fresh version of the cheese was accidentally left in storage for too long. The Italian-American community soon adopted it in place of the imported hard grating cheeses that were difficult to get during World War II.

Another California original, teleme cheese, was developed in Los Banos in 1920, by Giovanni Peluso. What had started as a crumbly fetalike cheese, made by a Greek cheese maker, was refashioned by the Peluso family into a smooth, creamy cow's milk cheese. Three generations later, the family is still producing this distinctive cheese with its lemony-yeasty tang.

About a decade later, Vella Cheese Company was started in Sonoma and is still family run. The company's dry Jack rounds, which come coated with a mixture of cocoa, black pepper, and oil, set the standard for aged Jack here and elsewhere.

To a state whose cheese legacy had long depended on cow's milk, the introduction of goat's milk cheeses in 1979 by Laura Chenel became almost synonymous with the evolving California cuisine. Chez Panisse baked Chenel's goat cheese and served it on lovely lightly dressed baby greens, creating a much imitated dish. Most experts credit Laura Chenel with being the single person most responsible for changing the way Americans taste cheese.

Because of innovators such as Chenel and because Americans were traveling more, palates became open to bolder-flavored aged cheeses. The century-old Marin French Cheese Company in Petaluma, the oldest continuously operating cheese company in the United States, is now releasing its French-style bloomy rind, soft-ripening Rouge et Noir cheeses a little later than they used to, respecting the informed taste of many of their customers.

The time was ripe in 1997 for cheese makers Sue Conley and Peggy Smith to open Cowgirl Creamery and make a place on the American cheese board for their prizewinning rind-washed Red Hawk cheese, as well as their other cheeses, all made with local organic milk. Many serious California (and other American) cheese makers have followed suit and are now crafting cheeses with milk from their own farm (farmstead cheeses) or from neighboring

ORGANIC

MT TAM

Triple Cream
made with pasteurized milk, cream,
salt, cultures and enzymes

A truly hand-crafted cheese from the

COWGIRL
CREAMERY

POINT REYES STATION, CA 94956

Plant # 06-00040

MADE WITH ORGANIC MILK FROM STRAUS FAMILY CREAMERY • CERTIFIED ORGANIC by MOCA

MT. TAM
A TRIPLE-CRÉME
COWS MILK CHEESE WITH
A BLOOMY RIND. CREAMY,
BUTTERY, EARTHY AND RICH

Pt. Reyes, CA

ORGANIC

MT TAM

Triple
made w
salt, cultures

A truly hand-crafted cheese from the

COWGIRL
CREAMERY

POINT REYES STATION, CA 94956

Plant # 06-00040

MADE WITH ORGANIC MILK FROM STRAUS FAMILY CREAMERY • CERTIFIED ORGANIC by MOCA

Cheeses from Cowgirl Creamery

Cheese

farms, in the European tradition. And if the crowds around the cheese stalls at the Ferry Plaza market are any indication, the knowing American cheese consumer is enthusiastic about these attentively made regional artisanal cheeses.

COWGIRL CREAMERY

This first-rate cheese operation has both an outside stall at the Saturday farmers' market and a permanent stall inside the Ferry Building. Indoors, Cowgirl Creamery provides one of the great San Francisco experiences: a full-service cheese shop featuring handpicked, attentively made, top-notch cheeses from all over Europe and highly regarded artisanal cheeses from the United States. They are made from all manner of milk—cow, goat, sheep, water buffalo—and are mindfully tended and cut to order by knowledgeable sellers. Selections range from English farmhouse cheeses from Neal's Yard Dairy (many in huge, mottled wheels) to the highly coveted offerings of Jean d'Alos of Bordeaux, one of France's best-known *affineurs* (specialists who age cheeses in their own cellars).

Cowgirl Creamery owners Sue Conley and Peggy Smith, veterans of the Bay Area food world for over two decades, sell their own award-winning cheeses made with local organic Straus cow's milk in both locations. Red Hawk, winner of the 2004 Best in Show award of the American Cheese Society, is an assertive, triple-cream, washed-rind cheese that is aged for six weeks. Mt. Tam, another triple cream, is ripened to a soft, buttery, earthy goodness. St. Pat, available only in the spring, is a soft round wrapped in stinging nettles (that have lost their sting). Rounds of Pierce Point, yet another seasonal cheese, this one sold only in the fall and winter, is washed in muscat wine and rolled in herbs harvested around Tomales Bay.

The cowgirls make these and other aged cheeses, as well as clabbered cottage cheese, crème fraîche, and *fromage blanc* daily in their cheese-making facility, a renovated barn, in Point Reyes Station. They also regularly sell other locally made cheeses at their stall, such as the nutty-flavored Portuguese-style St. George, made by the Matos family of Santa Rosa. Conley and Smith are intrepid supporters of other cheese makers, showcasing a local maker—novice or seasoned—every Saturday at the market.

ANDANTE DAIRY

Soyoung Scanlan, a trained scientist and classical musician, has brought a poetic intellectuality to her cheese making that shows in her delicate French approach. Her cheeses are named for musical terms—Nocturne, Adagio, Largo, Cadenza. Even the name of her dairy, Andante, located in Santa Rosa, refers to a musical composition in a moderately slow tempo. She works deliberately and always alone, and gets remarkable results. Restaurants beg to be on her delivery path, but she keeps her operation small and within her control. Her stand is always several people deep Saturdays at the market, as customers wait for a chance to buy one of her hard or soft cheeses, made from the milk of Jersey cows, of goats, or of a mixture.

Scanlan describes her soft-ripened, ash-covered cow's milk Nocturne cheese as having been inspired by Whistler's painting *Nocturnes* at London's Tate Museum, and by the look of the fog rising off of the Thames.

REDWOOD HILL FARM

Jennifer Bice has been making award-winning goat's milk cheeses and yogurt on a family farm in Sonoma Country since the 1970s. Bice and her late husband, Steven Schack, took over a dairy her parents had started in 1968. The dairy began with a small herd of goats, all of them 4-H projects owned by Bice and her ten siblings. The herd has grown to four hundred registered pure-bred, free-range dairy goats, each with its own name. Bice sells six hundred to seven hundred pounds of goat cheeses a week, along with yogurt (in five flavors) and soap.

Redwood Hill's animal husbandry practices include using organic feed when it is available, or feed that is free of preservatives, hormones, chemical additives, and antibiotics when it is not. Animals are treated with medication only in life-saving circumstances, and they are then watched carefully to ensure that no tainted milk enters the human food chain.

All of Bice's cheeses, which are handmade in small batches, are crafted from 100 percent goat's milk, nonbioengineered rennet, imported French cheese cultures, and sea salt. Foreign interns help with handling the farm details and selling at farmers' markets.

Redwood Hill Farm was present at the very first Ferry Plaza Farmers' Market. Bice has won an enthusiastic following for her cheeses, which include feta and Cheddar, and yogurts. Her three French-style rind-ripened cheeses are the most sought after: Camellia, reminiscent of Camembert with a thin, velvety white rind; California *crottins*, small cylinders that are mild and surprisingly light textured when young, aging to a pleasant intensity; and Bucheret, a rich, intense aged cheese inspired by the *bûcheron* of the Loire Valley.

POINT REYES FARMSTEAD CHEESE COMPANY

Since 2000, the Giacomini family—father Robert and three daughters, Lynn, Jill, and Karen— have been producing California's first commercial blue-veined cheese. Original Blue was born out of necessity. The family's dairy farm, located in rolling hills near Tomales Bay, needed to diversify in order to survive.

Bob Giacomini had been dairy farming since 1959, and though his daughters had moved away to pursue careers in marketing and sales, the idea of making cheese perked their interest enough to return. Next, the family together lured Monte McIntyre, who had worked at the highly successful Maytag blue cheese operation in Iowa for fifteen years, to the farm. And so,

Cheese

with excellent Holstein milk from a closed herd (in other words, all the cows are offspring of the dairy's original herd), salty Pacific breezes, and a cool, foggy coastal climate, an award-winning creamy, tangy, slightly acidic blue cheese was born.

The excellence of the final product, which is aged for five to six weeks, owes much to how the Giacomini family cares for its herd. "Our cows are pasture fed seasonally and silage fed the rest of the year," explains Lynn Giacomini. "When we separate the curds from the whey during cheese making, we pump the whey back to the barn, where it is mixed with the cow's dry feed. And all the manure is recycled to fertilize the grasses on which our 250 Holsteins graze."

BODEGA GOAT CHEESE

Patty Karlin and her former partner, Javier Salmon, worked together for twenty years to bring a light, luscious Peruvian-style goat cheese to market. The small farm, on just seven and a half acres in Bodega, on California's northern coast, is almost self-sufficient.

Karlin grows high-protein shrubs and trees—tagasaste and willows—for the goats to browse on. She ferments mangel beets as an excellent animal fodder. The farm's solar-power system provides three-quarters of the energy requirements of the farm, including the milking machines. A self-sustaining water system takes care of water needs, and as soon as Karlin can begin to grow her own grain, the milk will be certified organic.

The herd of 120 Alpine and Saanen goats, milked April through December, provide enough milk to make two hundred pounds of cheese a week. Among the cheeses made are the feta-style *queso fresco*; *queso crema*, reminiscent of crème fraîche; and *queso cabrero*, a Manchego-style raw milk cheese. Bodega Goat Cheese also makes *natilla*, a caramel dessert sauce made of goat's milk and molasses that is delicious drizzled over ice cream.

Season

Remember it is what the animal eats that makes a cheese taste the way it does, so many cheeses have a season. Some goat cheeses are only available after the doe's kids have finished nursing.

Choosing

If you are unsure what to buy when faced with a selection of cheeses, ask for help. Describe your preferences and allow sellers to assist with your choices. Do not be shy. Cheese makers and their sellers want you to love their cheeses and want to educate their customers.

To assemble your own cheese course, consider serving a selection that includes a sheep's milk cheese, a cow's milk cheese, and one made with goat's milk. Keep variety in mind: aged and runny, semisoft and hard, blue and triple cream.

Storing

Cheese does best wrapped in the sort of paper used at the Cowgirl Creamery stall in the Ferry Building: butcher paper on the outside, waxed paper on the inside. Or, wrap cheese in waxed paper and slip it into a plastic bag or plastic wrap. If a cheese develops a mold, scrape it off and taste the cheese. If it has a sour or off taste, it is over the hill. If it tastes good, it is good.

Serving

Bring cheese to room temperature before serving. Sue Conley says that takes between 3 and 5 hours if the cheese has been refrigerated. If the cheese is soft, unwrap it, put it on a plate, and invert a bowl over it. It will soften nicely and will not attract insects.

Olive Oil

Olives are native to the Mediterranean, where trees were first cultivated thousands of years ago. Olive culture in the Americas didn't begin until the mid-1770s, when Spanish Jesuits took the fruits to Mexico, and California's first trees were planted at Mission San Diego de Alcala not long after. Soon, the first California oil was being pressed at San Diego and at other missions.

In the early 1900s, the California olive industry was largely confined to table olives, with oil production relegated to a salvage operation dependent on olives that were too small for curing. Olive oil was used in immigrant communities, and didn't gain popularity in the wider population until the 1960s and 1970s, with the growth of the natural-foods movement. Americans soon began to travel more and to buy cookbooks on Mediterranean cuisines, which translated into a demand for olive oil. Within a few years, the United States was importing some twenty-two million gallons of olive oil a year.

Since California has a climate similar to that of the Mediterranean, it is well suited to the cultivation of olive trees. Today, California annually produces about 450,000 gallons of extra-virgin oil from olives harvested from four thousand to five thousand acres of trees. There are some three hundred olive-oil producers and about seventeen olive-oil mills—big and small—in the state.

It is only in the past two decades that California has been producing and marketing specialty extra-virgin oils that are beginning to compete with the oils of Europe. Much of the state's acreage planted with olive trees for oil production is devoted to old-growth Mission, Manzanillo, and Sevillano trees. Some growers are going beyond these traditional varieties, however. For example, McEvoy Ranch, which has a permanent retail space inside the Ferry Building, imports Italian cultivars and produces fantastic organic extra-virgin olive oil in the Tuscan style on the outskirts of Petaluma. Nan Tucker McEvoy's 550-acre ranch sustains eighteen thousand olive trees, and others are propagated in the ranch's nursery to sell to other growers.

On most Saturdays, Ferry Plaza Farmers' Market shoppers can choose from extra-virgin oils from three producers who reflect the scope of what is possible in California's olive oil world today. This range mirrors what is happening regionally in Italy and other Mediterranean countries, where each region produces its own distinctive oils.

BARIANI OLIVE OIL

In 1990, the large Bariani family moved from Lombardy, in northern Italy, to forty-five acres of olive trees near Sacramento, primarily to pursue two goals: education and economic opportunity. They succeeded at both. The younger family members pursued their educations, while the older ones revived the century-old Manzanillo and Mission orchards and began producing excellent-quality unfiltered cold-pressed olive oil.

Olive Oil

All the extra-virgin oil is estate grown, produced, and bottled. The family has successfully blended the two olive varieties at different stages of ripeness, using a mixture of green olives for a peppery assertive taste and ripe black olives for a sweet, fruity flavor. Family members and seasonal workers handpick the olives from October through December, working seventeen hours a day, seven days a week, and produce their organic oil using traditional stone crushers and old-fashioned mats for pressing. Every bottle features both a harvest date and a bottling date.

The clay soil in the orchards is amended with horse manure and olive paste residue scraped from the pressing mats, ensuring the trees have a healthy growing medium. The harvest is pressed into gallons of oil each year, which are sold not only at local farmers' markets but abroad as well.

NASH'S OLIVE OIL

A big basket of farm fresh eggs nestled in straw and hay immediately draws passersby to Nash Dweik's farmers' market stall, where his olives and olive oil are also available. His 150 laying hens forage throughout the farm's twenty acres in Corning, fertilizing Dweik's olive orchards as they pursue their sustenance.

A small group of seasonal laborers handpick Sevillano, Manzanillo, and Mission olives alongside Dweik. His Manzanillo olives produce a typically peppery oil, while the Missions yield a fruity oil. But it is his expensive-to-produce Sevillano extra-virgin olive oil, with its nutty, buttery, earthy flavor, that shines. Sevillanos are costly to process because they produce less oil than other olives, making limited production inevitable. Some of the olive harvest is pressed with roasted garlic, roasted onion, lemon, or orange to make his popular flavored oils. He also cures table olives. "I produce delicious brine-cured olives typical of those I learned to make as a boy growing up in Jerusalem," Dweik explains.

Dweik values his employees highly, claiming that they are probably the highest paid in his small farming community. He is also responsible for an increase in the number of female pickers, a job traditionally held by men.

While Dweik's oils are not certified organic, all of his farming practices are. He mows his fields and turns over the soil to manage weeds, uses no sprays or pesticides, and supplements domestic well water for drip irrigation with water from the local water district. His yearly output of oil is inconsistent, however, because his olive trees are alternate bearers.

NICK SCIABICA & SONS

Nick Sciabica & Sons is the oldest continuously existing olive oil–producing company in California. The family migrated from Sicily to Modesto, where they briefly farmed fruits and vegetables. Then in 1936, Nicola Sciabica started making olive oil, putting into practice what he had learned as boy in his homeland. When he was unable to sell all that he produced in California, he went to the East Coast to sell bottle by bottle—door to door—in Italian neighborhoods.

At first the family struggled with competition from cheaper imports from Italy and Spain. But slowly business improved, largely due to an increased interest in the health benefits of olive oil. The family eventually bought machinery and started to produce oil in a continuous process. Costs of harvesting by hand and of production (sorting, crushing, pressing, and bottling) plague all growers and producers; the Sciabica family is no exception. Today, the family cold presses their own olives and the olives of over fifty growers that market oils under their own labels.

The Sciabicas have over six hundred trees in Modesto, and an organic orchard of forty-four hundred trees in Calaveras County. Combined, the orchards yield twenty-five varieties of extra-virgin olive oil. Those include the typical California varieties and imported cultivars from Italy and France. The Sciabicas take to market one of the largest selections of extra-virgin olive oils available anywhere from one source. They have filtered and unfiltered versions of many of their single varietals, as well as oil flavored with garlic, rosemary, basil, lemon, or orange.

"In California, we don't have huge crops to process all at once," explains Dan Sciabica, grandson of the founder. "In fact, we are known for small pressings of single varietal oils. Here, we can pick the same variety of olives at different times of the year. Americans are used to having a selection, so we release early-, mid-, and late-harvest oils made from the same type of olive. The oil will taste different at each stage—one will be from olives that are green and underripe in the fall; the midseason oils will be from some green, some black, and some rosy olives; while the other extreme is pressed from sweet, very ripe black olives harvested well into spring. They don't usually have that luxury in Europe—their crops are too expansive and need immediate attention."

Pest management in the Sciabica orchards is basic. Annoying squirrels and rattlesnakes are kept under control with a .22-caliber rifle. Infestation from the dreaded olive fly has been avoided so far, but should the fly show up, it will be handled with an organic spray.

And no matter what the workday brings at the olive-pressing plant in Modesto, Gemma, Dan's mother, always cooks a huge, traditional midday Italian meal for the whole family.

Bibliography

Andrews, Colman, Dorothy Kalins, and Christopher Hirsheimer. *Saveur Cooks Authentic American.* San Francisco: Chronicle Books, 1998.

———. *Saveur Cooks Authentic French.* San Francisco: Chronicle Books, 1999.

———. *Saveur Cooks Authentic Italian.* San Francisco: Chronicle Books, 2001.

Davidson, Alan. *Fruit A Connoisseurs Guide and Cookbook.* New York: Simon & Schuster, 1991.

———. *The Oxford Companion to Food.* Oxford: Oxford University Press, 1999.

———. *The Penguin Companion to Food.* New York: Penguin Putnam, 2002.

Fletcher, Janet. *Fresh from the Farmers' Market.* San Francisco: Chronicle Books, 1997.

Foust, Clifford M. *Rhubarb The Wondrous Drug.* Princeton: Princeton University Press, 1992.

Green, Aliza. *Field Guide to Produce.* Philadelphia: Quirk Books, 2004.

Grigson, Jane. *Good Things.* London: Penguin Books, 1990.

———. *Jane Grigson's Fruit Book.* London: Penguin Books, 1983.

———. *Jane Grigson's Vegetable Book.* London: Penguin Books, 1980.

Hearon, Reed, and Peggy Knickerbocker. *The Rose Pistola Cookbook.* New York: Broadway Books, 1999.

Kipple, Kenneth F. and Ornalas, Kriemhild Conee. *The Cambridge World History of Food. Volumes One and Two.* Cambridge, England: Cambridge University Press, 2000.

Knickerbocker, Peggy. *Olive Oil from Tree to Table.* San Francisco: Chronicle Books, 1997.

Madison, Deborah. *Local Flavors.* New York: Broadway Books, 2002.

McGee, Harold. *On Food and Cooking.* Rev. ed. New York: Scribner, 2004.

Plank, Nina. *The Farmers' Market Cookbook.* London: Hodder and Stoughton, 2001.

Richter, Henry. *Dr. Richter's Fresh Produce Guide.* Apopka, Florida: Tri-Foods International, 2004.

Ritchie, Tori. *Party Appetizers.* San Francisco: Chronicle Books, 2004.

Root, Waverly. *Food.* New York: Simon & Schuster, 1980.

Schneider, Elizabeth. *Uncommon Fruits and Vegetables: A Commonsense Guide.* New York: Harper and Row, 1986.

———. *Vegetables from Amaranth to Zucchini: The Essential Reference.* New York: William Morrow, 2001.

Waters, Alice. *Chez Panisse Fruit.* New York: Harper Collins, 2002.

———. *Chez Panisse Vegetables.* New York: Harper Collins, 1996.

Werlin, Laura. *The All American Cheese and Wine Book.* New York: Stewart Tabori and Chang, 2003.

Web sites

Achadinha Cheese Company www.achadinha.com
The Apple Farm www.philoapplefarm.com
Bariani Olive Oil www.barianioliveoil.com
Bella Viva Orchards www.bellaviva.com
Brokaw Nursery www.willsavocados.com
Cache Creek Farm www.experienceanut.com
Capay Fruits and Vegetables www.farmfreshtoyou.com
CUESA www.ferryplazafarmersmarket.com
Cypress Flower Farm www.cypressflowerfarm.com
Dirty Girl Produce www.dirtygirlproduce.com
Eatwell Farms www.eatwell.com
Eatwell Farms Lavender www.lavenderfarm.com
Everything Under the Sun www.underthesunfoods.com
Fairview Gardens www.fairviewgardens.org
Fitzgerald's www.well.com/user/ecrane/peaches.html
Flying Disc Ranch www.flyingdiscranch.com
Frog Hollow Farm www.froghollow.com
G. L. Alfieri Farms www.alfierifarms.com
Green Gulch Farm www.sfzc.org
Happy Boy Farms www.happyboyfarms.org
Happy Quail Farms www.happyquailfarms.com
Highland Hills Farm www.highlandhillsfarm.com
Hog Island Oyster Company www.hogislandoysters.com
Honeycrisp Farms www.honeycrispfarm.com
Knoll Farms www.knollorganics.com
Lagier Ranches www.lagierranches.com
Marin Sun Farms www.marinsunfarms.com
Mariquita Farm www.mariquita.com
Marshall's Farm www.MarshallsFarmHoney.com
Nash's Olive Oil www.nashsoliveoil.com
Nick Sciabica & Sons www.sciabica.com
Oak Hill Farm www.oakhillfarm.net
Point Reyes Farmstead Cheese www.pointreyescheese.com
Redwood Hill Farm www.redwoodhill.com
Springhill Jersey Cheese www.springhillcheese.com
Star Route Farms www.starroutefarms.com
Swanton Berry Farm www.swantonberryfarm.com
Tierra Vegetables www.tierravegetables.com
VB Farms www.sunshineorganic.com

Frederico Yerena, 91, in his vegetable garden

Acknowledgments

Many thanks to Colman Andrews for your wonderful writing and all those bottles of wine • Dorothy Kalins for being the smartest and most generous person around • Paula Wolfert for holding the line when it comes to the recipe • Niloufer King for sharing your delicious recipes • David Tanis and Randal Breski for every exquisite morsel • Verity Liljedahl for stringing our words together so beautifully and making sure the t's were crossed and the i's were dotted • Thank you to Bill LeBlond and Amy Treadwell for being our steady editors • To Sharon Silva for her thorough copyediting • To Carole Bidnick for being a great agent • Thank you to the staff at CUESA • Dexter Carmichael for help with communication with the farmers • Christine Ferren for helping us in the CUESA office • Chris and Michelle Meany for making the Market possible • Sharon Lutz for farmer information • All the farmers • Beverly Mills for her past and initiating leadership and to Janet Griggs for her present leadership • Dave Stockdale for his organizational prowess and for strategic planning • Patty Unterman for her friendship and suggestions • Jessica Prentice for sustainable agriculture tutorials • Laurel Gonsalves, Bob and Mary Estrin for recipe tasting at the ranch • Alice Waters for her extraordinary example and her beautiful foreword • Bob Carrau for not being bourgeois • Tony Oltranti for help in the kitchen • Sue Moore for help with understanding grass fed beef • Jim Hirsheimer for his patience • Christina Salas-Porras for her unerring sense of style and her beautiful ways • Robert Schneider for the ongoing dialogue about food and movies • Terry Gamble for being my Market pal • Leslie Jonath for advice • Eleanor Bertino for advice and helping us to understand the politics of food • Garth Bixler for recipe testing • Barbara and Mendelsohn for their friendship and good cooking • Sibella Kraus for your amazingly told story of the history of the Market • The Board Members of CUESA for supporting us to write the official board-sanctioned *Ferry Plaza Farmers' Market Cookbook*

Index

Index

Index

Table of Equivalents

The exact equivalents in the following table have been rounded for convenience.

Liquid/Dry Measures

U.S.	Metric
1/4 teaspoon	1.25 milliliters
1/2 teaspoon	2.5 milliliters
1 teaspoon	5 milliliters
1 tablespoon (3 teaspoons)	15 milliliters
1 fluid ounce (2 tablespoons)	30 milliliters
1/4 cup	60 milliliters
1/3 cup	80 milliliters
1/2 cup	120 milliliters
1 cup	240 milliliters
1 pint (2 cups)	480 milliliters
1 quart (4 cups, 32 ounces)	960 milliliters
1 gallon (4 quarts)	3.84 liters
1 ounce (by weight)	28 grams
1 pound	454 grams
2.2 pounds	1 kilogram

Length

U.S.	Metric
1/8 inch	3 millimeters
1/4 inch	6 millimeters
1/2 inch	12 millimeters
1 inch	2.5 centimeters

Oven Temperatures

Fahrenheit	Celsius	Gas
250	120	1/2
275	140	1
300	150	2
325	160	3
350	180	4
375	190	5
400	200	6
425	220	7
450	230	8
475	240	9
500	260	10